New Casserole Cookery

Marian Tracy

NEW Casserole Cookery

INTRODUCTION BY

Phyllis McGinley

NEW YORK / *The Viking Press*

Text Copyright © 1968 by Marian Tracy
Illustrations Copyright © 1968 by The Viking Press, Inc.
Copyright 1941 by Marian and Nino Tracy, Copyright © renewed 1968 by
Marian Tracy, 1951, © 1956 by Marian Tracy
All rights reserved

Published in 1968 by The Viking Press, Inc.
625 Madison Avenue, New York, N.Y. 10022

Published simultaneously in Canada by
The Macmillan Company of Canada Limited
SBN 670-50654-0

Library of Congress catalog card number: 68-16626

Casserole Cookery, first printing 1941 (thirteenth printing 1952) ,

More Casserole Cookery, first printing 1951 (second printing 1952) ,

Casserole Cookery Complete, first printing 1956 (sixth printing 1967)

Reissued in this format in 1974

ILLUSTRATIONS BY JAMES AND RUTH MCCREA

Printed in U.S.A.

Author's Foreword

THE FIRST EDITION of *Casserole Cookery* appeared in bookstores on the day after Pearl Harbor in 1941. It seemed a most inauspicious time to be introducing a small cookbook, even with what was then a new idea. Looking back to that now distant time, I am amazed at how right the timing turned out to be. Formality in menus and meals such as I had grown up with was disappearing along with the maids who used to cook them. We were beginning a long period of shortages and rationing which lasted until sometime after World War II. Rationing was never really severe in this country, but it did make people rearrange their menus and ideas about food. The then small book fitted in somehow with the then current wave of social change and wartime pinch.

My husband — Nino — and I had written it to explain our own casual ways of cooking and entertaining, of cooking a casserole that burbled quietly in the oven until we had finished our drinks and come to a good break in the conversation. To me, although I had been used to a good Anglo-American table, it was exciting and adventurous to cook in this unfrantic, unfrightening, untedious, and unwearing way. I learned much from Nino's rich experience in eating and cooking in such gastronomic melting pots as Hawaii and New York City. Indeed, we have foods from many lands which more and more people know or want to know how to cook, since they have enjoyed them abroad. I was fascinated, and still am, by the heady aromas and lovely, rich, dark flavors of such modest things as beans, rice, and pasta mixed with small pieces of meat and some of the less well-thought-of vegetables — all inexpensive and easily obtainable ingredients. These dishes, served with the suggested salads and good breads, could make a meal in themselves or be part of a more elaborate meal with, perhaps, a dessert from a pastry shop.

As the French say, *"Plus ça change, plus c'est la même chose,"* or the more things change, the more they are the same. Twenty-seven years after the first *Casserole Cookery* was published, my way of life has changed much, as has that of most of the world, yet casserole cooking has become more and more the way to cook and serve, for me as well as for many others. The first edition contained a modest one hundred and fifty recipes; the present revision has four hundred recipes, all of which demonstrate relaxed and gracious ways of giving the food and the guests your entire attention, at separate times. The dish itself can be personal and a great pleasure to prepare; the recipes here are intended as suggestions rather than as rigid sets of rules to be followed like a doctor's prescription. Have a specialty of the house, based on some special perfection of ingredient ready to hand or equally readily obtainable—the freshest lump crab meat, sun-ripened tomatoes, fresh herbs—what this is will depend upon your own tastes and the region in which you live.

We do have very good, well-controlled quality food in our supermarkets, truly a treat for visiting queens and kings and heads of state, but perfection is still something rare and lovely. So find the very best country-cured ham, the freshest herbs, even among the dried ones on the market. Sometimes the essential oils of herbs are so volatile that the herbs do not keep well; check yours on your seasoning shelf and discard those that smell like the very best hay. (Hay is not good for seasoning.) I have talked to people at the McCormick Company in Baltimore, who package good seasonings of all kinds. It is the most exciting perfumed building I have ever been in; yet one of the men said sadly, "Yes, that is our cinnamon, mostly, evanescing." The men on the ships nearby, on days when the wind is going their way, are intoxicated with the aroma. Some herbs, such as dried mint, keep very well, even for several years; others, such as rosemary, should be checked from time to time, for they keep very poorly.

There is no such thing as a fool-proof recipe, as anyone who has been writing about food for even a short time can tell you (some very peculiar letters come in and, of course, some wonderfully warming ones) but casserole cooking is as nearly free from potential disaster as anything that involves the human element can be. It can be varied infinitely within the limits of good taste (in the figurative sense). We have good aids to skill, such as measuring cups and spoons, electric blenders, cooking thermometers, calibrated and easily controlled stoves, and authoritative cookbooks with explicit directions—and, of course, more and more casseroles, of all sizes, shapes, colors, and materials, and at assorted prices.

In French dictionaries, the casserole is defined as a flat-bottomed pan with a handle, often used on the top of the stove. But to us, it once meant an earthenware dish that was glazed inside, had a tight-fitting cover, and was used for both cooking and serving. Now, in a way disconcerting to purists in linguistics, "casserole" has come to mean in this country anything cooked in the oven and served in the same dish — which may be not only a large or small casserole of any shape or size but also such a dish as a ceramic quiche pan or a pottery loaf pan. Some casseroles will take top-of-the-stove heat for preliminary cooking; others, especially the pottery ones, will not, unless a fire tamer is used to temper the heat.

No one has *all* sizes and shapes on hand, but because some foods are bulkier than others, it is best to start with about three sizes, which will vary according to the size of your family and the way you entertain. For these reasons, exact cup sizes of casseroles have not been given in my recipes, but the directions do give some indication of what to reach for — a large, deep one, a shallow one, or a medium deep one. You will use what you have and have what you like best. There are very good electric casseroles and bean pots (good for stew also) that have well-controlled heat. For purely personal and aesthetic reasons, I do not care for them, partly because I do not wish to have my life overmechanized. Casseroles retain heat fairly well because of the heat of the ingredients; when more heat is needed, I use electric trays (now that is irrational!) or candle warmers. On the other hand, I do not like to contemplate a cooking life without an electric blender. It is used often in directions for these dishes.

These days, when one family in four has a freezer and most apartment refrigerators have freezing units, it is often convenient to freeze some of the long-cooking dishes. Line the casserole you plan to use with aluminum foil, and let it extend generously over the sides. Cook the food in the casserole thus prepared, cool it, and put it in the freezer. When it is solid, remove it from the casserole, fold the overlapping foil over, and seal. Cover with another layer, seal, and label as to contents and date. To serve, remove from freezer and wrappings, place in the same casserole, and let thaw somewhat before putting it in the oven. Allow some extra time for heating but not, of course, for cooking, which has been done.

Since Nino and I first compiled our book so long ago, many friends have helped first us and then me with their continuing interest and enthusiasm, and at times with the dull, tedious parts of getting a book together. Some of this has been above and beyond the call of friendship or family ties. My brother, Horace Coward, had always stood by with all kinds of help. In this edition, his daughter, Ellen Rogers Coward, also helped with some of her time. Caroline Ford, Mary Hamaker, Laulette Hanson, and Jean Evans have always been nearby with practical and kind advice, whatever their place on the map. The first book would never have come into being without the blind faith of Edward C. Delafield, Jr., and the help of his wife, Margaret.

Contents

POULTRY AND GAME

FISH AND SHELLFISH

VEGETABLES

DESSERTS

Introduction

By Phyllis McGinley

THE PUBLICATION OF AN EXEMPLARY COOKBOOK, either new or revised, is always an event; this justly famous collection of casserole dishes is no exception. In fact, good cookbooks, like good *juvenilia*, have recently become our true classics in the domestic reading field. Dog-eared and much thumbed, they outshine Dickens, dictionaries, even the Bible in household affection. On my own kitchen shelf stands a select row of them, shabby from much use, and I would sooner give up my set of Jane Austen than the half-dozen I most prize. I think a majority of housewives who care about cuisine would agree with me.

Yet few of these amateur chefs (devoutly consulting Marian Tracy or Julia Child or Craig Claiborne for something less trite on the evening menu than chops and mashed potatoes) realize how new is this interest in printed cooking guides. Women fifty, even thirty years ago, had few such counselors. They learned their art from their mothers, their grandmothers, their neighbors and contemporaries. They borrowed "receipts" or cut them out of magazines. Or else they simply relied on paid help to dish up their interminable roasts and fricassees and thick gravies. If they did own a bound volume of recipes it was almost certain to be one of two standard works — *The Settlement Cook Book* or that bearing the imprimatur of the Boston Cooking School. (And very respectable are these even today.) For the most part, however, they got along by trial, error, and traditional advice.

I lived at intervals in my childhood with two aunts, both locally famous for their admirable tables, and I never saw either of them consult so much as a slip of paper when they were beating up a sponge cake or marinating a sauerbraten. What they knew about food had been learned by ear and by heart. And of course they had talent. Talent then was vital. Deprived of our cunning stoves, blenders, beaters, automatic timers, unassisted by the world's fruits and vegetables in and out of season, they had to make do with wit and experience. They had to know how to test an oven's heat with the open hand, to sense exactly when an icing had been sufficiently boiled or a custard was ready to "coat the spoon." Take the matter of vegetables, for instance. In the summer they were forced to vary the redundant asparagus, beans, sweet corn—each as it came into the markets—by ingenuity of preparation. In the winter it was necessary that the inevitable beets, cabbage, carrots, be flavored and savored a dozen different ways. Their February strawberries, unlike ours, were preserved; their December salads chiefly slaw. They lacked our year-round variety. They lacked also our canned stocks, our frozen and packaged delights. (For let us not be snobbish about such staples. No family should be forced to exist on such dubious treats, but they are invaluable as pinch-hitters, as an ever present help in time of trouble.) That my aunts fed their families—and me—so well all through the year testified to their industry and native ability.

The weeping bride with her spoiled dinner was as much a stock character in that day as the domineering mother-in-law or the stage Irishman. And with good reason. It took years of training to make a veteran cook out of a novice. All that, now, has been marvelously changed. Equipped with one of the explicit, step-by-step manuals such as Mrs. Tracy's; assisted by ingenious mechanisms, and markets which stock an infinite variety of foods in every season, any willing and literate young woman who can follow directions ought to be able to compete with her mother by the time she has assembled around her a basic set of kitchen tools.

The tools, the written word, are her salvation. But another factor, almost a revolutionary one, increases her pleasure of performance. For necessity, as it so often does, has turned into a virtue, an enlargement of modern life. Servantless cooking has become chic.

Mrs. Tracy in her own introduction to this book mentions "the casual ways" brought in by World War II. At the time this collection was first published, "formality in menus and meals such as I had grown up with," she writes, "was disappearing along with the maids who used to cook them." Her personal answer was the "casserole that burbled quietly in the oven" while the hostess-cook gossiped over cocktails with her guests. She was the prophet of a new gospel. But even a prophet cannot always realize the impact of her soothsaying. For not only did this sort of meal-getting become necessary—it became and increasingly becomes, as I said, immensely stylish. Bridget and Willie-Mae have left the kitchen. Yet in spite of, or perhaps because of, their departure Americans eat better and more interestingly than they have ever done. (In their own homes, that is. It seems to me that in restaurants they eat worse.) And managing efficiently without help has grown to be as much a part of smart affluent modern living as buying antiques or going to the theater. The woman who used to boast she had never so much as boiled an egg is an anachronism along with bustles and antimacassars. She is rather pitied than admired.

Particularly to the young is food high fashion. Since theirs is the generation which understands that nourishing a family will probably forever wholly depend on them, they have risen brilliantly to the challenge. They contrive, they explore, they experiment. It is their way of removing drudgery from a daily task. They borrow from Italy, France, Greece, the Orient. They stock their cupboards with herbs and wine and esoteric seasonings. And among them food has become a social topic, engrossing as politics or sex. They discuss a new cooking directory with all the enthusiasm they might give to the opening of a Pinter melodrama. And their heroes, their heroines are the makers of those books. (I have no doubt that Mrs. Tracy has found and will find herself increasingly a celebrity with this sophisticated group.)

Not long ago my husband and I attended a party where lions roared and Names chatted with Names. There were present a United States Senator, a member of the Cabinet, a famous drama critic, any number of best-selling authors. Also invited was a journalist-chef, one at the moment in high public esteem. And who was it that even the thickest-maned lion wanted to meet? The food expert, of course. Pretty ladies and voluble men in black tie deserted the Senator, the critic, the Secretary, to flock about him, as fascinated by what he represented as are teen-agers by a new folk singer. That I was a friend of his and could introduce him to the company gave me all the cachet I needed for that night.

This blossoming interest in cuisine is a hopeful sign for the nation. An interest in any of the arts is good for a country, and food *is* an art — as France, Austria, China, demonstrated for centuries. But America stamps its own signature on all adventures. While we improve our tables, we also simplify our methods. It is not enough for today's housewives to entertain fastidiously without benefit of a servant. What is even more fashionable is to do the job without apparent effort. And that is where Mrs. Tracy's compendium makes its impact. She is nearly the inventor of the maidless festivity.

I am reminded by her advice of another dinner party in my neighborhood, an even more recent one. The guests were not so numerous as at the one I just described, but there were more than a dozen, all of them in a gala mood and looking forward to an excellent meal—since this hostess has a reputation for good food and wine. During the late afternoon I had occasion to telephone her on some small matter, probably on what people were wearing. One of her half-grown daughters reported that she, the hostess, was swimming at the Club pool, that her husband was out sailing, and that neither was expected home until five-thirty. Remembering what I am like before company arrives (for I belong to a different and elder tradition which goes in for "party nerves"), I thought fleetingly, She must be using a caterer for once.

Yet when we arrived a little after seven, the smiling pair were unaided as usual. Easy and assured, they presided over our cocktails, our canapés, our conversation. There were no sudden dashes to the kitchen, no flurry in the dining room. And presently when appetites had been sufficiently sharpened, as easily again they called us to dinner. It was, of course, a buffet. But everything was delicious, ample, magnificently served. To me the whole effect constituted a kind of suburban miracle. I expect, however, that the only miraculous thing about it was the clever planning it involved—the efforts of that morning or of the day before, but all behind the scenes.

Indeed, "the casserole burbling quietly in the oven" may be the magic all by itself. It has made such dinners possible, made entertaining the calm and charming affair it is, or at least can be. And for her part in the innovation, I give Mrs. Tracy the royal salute. Let the unreconstructed go on greasily frying chicken, over-thickening their sauces, adding sugar to the salad dressing. The enlightened will take another path and use this book as one of their invaluable guides. Surely the young in either years or curiosity will soon dog-ear it like their other treasures. They will also have added another dimension to their household life. For good cooking is not only an art, but the most urbane of them. Civilization, like an army, marches upon its stomach.

New Casserole Cookery

Meats

Meats

Beef Rolls

1½ lbs. rump beef, cut in four 4-inch squares about ¼ inch thick

2 small onions, chopped fine

¼ cup diced mushrooms

2 tablespoons butter

2 slices cooked bacon, crumbled

3 tablespoons breadcrumbs

1 tablespoon grated lemon rind

¼ teaspoon rosemary

flour

salt, pepper

½ cup beef bouillon

1 clove garlic, minced

1 tablespoon prepared French mustard

These have more exotic names, depending on the language you are using. The French call them *paupiettes de bœuf;* the Polish, *zrazi;* and so on. If veal is used, and it is in many European countries, there are still more names. Whatever called, they are slices of beef or veal rolled around a stuffing and cooked in their gravy. The best ones are made from slices of beef rump or round cut by either you or your butcher. Some frugal and fast ones may be made from what the supermarkets call minute steaks. *Serve with mashed potatoes; hot rolls; cucumber, onion, and chicory with oil-and-vinegar dressing; chocolate mousse.*

Flatten pieces of beef by pounding with a rolling pin or any blunt instrument. Sauté onions and mushrooms together in 2 tablespoons butter. Mix onions, mushrooms, bacon, breadcrumbs, lemon rind, and rosemary together. Put ¼ of mixture on each piece of beef, roll up, and secure with a toothpick or poultry nail. Dust lightly with flour, salt, and pepper. Brown the rolls in the rest of the butter. Transfer to a small shallow casserole, add beef bouillon and about ¼ cup water. Bake in a preheated 400° oven for about 30 minutes, adding more liquid if it starts to dry out. Add garlic and mustard and cook about 20 minutes more. Serve in the sauce. Serves 4. Time: 1¼ hours.

Beef Goulash with Sweet Red and Green Peppers

4 tablespoons butter
2 lbs. onions, sliced
1 clove garlic, minced
flour
1½ lbs. rump or round steak, cut
in chunks
salt, pepper
2 teaspoons marjoram
1 teaspoon caraway seeds
1 teaspoon grated lemon rind
1 tablespoon Hungarian sweet
rose paprika
1½ cup beef bouillon or water
2 lbs. mixed red and green
sweet peppers, seeded, cut in
½-inch pieces
salt, if necessary

All goulashes are not chicken, nor do all of them have sour cream. They are basically stews, cooked with real Hungarian paprika. Imported paprika is bought in speciality stores in several strengths. My Hungarian friends prefer the sweet rose paprika. The very hot is only for experienced addicts. Paprika Weiss, 1546 Second Avenue, New York, N. Y., among other places, carries Hungarian and other Middle European specialities and will send them by mail. *Serve with boiled potatoes or buttered noodles; red cabbage slaw with roquefort cheese dressing; lemon mousse.*

Sauté onions in butter. Add garlic for 1 or 2 minutes, then discard it. Flour beef, add to butter, and brown on all sides. Put in a casserole with onions, the marjoram and caraway seed crushed together, lemon rind, paprika, and bouillon or water. Cover and bake at 350° for 1½ hours or until tender. After cooking for about 1 hour, add pepper strips. Serves 6. Time: 2 hours.

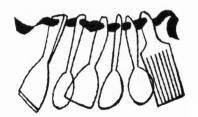

Steak with Jerusalem Artichokes

1½ lbs. round steak, cut in
2-inch squares
3 onions, sliced
3 tomatoes, sliced and seeded
6 Jerusalem artichokes,
scraped and sliced
½ teaspoon basil
½ teaspoon savory
salt and pepper

A Jerusalem artichoke, very different from the globe artichoke, is not unlike a Chinese water chestnut in its crisp emphasis. *Serve with salad of greens with French dressing; Italian bread; cherry pudding (see index).*

Arrange steak, onions, tomatoes in layers in a deep buttered casserole and top with sliced artichokes. Add seasonings, and ½ cup water. Cover tightly and bake in 350° oven for 50 minutes to 1 hour. Serves 4 or more. Time: 1 hour.

Beef Stroganoff

¼ lb. butter
1½ lbs. fillet of beef, cut in thin
strips
1 medium-sized onion, chopped
fine
½ lb. fresh mushrooms, wiped
with a damp cloth, sliced thin
1 tablespoon Italian tomato
paste
1 tablespoon Hungarian
paprika
juice of ¼ lemon
1 teaspoon salt
¼ teaspoon pepper
1 pt. sour cream

Of all the mélanges of meat simmered in liquid with assorted embellishments, one of the greatest is beef Stroganoff. This version, from the Plaza Hotel, has been modified slightly for home preparation and casserole use. *Serve with wild rice, kasha (see index), or hominy; cucumber sticks, peeled, salted, and sprinkled lavishly with freshly ground black pepper; French bread.*

Heat ⅓ the butter in a skillet over a full flame until golden brown. Add half the meat and brown on all sides. Transfer to large shallow casserole. Add another ⅓ of the butter to skillet and brown the rest of the meat. Add to casserole. Brown onion and mushrooms in the balance of the butter. Stir in tomato paste and paprika, add ½ cup water. Cover and simmer in 350° oven for 20 minutes. Add lemon juice, salt, pepper, and sour cream, and stir well. The meat is juicier, according to Plaza and general culinary beliefs, if seasoned at the last. Serves 4 generously. Time: 1 hour.

Meat Loaf with Apricots

1½ lbs. ground beef
1 egg
⅔ cup dried apricots, cut in
quarters
½ cup chopped green onion
⅓ cup chopped fresh parsley
1 teaspoon aromatic dried mint
½ teaspoon cinnamon
salt, pepper

This is for the ever-growing number of people who like meat loaf without tomatoes in any form. It is baked and served in a Mexican loaf pan. *Serve with spoon bread (see index); sliced-orange-and-sliced-onion salad with French dressing and a few black olives; coffee ice cream with chocolate syrup.*

Mix meat and egg with your fingers. Add the rest of ingredients and pat into buttered pottery loaf pan. Bake in preheated 350° oven for 1 hour or more. Serves 4 to 6. Time: 1¼ hours.

Steak and Onion Pie

1 lb. small white onions, peeled
¼ cup butter or bacon fat
½ cup flour
salt and pepper
1 lb. round steak, cut in 1-inch
  cubes
½ teaspoon ginger
¼ teaspoon allspice
4 medium-sized potatoes, boiled
  and diced
2 cups hot water
pie dough for 1 crust

You can use leftover steak in this if you have it; we never do. *Serve with sliced tomatoes with chopped parsley and basil and any dressing you prefer; hot poppy-seed bread (brown-and-serve kind).*

Cook onions slowly in butter until yellow, but not brown. Mix flour with salt and pepper and roll pieces of steak in it. Remove onions and put floured steak in pan. Add seasoning and brown. Remove steak, brown potatoes in same pan. Put all the ingredients in a low buttered casserole, add 2 cups hot water. Mix piecrust according to directions and cover casserole with crust, sealing the edges and making 3 small openings for the steam to escape. Bake in 425° oven for 30 to 40 minutes or until crust is brown. Serves 4. Time: 1 hour.

⅓ to ½ teaspoon of a dried herb equals 1 tablespoon fresh.

Roast Beef Stew in the Canadian Manner

3 tablespoons roast-beef fat
2 large onions, sliced
1 clove garlic, minced
½ cup fresh or frozen mushrooms, diced
cubed roast beef (at least 2 cups)
1 teaspoon Hungarian sweet
  rose paprika
½ teaspoon dried basil
¼ teaspoon ground cloves
1 cup clear part of roast beef
  gravy, or 1 can beef gravy
1 tablespoon brandy

A pleasing variation on a usual theme. *Serve with boiled potatoes; cold marinated okra; cherry pudding (see index).*

Melt meat fat and brown onions, garlic, and mushrooms. Add the beef, cook a few minutes more, add seasonings, beef gravy, and brandy. Put in a shallow casserole and bake in a pre-heated 400° oven for 30 minutes. Serves 4. Time: 50 minutes.

Steak and Kidney Pie

6 lamb kidneys
1 lb. beef—top round, cut into pieces about the size of a half-dollar
2 tablespoons fat, preferably bacon drippings
1 medium-sized bunch carrots, scraped and cut in 1-inch pieces
4 medium-sized potatoes, boiled and diced
1 lb. fresh, or 1 10-oz. package frozen, lima beans
3 medium-sized Bermuda onions, peeled and quartered
1/4 small bay leaf
1/4 teaspoon thyme
1/4 teaspoon sage
salt and pepper
2 cups prepared biscuit flour
1 cup milk

The lima beans and biscuit top are ethnically impure but pleasing touches added after this dish left England. *Serve with endive salad with French dressing; drop biscuits; lemon sherbet and bitter chocolate leaves from a French pastry shop.*

Prepare kidneys by splitting and removing white membrane; soak in cold salted water for 1/2 hour to 1 hour. Rinse well. Sear both kidnets and beef in fat in an iron skillet about 5 minutes, add 2 cups water and boil 6 minutes. Put meat, vegetables, and seasonings in low buttered casserole and cover with soft dough (2 cups biscuit flour, 1 cup milk, and *do not roll*). Bake about 20 minutes at 450°. Serves 4 lavishly, or 6 moderately. Time: 1 1/4 hours.

Steak and Oyster Pie

1 batch pie dough for a double crust
1 lb. round steak, cut in cubes
2 tablespoons butter or bacon fat
24 oysters, drained (save juice)
1/2 cup oyster liquor
1/2 cup port wine
1 tablespoon walnut or tomato catsup
juice from 1/4 lemon
pinch of mace
salt and pepper
white of 1 egg, slightly beaten

An elegant winy and aquatic twist on steak and kidney pie. *Serve with sliced avocado and grapefruit segments on romaine with French dressing.*

Line a decorative deep-dish pie plate or casserole with pastry. Brown the steak in the butter. Put it in the pie shell with oysters and all other ingredients except beaten egg white. Top with more pastry and brush with egg white. Bake in a 400° oven for 30 to 35 minutes. Serves 4. Time: 1 hour.

Beef Stew with Water Chestnuts

¼ lb. salt pork, cubed
1 clove garlic, chopped fine
1 large onion, sliced thin
2 lbs. lean beef, cut up for stewing
flour
1 cup beef bouillon
1 cup red wine
1 teaspoon Worcestershire
sauce
½ teaspoon orégano
3 large potatoes, peeled and
diced
12 small white onions
1 small can, or ½ large can,
water chestnuts, drained and
sliced thin
salt and pepper

This is an unusual dish; the crisp water chestnuts give a pleasing puzzling flavor and
texture. *Serve with Belgian endive; French bread;
black walnut pudding (see index).*

Sauté pork in a heavy skillet until crisp. Add
garlic and onion and cook until pale yellow.
Transfer pork, onion, and garlic to a casserole.
Dust beef with flour and brown on all sides in
the pork drippings. Drain and put in casserole
with bouillon, wine, Worcestershire sauce, and
orégano. Cover and bake in a 350° oven for
1½ hours. Remove from oven and add potatoes, small onions, water chestnuts, salt, and
pepper. Cover and bake 45 minutes longer.
Skim off any fat that comes to the top. Serves 4.
Time: 2½ hours.

Creole Beef

1 lb. round steak, cut in 2-inch
squares
3 tablespoons olive oil
1 green pepper, chopped, without seeds
1 clove garlic, minced
1 onion, chopped fine
1 12-oz. can whole-kernel corn,
or 1 10-oz package frozen cut
corn
2 cups (1-lb. can) tomatoes
2 tablespoons catsup
1 teaspoon celery salt
1 tablespoon freshly grated
horseradish root (you may use
2 tablespoons prepared, but it
is not as good)
salt and pepper
2 hard-cooked eggs, diced

A good spicy mélange. *Serve with French-fried
potatoes; salad of lettuce and thin slices sweet red
onion with French dressing; Vienna bread.*

Sauté steak on both sides in olive oil with pepper, garlic, and onion—the vegetables should
be slightly wilted but not browned. Put in low
buttered casserole. Add corn, tomatoes and
juice, catsup, seasonings, and eggs. Add to the
casserole. Bake 25 to 30 minutes in 350° oven.
Serves 4. Time: 50 minutes.

Chopped Beef Topped with Potato Soufflé

1 lb. chopped lean beef
3 tablespoons oil
salt, pepper
1 lb. yellow squash, sliced, but
   not peeled, or
   1 10-oz. package frozen sliced
   yellow squash
½ cup beef bouillon
2 cups hot fluffy mashed potatoes made with lots of butter
   (instant mashed potatoes may
   be used)
¼ teaspoon rosemary
3 egg whites, stiffly beaten
more salt, pepper
½ medium onion, finely
   chopped

Brown beef in oil. Season with salt and pepper. Add sliced yellow squash and bouillon. Cook for 3 or 4 minutes. Put in 8- or 9-inch casserole. Mix hot fluffy mashed potatoes with the rosemary and stiffly beaten egg whites and more salt and pepper if needed. Pile lightly on top of meat and squash, being careful to spread well to the edges. Sprinkle with chopped raw onion. Bake in a 350° oven until the top is lightly browned and puffy and the bits of onion are slightly charred, about 40 to 50 minutes. Serves 4. Time: 1¼ hours.

Spiced Chuck Steak

½ cup vinegar
2 teaspoons allspice
3 lbs. chuck or eye roast
4 medium-sized onions, peeled
   and sliced
3 tablespoons butter
¼ teaspoon sage
½ teaspoon savory
2 teaspoons salt
flour to thicken

This is a very good naturalized version of sauerbraten, without the wine and the long, long hours of marinating. *Serve with hot potato salad (peeled and diced potatoes cooked, with chopped onion, in chicken broth; pour hot crumbled bacon, a little bacon fat, and fresh lemon juice over all just before serving, while still warm); French bread.*

Heat vinegar and allspice with ½ cup water. Pour over meat and let stand for about 2 hours. From time to time turn meat over. Drain, but save the marinade. Brown onions and meat in fat in a flameproof casserole. Add the rest of the seasonings and marinade. Cover and simmer in a 350° oven for 2½ hours, adding a little water if it starts to dry out. Thicken sauce if desired by mixing 3 tablespoons flour with cold water to form a thin paste and then adding to the sauce. Serves 4 moderately for two nights, or 6 generously for one. Time: 5 hours.

Beef Pancake

2 onions, chopped fine
¼ cup parsley, chopped
2 to 3 cups diced roast beef, or
1 lb. ground beef, sautéed
3 tablespoons melted meat fat or
butter
2 cups milk
3 eggs, beaten
½ cup flour
tomato sauce

For those lucky ones who have some cold roast beef left. Freshly ground beef may be used if sautéed first briefly in butter. *Serve with green salad; baked pears with ginger marmalade and chopped nuts.*

Mix all the ingredients *except* the tomato sauce together. Put into shallow buttered casserole and bake in a preheated 375° oven for 25 minutes or until pancake is golden and puffy. Serve in wedges with hot tomato sauce, either canned or made according to the recipe for pasta with fresh tomato sauce (see index), omitting the bacon. Serves 4. Time: 45 minutes.

Caleb's Hungarian Goulash

1 lb. top round beef, cut in
1½-inch cubes
2 large or 4 small onions, sliced
thin
½ teaspoon Hungarian hot
paprika
2 tablespoons Hungarian sweet
rose paprika

This, quite literally, stews in its own juices. It is best made with two paprikas of different strengths, a hot and a sweet rose paprika from a good source, say Paprika Weiss (see p. 4). *Serve with boiled potatoes, salted well; watercress and romaine with French dressing; hot brown-and-serve rolls.*

Put a layer of beef cubes in a shallow casserole that has a tightly fitting lid. Add a layer of sliced onion and sprinkle with a little hot Hungarian paprika. Add a layer of beef and a layer of onions, and sprinkle the onions with sweet rose paprika. Repeat, adding layers of beef, then onions, and sprinkling the onions alternately with the two kinds of paprika, until all ingredients are used. Cover tightly and put in a 325° oven for 45 minutes. Serve, with the juices, over well-salted boiled potatoes (there is no salt in the goulash). Serves 4. Time: 1 hour.

Beat egg whites at Room temperature for greater volume.

Beef Stew with Garbanzos

1 lb. beef, round or chuck, cut
in pieces
2 tablespoons salad oil
½ can Italian tomato paste
1 small lemon, sliced thin
1 jar small boiled onions, with
juice
1 1-lb. can garbanzos, drained
(or 1 cup dried ones, soaked
overnight and simmered until
tender)
1 tablespoon allspice
¼ cup finely chopped parsley
salt and pepper

In Spanish they are garbanzos, in Italian ceci, in English chick peas. By one name or another, these round, wrinkled, nutlike legumes are available, dried or canned, most places. They may be eaten plain with salt, with a sauce, or in a stew. *Serve with mixed greens with French dressing; hot corn muffins.*

Sauté meat in oil, browning on all sides. Dump into a deep casserole that has a lid. Add the rest of the ingredients, cover, and let it burble in a 350° oven 1 hour, more or less, depending upon when you are ready. Serves 4. Time: 1¼ hours.

Persian Meat Loaf

1½ lbs. ground beef or lamb
1 medium onion, finely
chopped
½ cup chopped green onion
½ cup finely chopped parsley
3 whole pimientos, cut in pieces
1 orange, peeled, seeded, and
diced
2 eggs
juice of ½ lemon
1 teaspoon grated lemon rind
½ teaspoon cinnamon
1 teaspoon salt
½ teaspoon cracked peppercorns

The emphasis is on the delicate and fragrant seasonings with a little different twist, rather than on duplicating any dish in a regimented cuisine. *Serve with tiny new boiled potatoes; lettuce, onion, and grapefruit salad with an oil-and-vinegar dressing with a touch of mint; hot biscuits; cream puffs filled with coffee-flavored, sweetened whipped cream.*

Mix ingredients together in a bowl with your fingers. Pack into buttered pottery loaf pan. Bake in 350° oven for about an hour. Before serving, pour off superfluous juices. Serves 4 to 6. Time: 1½ hours.

Beef with Dried Lima Beans

1 lb. large dried lima beans, or
1 1-lb.-14-oz. can cooked dried
   lima beans
2 lbs. beef, cut in 1½-inch
   squares
2 tablespoons bacon drippings
2 onions, sliced
3½ cups tomatoes (1-lb.-12-oz.
   can)
2 cloves garlic, minced
½ cup Burgundy
1 teaspoon Worcestershire
   sauce
salt and pepper

Serve with salad of romaine with julienne strips of cooked pickled beets, red onion and green pepper rings, with French dressing (2 parts olive oil, 1 part wine vinegar, ½ anchovy, mashed); French bread.

If using uncooked lima beans, soak them overnight and simmer in same water until tender, or cook in a pressure pan according to directions. Sauté pieces of beef in bacon drippings until browned. Transfer to a bean pot or deep casserole with lid. Add beans and their liquid, onion, tomatoes, garlic, red wine, Worcestershire sauce, salt, and pepper. Cover and bake in 350° oven about 1½ to 2 hours. Serves 6. Time: 3½ hours, plus preparation time for uncooked beans.

Pigs in the Blanket

1 lb. round steak, cut ¼ inch
   thick and then cut in rec-
   tangles 2 x 4 inches
½ lb. bacon
8 small onions
2 tablespoons butter
2 bunches small carrots, scraped
   and cut in 1-inch lengths
2 cups milk (or cream if you
   want to splurge)
salt and pepper
1 teaspoon good paprika

"Pigs" seem to rate quite a variety of "blankets." In this recipe the blanket outrates the pig, but it's a good arrangement anyway. *Serve with potato salad on a bed of chicory; hot rolls.*

Roll each piece of steak around a rolled piece of bacon. Sauté steak rolls and onions in butter. Place steak, onions, and carrots in low buttered casserole. Add milk, salt, pepper, and paprika. Bake in a 350° oven 1 hour. Serves 4. Time: 1¼ hours.

Braciuola

1 lb. lean top round beef, cut in thin pieces and pounded
1 clove garlic, cut in half
1/3 cup freshly grated Parmesan cheese
salt and pepper
1/3 cup chopped fresh parsley
1 cup diced soft bread
1/4 cup pine nuts or pignolias (nice but not obligatory)
2 tablespoons olive oil
2 cups (1-lb. can) tomatoes
2 tablespoons Italian tomato paste

Braciuola is a pleasant Italian dish of thin pieces of lean beef rolled about a stuffing and baked in tomato sauce. *Serve with dandelion, curly endive, rugula, escarole (any two of these), with sour-cream dressing (1/2 cup sour cream, 1 teaspoon tarragon vinegar, 1/2 teaspoon dry mustard) and sprinkled with finely chopped hard-cooked egg; French bread, sweet butter; Bel Paese cheese.*

Rub each piece of beef with one of the halves of garlic clove. Spread cheese on each piece, salt and pepper, then spread parsley and bread cubes over the cheese. Add pine nuts at this time, if they are used. Roll up pieces of beef and secure with toothpicks, or tie with string. Sauté in olive oil. Meanwhile, simmer tomatoes and tomato paste together for a few minutes. Transfer beef rolls to a casserole and pour the tomato sauce over them. Cook in a 350° oven until tender when poked with a fork—about 35 to 40 minutes. Serves 4. Time: 1 1/4 hours.

Persian Meat Casserole

1 1/2 lbs. ground beef
3 tablespoons melted butter
1 large onion, chopped
3 whole canned pimientos, cut in large pieces
2 cups, or 1 package frozen, chopped spinach
1/2 cup chopped green onions
1/3 cup chopped parsley
1 teaspoon curry powder
1/2 teaspoon cinnamon
1/2 cup chopped walnuts
salt, pepper
4 eggs, slightly beaten
yogurt

The Persian part is the seasoning and the egg top. However, such distant and disparate people as the Spaniards and the Brazilians are also inclined to top baked meat or fish mélanges with beaten eggs. The emphasis changes from country to country but "it's the syme the 'ole world over." *Serve with baked potatoes; leaf lettuce with lemon dressing; pideh, the flat Near Eastern bread; boysenberry sherbet with cointreau; crisp thin cookies.*

Mix all ingredients except the yogurt. Put into buttered round 9-inch casserole about 1 1/2 to 2 inches deep. Bake at 325° for 35 to 45 minutes. Pour off surplus juices and serve hot. Pass a pitcher of cold yogurt. Serves 4. Time: 1 hour.

Macaroni with Chopped Meat and Chick Peas

1 6-oz. can Italian tomato paste
2 cups chopped leftover meat and gravy
1 green pepper, chopped, without seeds
1 8-oz. package elbow macaroni, cooked but slightly underdone
2 cups (1 lb.) canned chick peas
salt and pepper

This is one of those mishmashes that sounds awful but tastes awful good. *Serve with tossed greens with smoked oysters cut in tiny pieces, and the oil from the oysters; pumpernickel.*

Dilute the tomato paste with 3 cups water. Mix all ingredients together and put in a greased casserole. Bake in a 350° oven for 1 hour. Serves 4. Time: 1¼ hours.

Roquefort Meat Loaf

2 lbs. ground chuck or round beef
1 pie wedge (1¼ oz.), or ⅛ cup, Roquefort cheese, crumbled
1 teaspoon Worcestershire sauce
salt and pepper
paprika

Eight to five will get you plenty of takers that there will be no leftovers when you serve this meat loaf, with its strange and beguiling flavor. *Serve with baked potatoes; salad of parsley pulled apart, but not chopped, in individual bowls with a light French dressing.*

With the fingers mix the ingredients together and pat into a buttered shallow pottery loaf pan. Bake in a 350° oven 45 to 60 minutes. Serve hot or cold. Serves 6. Time: 1 hour.

Beef Stew in the Scandinavian Manner

2½ lbs. beef chuck, cut in large squares
2 teaspoons salt
freshly ground black pepper
3 tablespoons flour
2 tablespoons butter
4 medium onions, preferably red, cut into sixths
½ teaspoon whole allspice
2 bay leaves, crumbled
1½ cup boiling beef bouillon or water

Sweet red onions taste and look best in this. *Serve with boiled potatoes; spiced crab-apples or pickled beets; pumpernickel bread; ambrosia.*

Dust pieces of beef with salt, pepper, and flour. Brown lightly in butter. Put in a medium casserole that has a lid. Add onions, allspice, bay leaves, and bouillon or boiling water. Cover and bake in preheated 350° oven 1½ to 2 hours, or until meat and onions are tender. Add more liquid from time to time if it becomes too dry, but it should not be sloshy. Serves 6 to 8. Time: 2½ hours.

Macaroni and Diced Beef Baked in Cheese Sauce

½ lb. macaroni
4 tablespoons butter
4 tablespoons flour
2 cups milk
salt, pepper
1½ cups grated Swiss cheese
2 cups diced cooked beef
2 tomatoes, skinned, seeded, and
  cut in pieces
½ lb. mushrooms, sliced and
  sautéed
breadcrumbs
butter

Most countries have a version of this. This is the Belgian. *Serve with cucumber and dill salad; hot party rolls; lemon chiffon pie.*

Cook macaroni in boiling salted water until barely tender. Drain. Heat butter in a saucepan, add flour, and cook over low heat until almost dry. Add milk, a little at a time, stirring constantly until smooth and thickened. Season with salt and pepper. Stir in grated cheese. Put macaroni in a deep casserole with beef, tomatoes, and mushrooms. Add cheese sauce and stir to mix with the other ingredients. Sprinkle the top with breadcrumbs and dot with butter. Bake in 350° oven 35 to 45 minutes or until brown and crusty on top. Serves 4 to 6. Time: 1¼ hours.

Swedish Onion Casserole

2 tablespoons butter
4 cups sliced or frozen chopped
  onions
2 teaspoons sugar
1 lb. ground beef
½ lb. Italian sweet sausages
salt and pepper
1½ cups beef bouillon
½ cup red wine (if you wish — if
  not, more bouillon)

This is a smorgasbord favorite. It may also be served for supper or any light meal. *Serve with boiled new potatoes; mixed green salad; Swedish pancakes with lingonberries.*

Sauté onions in butter and sprinkle with sugar for a nice brown color. Pull sausage from casing and mix with beef. Put half cooked onion on bottom of a casserole. Spread beef mixture over onions, sprinkle with salt and pepper, and top with the rest of the onions. Poke holes in the mixture with a spoon handle or finger and pour in stock and wine. Bake in preheated 375° oven 40 to 50 minutes. Serves 4. Time: 1¼ hours.

Belgian Beef Stew

1½ lbs. beef round, cut in 2-inch cubes
1 cup chopped onions
2 tablespoons fat, preferably bacon
salt, pepper
2 tablespoons floor
1 tablespoon brown sugar
2 cups beer
1 cup beef consommé
½ teaspoon anise seeds (if you wish)

A stew is indeed a stew is a stew, but there are interesting differences in the emphasis of the seasonings. *Serve with noodles; diced cucumber, radish, and onion salad covered with sour cream.*

Sauté beef and onions in fat. Put in a casserole that will take top-of-the-stove heat or use an asbestos pad. Sprinkle with salt, pepper, flour, and brown sugar. Add beer and consommé and anise seeds if used. Bring to a boil, then cover and bake in a preheated 375° oven 1½ hours or until beef is tender, stirring occasionally. Serves 4 or 5. Time: 2 hours.

To clarify bacon fat for cooking, pour while liquid but slightly cooled into can with cold water. Burnt part will drop to bottom, and clear bacon fat can be removed from water and stored in refrigerator.

Swiss Meat Loaf

½ lb. chopped beef
½ lb. chopped veal
½ lb. chopped pork
1 cup quick oats, soaked in milk
2 eggs
1 orange, tangerine, or green apple, peeled and chopped
½ cup (4 oz.) chopped pitted green olives, or 2 whole pimientos, chopped
¼ lb. sliced fresh mushrooms (if you wish)
salt and pepper, generous amounts

This recipe is from Fritz Glarner, the non-objective painter, who is not in the least abstract about food. *Serve with watercress and pot or cottage cheese, with a pinch of mixed herbs stirred in, allowed to stand in the refrigerator long enough for the flavors to permeate the cheese; hot rolls (brown-and-serve); lemon pudding (see index).*

Mix thoroughly. Spoon into an oblong Mexican pottery casserole that has been well greased, being careful not to pack. Bake for at least 1 hour in a preheated 350° oven. Serve from the baking dish, either hot or cold, after pouring off surplus juice. Serves 4. Time: 1¼ hours.

Enchiladas

3 medium-sized onions,
  chopped
bacon fat
2 lbs. chopped beef
1 clove garlic
salt and pepper
chili powder—for experienced
  Mexican food eaters, chili
  pods mashed to a paste
1 cup canned tomatoes (or 1 cup
  water) cumin, cardamom,
  orégano, or all three
12 tortillas
½ lb. grated Cheddar cheese

This is a most controversial dish. A friend, well versed in Mexican cookery, gave me this recipe, but another, equally knowledgeable, says you don't bake enchiladas. *Serve with bunches of crisp parsley with French dressing; more tortillas (canned or homemade).*

Cook 2 onions in bacon fat until transparent, then add beef and garlic. Salt and pepper heavily and add as much chili powder as you can stand—at least 3 tablespoons. Add either water or tomatoes (water makes the chili more fiery) and let simmer until there is a gloppy mixture. Add the rest of the seasonings and simmer some more. Sauté tortillas a minute or two in bacon fat. Spread each tortilla with some of the beef mixture and roll them up. Lay side by side in a shallow casserole—Mexican, naturally—and cover with the rest of the meat mixture. Sprinkle the top with the grated cheese and the third chopped onion. Bake in a 350° oven just until the cheese is melted, about 15 minutes. Serves 4. Time: 50 minutes.

Tamale Pie

1 cup corn meal
salt
1 lb. round steak, ground
2 onions, minced
2 tablespoons olive oil
2 cups (1-lb. can) tomatoes
1 8-oz. can ripe olives, chopped
2 teaspoons, or 1 tablespoon,
  chili powder
½ teaspoon dried basil
pepper

Filling, fattening, and highly seasoned. *Serve with endive with French dressing (2 parts olive oil, 1 part lemon juice, salt and pepper); Italian bread.*

Stir corn meal and 1 tablespoon salt into 1 quart boiling water. Cook for about 20 minutes, stirring constantly to keep it from lumping. Meanwhile sauté round steak and onion in olive oil in a large skillet. Add tomatoes, olives, chili powder, basil, salt, and pepper. Cook until somewhat thickened. Add water if it starts to get dry. When corn meal has become thick and mushy, put half of it on the bottom of a low buttered casserole, then spread meat mixture on it and top with the other half of the corn meal. Bake in a 350° oven 40 minutes or until the top is slightly browned. Serves 4 or more. Time: 1¼ hours.

Chili con Carne

3 spring onions, tops and bulbs chopped
2 tablespoons olive oil
1½ lbs. round steak, cut in 1-inch squares
¼ cup fat from steak, chopped
salt
2 cups hot water
chili powder — 1 to 5 tablespoons
1 clove garlic, chopped
2 1-lb. cans kidney beans

In Mexico the chili and meat are served separately, as in Chili con Carne for a Party (see below). Here they are together, American fashion. *Serve with escarole salad with a little olive oil and salt — no vinegar, the chili is hot enough; tortillas (if available); beer.*

Cook onion in olive oil until yellow. Add meat, fat, and salt. Stir until meat is brown, then add water, chili powder, and garlic. Cook about 10 minutes. Put in deep buttered casserole, add kidney beans, cover, and cook in 350° oven 40 minutes. Serves 4 or more. Time: 1 hour.

Chili con Carne for a Party

6 large chili peppers (for the true addicts)
hot water
1 lb. coarsely ground suet
1 large onion, chopped
3 cloves garlic, minced
5 lbs. coarsely ground beef
½ lb. best chili powder
2 tablespoons ground cumin
1 scant tablespoon orégano
salt

Serve with red chili beans or kidney beans, slightly mashed; mixed greens with Roquefort dressing; onion bread (made like garlic bread, but with finely chopped onions); beer.

Soak chili peppers 15 minutes in hot water, remove seeds, and run peppers through a food chopper. Render suet by heating in a large, heavy pan (or 2 skillets), drain off fat, and return suet to pan. Add onion and garlic and brown lightly. Add meat slowly and brown, stirring constantly. Transfer to a large, deep casserole and add remaining ingredients. Pour in enough hot water barely to cover. Mix well and cover with a tightly fitting lid. Bake in a 325° oven for at least 2 hours — the longer it cooks the better. Serve in pottery bowls or soup plates. It's pretty runny for plates. Serves 16 to 20. Time: 3 hours.

Corned-Beef Hash

4 medium-sized potatoes,
  boiled, peeled, and diced
1 cup milk
2 eggs
1 12-oz. can corned beef (just
  the meat, not the hash),
  chopped fine
1 onion, chopped fine
salt and pepper

Corned-beef hash varies from nondescript conglomerations from a can to a fascinating pudding-like affair such as this. *Serve with mixed greens sprinkled with finely chopped hard-cooked egg and French dressing; Ry-Krisp.*

Mix together and pour into a greased casserole. This makes a rather sloshy mixture. Bake in a 350° oven for about 1 hour, or until firm and crusty. Serves 4. Time: 1¼ hours.

Beef, Pork, Veal, and Mushrooms with Rice

½ lb. lean beef, diced
½ lb. lean pork, diced
½ lb. lean veal, diced
2 spring onions, tops and
  bottoms chopped
¼ cup butter
½ lb. fresh, or 1 6-oz. package
  frozen, mushrooms, sliced
1 cup uncooked rice
3 cups beef bouillon
salt and pepper

Serve with salad of escarole, white grapes, orange sections, with French dressing; poppy-seed bread (the brown-and-serve kind).

Sauté meats and onions briefly in butter in a skillet; then sauté mushrooms. Place uncooked rice in the bottom of a deep buttered casserole. Add other ingredients. Cover tightly and bake in 350° oven 45 minutes to 1 hour. Serves 4. Time: 1¼ hours.

Red-Flannel Hash

1½ lb. round steak, ground
salt and pepper
3 tablespoons fat
4 medium-sized potatoes,
  boiled, peeled, and diced
2 cups (1-lb. can) diced beets,
  drained, or 1 bunch small
  beets, boiled, skinned, and
  diced
1½ cups milk

New England washday special that appeals to those who have never even entered a laundromat. *Serve with mixed green salad with sliced radishes, pickled onions, and French dressing; hot buttered toast; blue cheese and crackers.*

Season round steak with salt and pepper and sauté in fat. Mix potatoes, beets, and round steak. Put in low buttered casserole. Pour in milk and bake in a 350° oven 30 minutes, until crusty on top. Serves 4. Time: 45 minutes.

Corned Beef with Brussels Sprouts

1 pt. fresh, or 1 10-oz. package
    frozen, Brussels sprouts
4 medium-sized potatoes, boiled
    and diced
salt and pepper
¼ teaspoon thyme
1 12-oz. can corned beef, cut in
    ¼-inch slices
1½ cups beef bouillon

A dish with positive flavor for rugged palates. *Serve with raw onion rings marinated in anchovy dressing (2 parts olive oil, 1 part vinegar, 1 teaspoon anchovy paste); corn muffins.*

Wash Brussels sprouts, if fresh, and remove frayed outer leaves. Take a deep casserole, butter it, and place a layer of potatoes on the bottom, then a layer of Brussels sprouts. Sprinkle with salt, pepper, and thyme, place a few slices of corned beef, and repeat in this order. The layers should be thick enough so that there are only two layers of each ingredient. Bake in a 350° oven about 35 minutes, or until the Brussels sprouts are tender. Serves 4. Time: 1 hour.

Zucchini with Meat Sauce

½ lb. chopped meat
¼ cup melted butter
6 tomatoes, skinned, seeded,
    and chopped
salt
3 cups sliced zucchini (do not
    peel)

Either zucchini or yellow summer squash may be used in this dish, a light and lovely one for a hot day. *Serve with Caesar salad; Italian bread; granita di caffe (Italian coffee sherbet).*

Sauté meat in butter until brown, add tomatoes and salt, and sauté for a few minutes. Turn heat down and cook until thickened, about 15 minutes. Arrange zucchini slices in a shallow casserole. Pour meat sauce over them. Bake in preheated 350° oven about 30 minutes or until the zucchini is tender. Serves 4. Time: 1 hour.

Beef with Tiny New Potatoes in Horseradish Sauce

2 tablespoons butter
2 tablespoons flour
1 cup milk
salt
2 tablespoons freshly grated, or 4 tablespoons bottled, horse-radish
2½ cups diced cooked beef
12 tiny new potatoes, boiled and peeled

The horseradish that comes pickled in vinegar is a weak and nondescript version of this sharp and pungent herb freshly grated. *Serve with small cherry tomatoes with a small dish of heavily salted and peppered oil; pumpernickel and sweet butter.*

Melt butter and blend in flour. Add milk slowly, stirring, and cook until thickened. Add salt. Add horseradish. Toss beef and potatoes together gently. Pile into a casserole and pour in the sauce. Bake 20 to 25 minutes in a 350° oven or until the dish is bubbling gently and the top is a nice golden brown. Serves 4. Time: 45 minutes.

Swedish Stuffed Cabbage

½ cup uncooked rice
1 cup milk
¼ lb. beef
¼ lb. pork
⅛ lb. veal
12 cabbage leaves
1 egg
¼ cup cream
salt and pepper
2 tablespoons melted butter
3 tablespoons flour
1 cup beef bouillon

This makes addicts out of even those who know they don't like cabbage. *Serve with sliced fresh tomatoes with horseradish dressing (mix ¼ cup sour cream with 1 tablespoon of the freshest horseradish you can buy); dark pumpernickel bread and sweet butter.*

Cook rice in milk for about 20 minutes. Put the meat together through the grinder twice. Drop cabbage leaves in boiling water for a minute to make them pliable. Mix meat, egg, cream, and cooked rice together with salt and pepper. Divide meat mixture into 12 portions and put one on each cabbage leaf. Roll leaves up and put side by side in butter in a heavy skillet. Brown and transfer to a shallow casserole. Sprinkle flour into the skillet with the fat and juices from the meat, and stir. Add bouillon and stir till thoroughly blended. Pour over cabbage rolls and bake in 350° oven 25 to 30 minutes—time enough for the flavors to mingle. Serves 4. Time: 1¼ hours.

Veal Shanks in the Provençal Manner

1 clove garlic, cut in half
2 tablespoons olive oil
4 thick slices veal shank (1½ to 2 lbs.)
⅔ cup chopped onion
3 tomatoes, skinned, seeded, and chopped, or 1 cup tomato purée
½ cup white wine
salt, pepper
1 teaspoon sugar
½ teaspoon ground and still aromatic rosemary, or 1 teaspoon fresh chopped rosemary
¼ teaspoon thyme
2 tablespoons finely chopped parsley
1 tablespoon grated lemon rind

Much like the Italian osso bucco except that the veal shanks are cut in thick slices. *Serve with buttered noodles; tossed green salad; French bread; lemon mousse.*

Brown garlic in oil and discard. Brown veal shanks in oil and transfer meat to casserole. Sauté onion in oil. Add to the casserole with tomatoes or purée, wine, and seasonings. Cover and bake in preheated 350° oven 1½ to 2 hours or until tender. Add more liquid— wine or beef bouillon—if necessary. Sprinkle with parsley and lemon rind before serving. Serves 4. Time: 2¼ hours.

Rip's Veal Paprika

1 veal steak, 1 inch thick (the weight will vary according to the size of the calf)
3 tablespoons bacon fat
3 medium-sized onions, minced fine
2 tablespoons flour
1 tablespoon prepared mustard
1 cup canned tomatoes
salt
1 teaspoon Hungarian paprika (see p. 4)
½ cup sour cream

The mustard that Helmut Ripperger puts into his version of veal paprika makes it a little different from and a little better than most versions of this Hungarian dish. *Serve with noodles—homemade, if possible; mixed greens with French dressing; salt sticks.*

Brown veal in bacon fat. Transfer to a shallow casserole that has a lid. Brown onions in the same fat. Sprinkle flour over onions in skillet and stir well. Add mustard, tomatoes, salt, and about ½ cup water. Mix well and pour over veal. If it doesn't cover the veal, add more liquid—water or tomato juice. Cover casserole and bake in 350° oven 30 to 45 minutes, or until veal is tender. Then add paprika and sour cream, mixing well with the gravy. Do *not* cook after sour cream has been added, and do not strain gravy. The onions and tomatoes give an interesting texture. Serves 4. Time: 1 hour.

Veal Birds

1½ lbs. thin veal steak, cut in 2-x-4-inch pieces (save the scraps and chop fine)
3 tablespoons butter
½ pt. fresh, or 1 7-oz. can frozen, oysters
breadcrumbs, preferably coarse homemade ones
2 tablespoons melted butter
1 tablespoon lemon juice
1 egg, slightly beaten
1 tablespoon chopped parsley
1 small onion, minced
½ teaspoon marjoram
salt and pepper

Somewhat inhibited in title, but more emancipated in treatment. *Serve with baked rice pilaf (see index); cucumbers, radishes, and onions sliced thin in individual bowls with fresh sour cream; hot rolls; Belgian hothouse grapes.*

Sauté pieces of veal briefly in butter. Make a dressing, mixing oysters, veal scraps, breadcrumbs, melted butter, lemon juice, egg, parsley, onion, and seasoning. Divide filling and put on oblongs of veal, roll them, and secure with toothpicks or poultry nails. Salt and pepper. Place in low buttered casserole and pour in any remaining oyster liquid and water enough to reach halfway up the rolls. Cover tightly and simmer in 350° oven 20 to 25 minutes, or until veal is tender. Serves 4. Time: 1 hour.

Veal Viennese

1 lb. tender veal, cut in 1¼-inch squares
2 tablespoons butter
1 cup beef bouillon
1 tablespoon flour
1 cup sour cream
½ lb. noodles
1 tablespoon poppy seed
¼ cup toasted slivered almonds

The mildly tangy sour cream, the pungent poppy seeds, and the crisp taste and texture of the almonds point up the delicate flavor of the veal and the even blander noodles. *Serve with lettuce and thin slices of cucumber and radish, with French dressing; Melba toast.*

Sauté the squares of veal in butter until quite brown. Add bouillon. Mix flour with sour cream and add to bouillon and meat. Simmer until meat is tender, about 30 minutes. Meanwhile cook noodles until just barely tender. Rinse them with cold water, drain, and put in a medium-sized greased casserole. Pour in meat and sauce. Sprinkle with poppy seeds and toasted almond slivers. Bake in 350° oven just long enough for the flavors to mingle, about 15 minutes. Serves 4. Time: 50 minutes.

Veal with Squash

1½ lbs. veal, cut in ½-inch slices
3 tablespoons bacon drippings or olive oil
1 large onion, sliced thin
1½ lbs. yellow squash, sliced thin but not peeled
½ cup beef bouillon or broth
¼ teaspoon marjoram
salt and freshly ground black pepper
2 tablespoons butter

Serve with French-fried potatoes; cucumber sticks with salt and pepper; hot drop biscuits.

Sauté pieces of veal in fat in a skillet. Line a shallow casserole with the meat. Cover with thin onion rings. Brown squash lightly in the same fat, same skillet. Cover casserole with circles of squash. Pour in bouillon. Sprinkle top with seasonings and dot with butter. Bake in 375° oven until veal is fork-tender, about 45 minutes. Serves 4. Time: 1 hour.

Veal Loaf

3 lbs. veal, ground
2 cups soft homemade bread-crumbs
4 medium-sized onions, chopped fine
4 eggs
salt and lots of freshly ground black pepper

The veal stands alone in this old Pennsylvania meat loaf. *Serve with tomato pilaf (see index); hot rolls; rhubarb custard with meringue.*

Mix the veal, breadcrumbs, onion, eggs, salt, and freshly ground pepper. Put in a small loaf-shaped casserole and bake in a 300° oven for 1 hour. Serves 7 or 8. Time: 1¼ hours.

Veal with Tuna-Fish Sauce

1½ lbs. stewing veal, cut in pieces
4 anchovies
1 onion, minced
1 piece bay leaf
3 cloves
½ teaspoon salt
1 7-oz. can tuna fish in oil
1 tablespoon capers, drained
¼ cup olive oil

Veal with tuna fish is an Italian combination — though the Italians usually cook the meat in one piece and serve it cold, sliced. *Serve with escarole and 2 pieces of hearts of palm, sliced thin, with French dressing; hot poppy-seed rolls.*

Simmer veal in 1 cup water with 2 anchovies, onion, bay leaf, cloves, and salt, about 30 minutes or until veal is barely tender. Drain. Mix and beat tuna fish with the other 2 anchovies, capers, and olive oil, until mixture is smooth. Put veal in a shallow casserole with the tuna-fish sauce. Bake in 350° oven 15 to 20 minutes. Serves 4. Time: 1 hour.

Veal Curry

1½ lbs. veal, cut in 2-inch
  squares
¼ lb. butter
4 spring onions, tops and bottoms, chopped, or 1 medium-
  sized onion, chopped
1 tablespoon curry powder
1 clove garlic, minced
1 tart apple, cored and diced
1 cup uncooked rice
1 tiny package seedless raisins
½ teaspoon powdered ginger
salt and pepper
3 cups chicken broth

Strictly speaking, this is a curried risotto. No proper curry is ever baked with the rice, but this works and even tastes good. *Serve with mixed greens with French dressing; Vienna bread.*

Sauté veal on both sides in butter. Add onion, curry powder, garlic, apple, and rice. Cook until pale yellow. Transfer this buttery conglomeration to a casserole, add raisins, other seasonings, and broth. Cover tightly and bake in 350° oven 45 to 55 minutes or until veal is tender and liquid absorbed. Fluff with a fork. Serves 4 or more. Time: 1¼ hours.

Rub ½ lemon on your hands or chopping board to remove garlic, onion, or fish odors.

Babotee

4 tablespoons butter
1 tablespoon or more curry
  powder
1 medium-sized onion, chopped
1½ cups chopped cooked meat
  (beef, lamb, or what will you)
1 slice bread, crumbled and
  soaked in the juices from the
  meat
½ cup blanched and slivered
  almonds
juice of 1 lemon
grated peel of ½ lemon
salt and pepper
1 cup milk, scalded
1 bay leaf, crumbled
2 eggs, beaten

Now in South Africa many of the Dutch families, and some of the others, too, put their chopped meat in a curried custard. *Serve with rice, chutney, and baked apples.*

Melt butter. Sauté onion and curry powder in it and add to meat with crumbled bread. Mix and add almonds, lemon juice, grated lemon peel, salt, and pepper. Mix thoroughly and put in a shallow buttered casserole. Add scalded and slightly cooled milk and crumbled bay leaf to the beaten eggs and pour over meat. Put casserole in a pan with 1 inch water and bake in 350° oven until custard is firm and a knife inserted comes out nice and clean—about 40 to 55 minutes. Serves 4. Time: 1 hour.

Lamb Shanks with Dried Fruits

4 lamb shanks
salt and pepper
flour
2 tablespoons butter
2 large cloves garlic, minced
1 package mixed dried fruits
½ cup sugar
1 teaspoon cinnamon
½ teaspoon allspice
½ teaspoon ground cloves
¼ cup tarragon vinegar

Serve with nut and currant pilaf (rice cooked in chicken broth with currants and sprinkled with slivered almonds); watercress; brownie pudding (see index).

Dust lamb shanks with salt, pepper, and flour. Brown with garlic in butter. Put in a large casserole with dried fruits, sugar, seasonings, vinegar, and 3½ cups water. Cover tightly and bake in 350° oven about 1½ to 2 hours or until lamb shanks are tender. Serves 4 to 6. Time: 3½ hours.

Bacon and Veal Pie

1 lb. veal steak, cut in 2-inch squares
½ lb. lean bacon, sliced, and cut in 1-inch squares
3 eggs, hard-cooked and sliced
⅓ cup chopped parsley
¼ teaspoon marjoram
¼ teaspoon thyme
⅔ cup beef bouillon
salt and pepper
pie dough for 1 crust

Serve with potato salad garnished with chopped Pascal celery, sliced radishes, and cherry tomatoes; Swedish bread.

Sauté veal on both sides with bacon in bacon fat. Drain on paper towels. Arrange pieces of veal, bacon, and hard-cooked eggs in shallow casserole. Sprinkle with herbs. Add bouillon. Cover and bake in 350° oven about 50 minutes or until veal is tender. Season with salt and pepper and top with pastry. Increase heat to 400° and bake 15 to 20 minutes, or until browned. Serves 4. Time: 2 hours.

Shoulder Lamb Chops with Mandarin Oranges

4 thick shoulder lamb chops
1 cup uncooked rice
2 tangerines, peeled, separated in segments, or 1 buffet-sized can Mandarin oranges.
2½ cups beef bouillon
½ teaspoon dried mint
salt and pepper

Serve with romaine and cucumber sticks with French dressing; hot rolls.

Sear lamb chops briefly in their own fat. Place uncooked rice in the bottom of a low buttered casserole. Place chops over rice and arrange oranges on top. Pour in bouillon and sprinkle mint, salt, and pepper on top. Cover and bake in 350° oven 45 minutes. Serves 4. Time: 1 hour.

Saltimbocca Florentine

12 thin slices prosciutto (or
    Dutch or Danish ham), cut to
    fit the veal
1 lb. veal for scaloppine,
    pounded thin and cut in
    about 12 3-inch pieces
2 tablespoons butter or olive oil
1 clove garlic
1 package frozen spinach,
    cooked and drained
½ cup white wine
½ cup beef bouillon
salt and pepper

Prosciutto is a delicate and lightly smoked raw Italian ham. Canned cooked Danish or Dutch hams, also lightly smoked, may be used if no prosciutto is available. Our own hams are a little too bland for best results in this dish. *Serve with mixed greens with slivered Swiss cheese and salted almonds and French dressing; Italian bread.*

Put ham on veal pieces and roll them up, securing with toothpicks. Sauté in melted butter or oil. When browned remove and place to one side. Sauté garlic clove and spinach in the same oil until it is almost absorbed. Remove garlic and put spinach on the bottom of a shallow oiled casserole. Arrange meat rolls on top, and pour wine, bouillon, and seasonings over all. Bake about 30 minutes in a 350° oven, or until veal is tender. Serves 4. Time: 1 hour.

Lamb Shanks

4 meaty lamb shanks
2 large onions, in thick slices
2 cups milk
⅔ cup vinegar
½ lb. mushrooms, sliced
2 tablespoons butter
½ cup sour cream
salt and pepper

Lamb shanks are usually cheap, no matter how other meat prices fluctuate. Marinated in a milk and vinegar mixture overnight and cooked with sour cream and mushrooms, they make an extra special dish. *Serve with salad of grapefruit segments, sprinkled with celery seeds, on lettuce torn into pieces, with French dressing; salt-stick rye bread with sweet butter; good cold ale; apple crumb pie.*

Put lamb shanks in a casserole with onion slices and soak them overnight in milk mixed with vinegar. Next day cover and bake in a 325° oven for 2½ hours, cooking with the cover off the last ½ hour, to brown the meat. Sauté mushrooms in butter and add with sour cream, salt, and pepper to the casserole 5 minutes before serving. Serves 4. Time: 12 hours.

Lamb with Red Onions and Chick Peas

3 tablespoons bacon drippings
    or olive oil
1 clove garlic, minced
2 red onions, sliced
2 cups diced cooked lamb
½ teaspoon cinnamon
½ teaspoon turmeric
1 teaspoon grated lemon rind
1 teaspoon dried mint, crum-
    bled
½ cup beef bouillon
2 1-lb.-14-oz. cans chick peas,
    drained
⅓ cup chopped parsley
salt, pepper

A nice variation on the usual theme. *Serve with pilaf; chopped cucumbers; fresh mint and yogurt; pideh, the flat Near Eastern bread; boysenberry sherbet; macaroons.*

Sauté garlic and onions in bacon fat until limp. Discard the garlic and add lamb. Add cinnamon, turmeric, lemon rind, and mint. Transfer to a small casserole, add bouillon, chick peas, and parsley; season with salt and pepper. Heat in preheated 350° oven 20 to 30 minutes. Serves 4 to 6. Time: 50 minutes.

Stuffed Lamb Chops

4 thick loin lamb chops
1 lb. fresh green beans, broken
    into pieces, or 2 9-oz. packages
    frozen cut green beans,
    parboiled
2 tablespoons butter
2 tablespoons flour
salt and pepper
1 cup milk
1 small horseradish root,
    grated, or 4 tablespoons
    prepared horseradish
2 egg yolks
¼ cup breadcrumbs
3 tablespoons grated Parmesan
    cheese

We call them "stuffed" because that's the way we learned it and it's almost easier to remember than if they really were. *Serve with hot potato salad with French dressing; biscuits.*

Sauté lamb chops in their own fat on one side only. Place in low buttered casserole with sautéed side down and place green beans around them. Make a cream sauce, melting butter, adding flour, then salt, pepper, and milk very slowly, stirring until smooth and thick. Remove sauce from fire, cool slightly, add horseradish, and stir in yolks of eggs. Pour sauce over chops and beans, top with breadcrumbs mixed with cheese, and bake in 350° oven 45 minutes. Serves 4. Time: 1 hour.

Veal Batter Pie

1 egg
2 cups milk
½ teaspoon salt
½ teaspoon thyme
1 cup flour, sifted before measuring
2 cups tender cooked veal (about 1 lb.), cut into small cubes
2 tablespoons fat, preferably bacon fat
salt and pepper

Veal batter pie is an old-fashioned dish new to most people. It's a substantial and savory food, so go easy on the rest of the meal. *Serve with small individual bowls of chopped cucumber, sliced radishes, and chopped onion, covered with sour cream; Melba toast.*

Beat egg until light and then add milk, ½ teaspoon salt, and thyme. Make a well in the flour and stir in egg-and-milk mixture. Sauté pieces of veal briefly in the fat. Place veal in the bottom of a medium-sized buttered casserole. Season well with salt and pepper. Pour batter over the meat. Bake in 350° oven about 1 hour. Serves 4. Time: 1¼ hours.

Lamb Chops and Mashed Potato Pie

4 thick loin lamb chops
4 anchovies – preferably the curled ones
8 to 10 small white onions or 1 1-lb. can small boiled onions
2 tablespoons flour
1½ cups mashed potatoes
2 egg yolks, slightly beaten
salt and pepper
1 tablespoon chopped parsley and chives

This is really gilding the lily – a shepherd's pie with a fishy touch. *Serve with endive, lettuce, chopped chives, tarragon leaves, and French dressing; hot rolls.*

Make a slit in each chop and insert one anchovy. Sauté in lamb fat for 5 minutes on each side. Place in bottom of a low buttered casserole. Add onions. Make a gravy of lamb juices in pan, thickened with flour and thinned with water or juice from canned onions, and seasoning. Add to casserole. Add egg yolks to mashed potatoes. Place gently on top of casserole and sprinkle with parsley and chives. Bake in 375° oven 40 minutes or until top is puffy and brown and chops are tender when gently pierced with fork. Serves 4. Time: 1 hour.

Lamb Patties with Glazed Carrots and Italian Green Beans

2 cups raw carrots, peeled and diced
3 tablespoons melted butter
½ teaspoon salt
pinch of pepper
1 tablespoon sugar
1 tablespoon cornstarch
1½ tablespoons lemon juice
1 10-oz. package frozen Italian green beans, cooked
4 lamb patties
1 teaspoon dried mint

A pleasing combination of flavors, textures, and colors. *Serve with Boston lettuce with marinated red onion rings; hot corn sticks; pineapple cheesecake.*

Put carrots, water, melted butter, salt, pepper, sugar, cornstarch, and lemon juice in electric blender. Blend on high until carrots are all grated. Brown lamb patties on one side in a skillet. Arrange drained cooked green beans in a small shallow buttered casserole. Spoon carrot mixture over. Top with lamb patties, browned side down, and pour any juice from the pan over the casserole. Crush mint in your hand and sprinkle over the dish. Bake in preheated 350° oven 50 minutes to 1 hour, or until carrots taste cooked. Serves 4. Time: 1½ hours.

Lamb, Sweet Red Peppers and Prune Pilaf

1 medium onion, chopped
1½ lb. lean lamb, cut in stew-sized pieces
3 tablespoons bacon fat
3 cups beef bouillon
½ lb. prunes, soaked, seeded, and quartered
1 cup uncooked rice
½ lemon, sliced thin
½ teaspoon orégano
pepper
2 large sweet red peppers, cut in chunks, seeds and white part discarded

It is a good idea to add the sweet red peppers about 10 to 15 minutes before the end of the cooking time for a crisper texture. *Serve with poppy-seed rolls and a fruit compote.*

Sauté onion and lamb in bacon fat over low heat for about 10 minutes. Add 1 cup bouillon and simmer about 20 minutes. Transfer to a deep casserole with a lid. Add prunes, rice, lemon, seasonings, and the rest of the bouillon. Most bouillon has enough salt. The sweet red peppers may be added now or 30 minutes later. Cover and bake in 350° oven 45 minutes or 1 hour, or until lamb is tender (it varies) and rice has absorbed all the bouillon. Fluff with a fork. Serves 4. Time: 1½ hours.

Lamb Stew

1½ lbs. lamb shoulder, cut in 2-inch squares
salt and pepper
3 tablespoons olive oil
1 clove garlic, minced
6 spring onions, tops chopped but not the bottoms
2 medium-sized turnips, peeled and diced
6 small carrots, scraped and sliced
4 medium-sized potatoes, peeled and cut in ½-inch slices
2 cups beef bouillon
½ cup white wine
¼ teaspoon thyme
½ teaspoon marjoram
1 small bay leaf
flour

Serve with cottage cheese chilled with chopped chives, parsley, and fresh basil; hot butterflake rolls.

Season lamb with salt and pepper and sauté in olive oil with garlic and onions. Remove lamb and garlic. Cook turnips and carrots for a few minutes in the same skillet, until lightly browned. Place all the vegetables and lamb in a deep buttered casserole and mix well. Pour in bouillon, wine, and herbs. Cover tightly and simmer in 375° oven 1¼ hours or until lamb is tender. If a thickened gravy is desired, stir in flour and water mixed to a thin paste. Serves 4 or more. Time: 1¾ hours.

Lamb Stew with Fresh Pears

1½ lbs. lean lamb, cut in chunks
6 medium-sized, slightly green pears, quartered, cored
1 tablespoon ginger
1 9-oz. package frozen, or ¾ lb. fresh, green beans, frenched
salt and pepper
white wine

Serve with young leaf lettuce with sour-cream and poppy-seed dressing (½ cup sour cream, 1 teaspoon fresh lemon juice, ½ teaspoon dry mustard, 1 tablespoon poppy seeds); hot biscuits; Italian cheese cake (see index).

Trim excessive fat from lamb and brown the meat in its own remaining fat. Transfer to a casserole with a tightly fitting lid and add all ingredients except the wine. Cover and cook for about 1 hour in 350° oven. The juice from the pears should provide sufficient liquid, but add a little white wine if the stew starts to dry out. Serves 4. Time: 1¼ hours.

Lamb Stew with Dill

2 lbs. lamb shoulder or breast, cut in pieces
8 small whole onions, peeled
3 large turnips, peeled and diced
1 teaspoon Kitchen Bouquet
1 tablespoon salt
4 peppercorns
1 bay leaf
2 sprigs fresh dill, slightly crushed, or ½ teaspoon dried dill

DILL SAUCE

2 tablespoons butter
2 tablespoons flour
2 cups broth drained from stew
2 tablespoons chopped fresh dill or 1½ teaspoons dried dill
1 tablespoon vinegar
1 tablespoon sugar
salt and pepper
1 egg yolk, slightly beaten

When you are bored with the cooking and the family is bored with the food, sometimes all that is necessary is a change of seasoning. *Serve with slices of raw apples and oranges with sour-cream dressing (½ cup sour cream with 1 teaspoon lemon juice); Swedish flat bread.*

Cover meat, onions, and turnips with boiling water. Bring to a boil and skim. Add seasonings. Cover and cook in a 325° oven about 1 hour, or until the meat and vegetables are tender. To make the sauce, melt butter, add flour, and stir over low heat until well blended. Add broth slowly, stirring, until sauce is smooth and thick. Add dill, vinegar, sugar, salt and pepper to taste. Simmer 3 or 4 minutes. Remove from fire and stir in egg yolk. Stir into the casserole. Serves 4. Time: 1½ hours.

Lamb and Okra

2 lbs. lamb shoulder, cut in 2-inch squares
3 tablespoons olive oil
3½ cups (1-lb.-12-oz. can) tomatoes
1 cup bouillon
2 tablespoons grated lemon peel
1 lemon, sliced thin
8 to 10 tiny onions, peeled, or 1 1-lb. can small boiled onions
1 qt. fresh young okra, or 2 10-oz. packages frozen okra, tips and stems removed
¼ teaspoon thyme
salt and pepper

One of the prettiest of all stews of Balkan derivation. *Serve with hot potato salad with wine dressing (½ cup sauterne, ¼ cup olive oil, 3 tablespoons vinegar, 1 tablespoon sugar, 3 tablespoons chopped chives, salt and pepper; warm and add to warm potatoes); hot poppy-seed rolls (brown-and-serve kind).*

Sauté lamb in olive oil. Transfer to a deep buttered casserole. Add tomatoes, bouillon, grated peel, lemon slices, onions, and okra. Add seasoning and simmer gently in 350° oven for about 1 hour or until lamb is tender. Serves 4 or more, depending on your friends' appetites. Time: 1½ hours.

Yellow Squash with Armenian Lamb

2 medium-sized yellow squash (lucky home gardeners can use 8 tiny ones about 2 inches long)
2 tablespoons olive oil
½ lb. chopped lamb
1 tablespoon minced onion
¾ cup cooked rice
½ lemon, juice and grated peel
1 teaspoon ground cinnamon
salt and pepper

This is a Balkan recipe is unusual in its combination of seasonings. *Serve with artichoke hearts in French dressing; hot salt sticks (brown-and-serve); fresh figs and cream (or stewed black mission figs or canned Kadota figs).*

Parboil squash, halve them, and hollow out with a melon-ball scoop until the shells are ¼ inch thick. Heat oil. Sauté lamb and onion in it. Mix with cooked rice, lemon juice, grated peel, ground cinnamon, salt, and pepper, stirring enough to blend flavors thoroughly. Fill the cavities in the squash halves with the lamb mixture, being careful not to pack. Put in a large shallow casserole with ½ inch water in the bottom. Cover and bake in 350° oven ½ hour. Pour off surplus water before serving. Serves 4. Time: 1 hour.

Lamb Curry Pie

1½ lbs. shoulder lamb, cut in 2-inch pieces
10 small onions, or 1 1-lb. can small boiled onions
¾ teaspoon curry powder
1 tablespoon flour
½ cup seedless raisins
8 to 10 tiny new potatoes
salt and pepper
1 tube prepared biscuits

This is one to add your own flourishes to. *Serve with Russian radishes (radishes sliced lengthwise, buttered, and put together); hot rolls; apricot soufflé (see index).*

Simmer lamb and onions in 2 cups water, or water and canned onion juice, until tender. Mix curry powder and flour with water into a thin paste before adding to the stew, and stir in until smooth. Add raisins, potatoes, and seasoning. Put in casserole and cover with small biscuits. Bake at 425° for 20 minutes. Serves 4. Time: 1½ hours.

Shepherd's Pie No Shepherd Ever Saw

2 cups diced cooked lamb
2 1-lb. cans small boiled onions, drained (save juice)
1 cup grape jelly or spiced grape jam
1 teaspoon dry English mustard
salt and pepper
1½ cups mashed potatoes
1 package frozen French-fried onions

Serve with mixed greens and raw, peeled, sliced Jerusalem artichokes, with Roquefort cheese dressing; hot salt sticks (brown-and-serve).

Put lamb, onions, and grape jelly in the bottom of a shallow buttered casserole. Sprinkle with mustard, salt, and pepper. Top with mashed potatoes. Arrange rings of French-fried onions decoratively on top of the mashed potatoes. Put in a 350° oven 15 to 20 minutes, or until the top is slightly browned. Serves 4. Time: 30 minutes.

Tuscan Pancakes

1½ cups ground cooked lamb
1 teaspoon cinnamon
1 teaspoon salt
12 very thin pancakes about 4 inches in diameter, sautéed in butter (see index)

TOMATO SAUCE

3 tomatoes, peeled, seeded, and chopped fine
1 teaspoon sugar
1 teaspoon salt
1 tablespoon cognac

In most European countries pancakes are served many ways, as main dish or dessert. These are Italian pancakes with a Balkan touch in the seasoning. The recipe is from a Greek chef on an Egyptian ship. *Serve with canned hearts of artichokes, marinated in French dressing, drained, sprinkled with cooked peas; French bread;* crème Chantilly.

Mix lamb with cinnamon and salt. Put a spoonful on each pancake, roll pancakes up, and place side by side in a shallow casserole. Mix all sauce ingredients together and simmer until thick and smooth. (This can be done before making the pancakes if desired.) Pour sauce over rolled pancakes and bake in 350° oven about 20 minutes. Serves 4. Time: 1 hour, including pancake time.

Roast Pork with Kasha, Sour Cream, and Sour Cherries

1 cup medium-grind kasha
6 tablespoons butter
1 teaspoon salt
2 cups diced roast pork, turkey, duck, or chicken
½ cup chopped green onions
1 1-lb. can sour red pitted cherries, drained
1 pint sour cream
juice from cherries
2 tablespoons prepared horseradish

This can be made with equal pleasure with cooked turkey, duck, or chicken. *Serve with marinated red onion rings; hot poppy-seed rolls; wine sherbet with chocolate-nut meringues.*

Cook kasha in 3 tablespoons butter, stirring until all kasha has been well coated. Add the salt to 2 cups water and pour over kasha. Bring to a boil, cover, turn heat down, and cook 25 to 30 minutes. Fluff kasha with a fork and put in a shallow buttered casserole. Strew pork over kasha. Cook onions in the rest of the butter until limp. Mix with cherries and pour with the cooking butter over the pork. Thin sour cream with 2 or 3 tablespoons juice from cherries and add prepared horseradish. Pour over the casserole. Bake in preheated 350° oven about 30 minutes. Serves 4 to 6. Time: 1½ hours.

Pork Chops with Chestnuts and Red Cabbage

1 lb. pork, cut for stew
1 lb. sweet Italian sausage, cut in halves
1 medium head red cabbage, shredded
¾ cup red wine
½ cup wine vinegar
12 chestnuts, peeled and cooked
1 lb. cooking apples, cored and sliced but not peeled
1 lb. onions, sliced
¼ cup brown sugar
¼ cup chopped parsley
½ teaspoon cloves
½ teaspoon cinnamon
salt, cracked black pepper
⅓ cup currant jelly

Freshly roasted chestnuts sold from pushcarts in New York City provide one of the exciting and indigenous cold-weather aromas that tempt one to buy, much as does the smell of freshly roasted coffee or the too rare smell of a good bakery that still bakes its own bread. Chestnuts may be prepared at home by cutting a cross in the top and roasting in the oven, or by soaking Italian dried ones and then simmering until tender. *Serve with poppy-seed rolls; marinated beet-and-celery salad; caramel custard.*

Brown pork and sausages in their own juices or fat. Put in a deep casserole with cabbage, wine, vinegar, chestnuts, apples, onions, sugar, parsley, and seasonings. Cover and bake in preheated 350° oven about 1½ hours. Just before serving, stir in the currant jelly. Serves 6 to 8. Time: 2 hours.

Pork Chops Baked in Sour Cream

4 thick loin pork chops
flour
²/₃ cup sour cream
2 tablespoons lemon juice
½ teaspoon grated lemon peel
1 teaspoon sugar
salt and pepper
½ teaspoon thyme

For some there is ambrosia. For others there are pork chops baked in sour cream and served with hot broiled fruit. It is all a matter of opinion. *Serve with broiled fruit (brush slices of orange and grapefruit with honey and put them in a pie plate, or a fireproof platter, with whole strawberries; broil about three inches from the flame until brown); hot poppy-seed rolls (brown-and-serve); warm gingerbread.*

Dredge chops lightly with flour. Melt a small amount of pork fat in a skillet and brown chops on both sides. Put chops in a shallow casserole. Mix sour cream, lemon juice, grated lemon peel, sugar, salt, pepper, and thyme. Dilute with ½ cup water and pour over chops. Cover and bake in preheated 350° oven 50 mintues or until chops are tender. Serves 4. Time: 1 hour.

Pork Chops and Rice

4 thick loin pork chops
¼ cup uncooked rice
4 thick slices Bermuda onion
4 thick slices green pepper, without seeds
4 thick slices fresh tomatoes
2½ cups beef bouillon — water may be used but never adds anything but water to a dish
¼ teaspoon thyme
½ teaspoon marjoram
salt and pepper

This is really a mixed grill that doesn't need to be watched. *Serve with pickled beets; very thin rye-bread toast; cinnamon roll and apple pudding (see index).*

Sauté chops on both sides in their own fat. Place chops in a low buttered casserole and place on each chop 1 tablespoon dry rice, 1 slice onion, 1 slice pepper, 1 slice tomato. Pour bouillon over all and sprinkle with herbs, salt, and pepper. Cover and simmer in 350° oven about 50 minutes or until chops are tender and most of the liquid is absorbed. Serves 4. Time: 1 hour.

Szekely Goulash

3 tablespoons oil
1 lb. lean veal, cut for stew
1 lb. lean pork, cut for stew
2 lbs. bulk sauerkraut or 2 lbs.
  canned sauerkraut
1 cup canned tomatoes
2 tablespoons caraway seeds
salt, pepper
1 pint sour cream

Most Americans who think they don't like sauerkraut do when it is muted by sour cream and caraway seed. *Serve with boiled new potatoes; mixed green salad; French bread; apple crisp.*

Brown veal and pork in the oil. Rinse sauerkraut with cold water and squeeze out most of the juice. Put in a deep casserole with veal and pork. Mix tomatoes, caraway seed, salt and pepper, and add to casserole. Cover and bake in 350° oven 1 to 1½ hours or until meat is tender. Just before serving, stir in sour cream. Serves 4. Time: 2 hours.

Pork Chops with Curried Apples and Celery

4 thick rib or loin pork chops
  (about 1½ lbs.)
⅓ cup chopped onion
3 tablespoons butter
1 teaspoon curry powder
¼ teaspoon cinnamon
2 cups diced celery
1½ cups diced cooking apples
  (do not peel)
1½ cups chicken broth
salt, pepper

When curry powder is cooked briefly with fat, the flavor is released in a special way and the aroma is intoxicating. *Serve with tossed green salad; hot cornsticks; cherry pudding.*

Brown chops on both sides in their own fat. Remove and drain on paper. Sauté onions in butter, add curry powder and cinnamon, and cook until onions are translucent. Put in a casserole with celery and apples. Add broth, salt, and pepper. Top with pork chops. Bake in a preheated 350° oven 1 hour or more. Serves 4. Time: 1½ hours.

Pork Chops and Sauerkraut

4 thick pork chops
1 qt. sauerkraut, or 3 cups
  canned sauerkraut, drained,
  rinsed, and squeezed
3½ cups (1-lb.-12-oz. can) tomatoes
1 tablespoon paprika
salt but *no* pepper

Most of you know these separately, but until you combine them in your casserole their harmonious blending may have escaped you. *Serve with potato salad with chopped green peppers; pumpernickel; fresh cherries.*

Sear chops in frying pan. Place chops on bottom of deep buttered casserole, cover with sauerkraut, add tomatoes, paprika, and salt. Cover and simmer slowly in 350° oven for 1 hour. Serves 4. Time: 1¼ hours.

Pork Chops with Sour Cherries

4 thick loin pork chops
1 cup uncooked rice
2 cups canned sour cherries
1 tablespoon sugar
grated peel of ½ lemon
pinch of cinnamon
salt and pepper

Serve with salad of thin slices of sweet Bermuda onion pulled into rings, lettuce, and French dressing; hot rolls.

Brown pork chops on both sides in their own fat. Place rice in bottom of casserole, pour cherries and their juice over it, plus ⅔ cup water. Sprinkle sugar, lemon peel, and cinnamon over this, arrange pork chops on top, salt and pepper, and cover. Bake in 350° oven 1 hour or until liquid is absorbed. Lift chops and fluff rice with a fork. Replace and serve. Serves 4. Time: 1¼ hours.

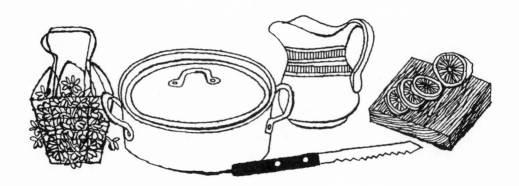

Pork Chops and Spinach

4 thick pork chops
8 to 10 tiny new potatoes, fresh or frozen
1 10-oz. package frozen chopped spinach, thawed
2 tablespoons butter
2 tablespoons flour
salt and pepper
¼ teaspoon nutmeg
1 cup milk
grated cheese

Very simple. Very hearty. *Serve with salad of lettuce, yellow plum tomatoes, with French dressing; whole-wheat muffins; brandied black Bing cherries.*

Sauté pork chops and new potatoes in the fat from chops. Mix potatoes with spinach in the bottom of low buttered casserole. Place pork chops on top. Make a cream sauce: melt butter, blend in flour, add the seasonings and milk very slowly. Cook and stir until smooth and thickened. Pour over chops and sprinkle grated cheese on top. Bake in 375° oven 50 minutes. Serves 4. Time: 1¼ hours.

Pork Pie with Cauliflower

1½ lbs. pork, cut in 1-inch pieces
flour
2 tablespoons butter
1 small cauliflower or 1 10-oz. package frozen cauliflower
1 8-oz. can tomato sauce
¼ green pepper, chopped, without seeds
salt and pepper
thyme
2 cups prepared biscuit flour
¾ cup milk

If the odor of cauliflower cooking offends you, this is not for you. *Serve with salad of cottage cheese, sour cream, chopped green peppers, chopped stuffed olives; crusty rolls.*

Dust meat with flour and brown in butter. Barely cover with water and simmer ½ hour. Parboil uncooked cauliflower and break into flowerets. Put in casserole with pork. Add tomato sauce, pepper, and seasoning. Mix biscuit flour with milk and roll it gently. Cover casserole with dough, leaving a hole in the center for steam. Bake 20 minutes in 450° oven or until biscuit top is done. Serves 4. Time: 1 hour.

Pork Chops Baked in Winy Plum Sauce

4 thick loin pork chops, excess fat trimmed off
salt and pepper
pinch of sage
flour
1 jar strained plums for babies
½ cup port wine
1 teaspoon grated lemon peel
½ teaspoon cinnamon
¼ teaspoon ground cloves

There is a natural and almost obligatory affinity between the rich, bland taste of pork and the flavor of mildly acid fruits—apples, cherries, plums, and, of course, oranges, limes, and tangerines. On a night when all monetary caution has been thrown to the winds, vary this dish by using a jar of brandied black Bing cherries instead of the plums, wine, and spices. *Serve with potato and watercress salad (equal parts of fresh chopped watercress and diced boiled potatoes marinated in French dressing); Swedish bread; rhubarb pudding with meringue (see index).*

Season chops on both sides with salt and pepper and a very tiny pinch of sage. Flour lightly and brown on both sides, using no fat but that on the chops. Transfer to a shallow buttered baking dish. Mix plums with wine, lemon peel, cinnamon, and cloves, and pour over chops. Bake in 325° oven 50 minutes, or until tender. If the sauce starts to dry out, add a little, very little, water. Serves 4. Time: 1 hour.

1 lemon gives 2-3 Tablespoons juice and 2 teaspoons rind.

Pork Tenderloin with Apples and Prunes

8 prunes, scalded and pitted
1 large apple, peeled, cored, and diced
1 pork tenderloin, split lengthwise but not cut all the way through
1 tablespoon cinnamon
salt
3 tablespoons butter
1 cup apple cider or apple juice

Pork tenderloin is pork concentrate; there should be no bony dilution of the meat, so have the butcher remove the bone from a rack of chops, or do it yourself. *Serve with sliced escarole and water chestnuts with French dressing (3 parts olive oil, 1 part fresh lime juice, grated lime peel, and salt); spoon bread (see index); Italian cheesecake (see index).*

Mix the two fruits and stuff mixture into the split in the tenderloin. Sprinkle with cinnamon and salt. Wrap string around tenderloin, roll and tie, or skewer with poultry nails. Sear in butter in a skillet. Put in an oblong or oval casserole with cider. Bake in 325° oven at least 50 minutes, until the meat is tender and the juices slightly thickened. Serve in the juices, but do not thicken them any more. Serves 4. Time: 1¼ hours.

Burgundy Spareribs with Apples

2 lbs. pork spareribs, cut apart
salt and pepper
⅓ cup chopped onion
⅓ cup chili sauce
¾ cup burgundy
4 tart apples, cored and halved
2 tablespoons brown sugar

A moist version of barbecued spareribs. *Serve with French-fried sweet potatoes; chicory with French dressing; Swedish bread.*

Wipe spareribs with a damp cloth and sprinkle them with salt and pepper. Place in a large shallow buttered casserole with a lid. Strew chopped onion over them. Mix chili sauce with burgundy and spread half the mixture over the ribs as evenly as possible (a pastry brush is best for this). Cover and bake 30 minutes in preheated 400° oven. At the end of this time surround meat with apple halves and spread the rest of the wine sauce over the apples. Sprinkle brown sugar on top, cover, and bake for 15 minutes. Uncover and bake 15 minutes more. Baste once or twice with the sauce in the pan during this period. Serves 4. Time: 1¼ hours.

Cassoulet

2 lbs. pork loin (See note above)
2 lbs. lamb shanks
2 lbs. dry Great Northern beans
½ lb. salt pork, diced
2 cloves garlic, minced
1 large onion, quartered
½ teaspoon thyme
2 bay leaves
¾ lb. Italian sweet sausage, Polish kielbasa, or homemade sausage with garlic
1 cup beef bouillon
salt
breadcrumbs

The exact combination of ingredients for Cassoulet is apt to make Frenchmen, especially those from the South of France, where the dish is said to have originated, very contentious. It is, basically, dried white beans baked slowly with various meats and their juices until the juices have permeated the beans and the flavors intermingled. There should always be pork or lamb, salt pork, and some garlic sausage. In Toulouse, where there are a lot of geese left over from making *foie gras,* goose fat preserved with pieces of geese, called *confit d'oie,* is considered obligatory, but the salt pork does as well. A roast duck, cut up and boned, with its juices, is an admirable alternate for the lamb. Vary your meat according to your wishes and supplies.

One of the rich and wondrous dishes in the French cuisine, with its many meats buried in the beans. This is a good robust dish for a buffet or an after-football dinner, or whenever lusty food is wanted that may be prepared ahead. Except for the shopping and the soaking of the beans, the over-all time is not excessive nor is the preparation at all arduous. *Serve with a light red wine; tossed green salad; French bread; platter of fruit.*

Roast pork and lamb shanks about 1 hour in a preheated 350° oven. Put beans and salt pork in a pan of boiling water, bring back to a boil for exactly 2 minutes. Remove from heat and let stand in water for 1 hour. As it cools, the beans will soak. When meat is cool enough to handle, cut in chunks; save all the juices and rind or skin. Discard bones. Drain beans, cover with fresh water, add salt pork, garlic, onion, thyme, and bay leaves. Simmer until beans are tender or the skin curls back when a few in a spoon are blown upon. Drain beans and salt pork and save liquid. Strain the liquid, discarding onion, garlic, and herbs. Put a layer of beans in a large deep casserole with a capacity of at least 4 quarts — preferably 6. Sprinkle with pieces of salt pork and any rind available, sausage cut in 1-inch pieces, and chunks of pork and lamb. Add the rest of the beans and pour in 1 cup bean liquid, 1 cup bouillon, and salt to taste. This much may be done a day or two ahead. Sprinkle the top with breadcrumbs and dot with butter or bacon drippings. Bring to a boil. Bake in a preheated 375° oven for 1 hour. As a crust forms, after about 20 minutes or so, break it and stir it into the bean mixture. You may do this twice more, turning in 3 crusts in all. On the other hand, you can just keep the first one if you wish, and not bother. Serve immediately. Serves 8 to 10. Time: 5 hours.

Spareribs and Lentils

1 lb. lentils
1½ lbs. spareribs, cut apart
2 tablespoons fat, preferably bacon drippings
6 carrots, scraped and sliced
2 onions, sliced thin
⅓ cup finely chopped parsley
3 cups or more beef bouillon (cubes and hot water may be used)

We do this with any kind of dried beans if we're out of lentils, or with the end of the ham if we've one to use up. But lentils and spareribs always taste the best. *Serve with watercress with French dressing; Italian bread.*

Soak lentils 2 or 3 hours in 2 cups water. Drain. Brown spareribs in fat in skillet. Put soaked lentils, spareribs, carrots, onions, parsley, in deep casserole with bouillon enough to cover. Cover and bake in 375° oven 2 to 3 hours or until lentils are tender. Serves 8. Time: 5 hours.

Cassoulet — Naturalized Version

1 lb. dried black-eyed peas or 2 1-lb. cans black-eyed peas
1 very small fresh pork shoulder
12 small white onions, or 1 1-lb. can small boiled onions
2 cloves garlic, minced
1 cup beef bouillon
1 cup white wine
2 tablespoons soy sauce (you need no salt when you use this)
bay leaf
½ teaspoon thyme
pepper

A robust but much, much modified version of the classic French dish. *Serve with salad of endive with white grapes, orange segments, and French dressing; corn bread.*

Soak peas overnight, if you use dried ones. Simmer them 30 minutes or until the skins curl back when a few are blown upon. Bake shoulder of fresh pork 30 minutes in a 450° oven. Place in bottom of casserole. Add peas, onions, garlic, bouillon, wine, soy sauce, bay leaf, thyme, and pepper. Cover and bake in 350° oven 3 hours. Serves 6. Time: 12 hours — 2 hours if canned peas are used.

Ham and Cauliflower

1 head cauliflower, pulled apart
1 cup diced cooked ham
½ cup grated sharp Cheddar
   cheese
3 eggs
1 tablespoon flour
2 cups half-and-half
salt, pepper

Serve with sliced orange-and-watercress salad; hot corn bread.

Cook the flowerets in salted water until almost tender. Drain. Arrange in a shallow buttered casserole and strew ham on top. Sprinkle with cheese, saving a bit for the top. Put eggs, flour, and half-and-half in the blender with seasoning and buzz briefly. Pour over cauliflower and ham. Sprinkle with the rest of the cheese. Bake in a preheated 325° oven until the mixture thickens and sets, about 30 minutes. Serves 4. Time: 50 minutes.

Wipe mushrooms with damp cloth; don't wash or peel unless tough or dirty. When slicing, cut off ends, slice through caps and stems.

Hominy and Ham in Cheese Sauce

½ lb. mushrooms, sliced
4 tablespoons butter
3 tablespoons flour
1½ cups milk
1 tablespoon prepared mustard
¾ cup grated Parmesan cheese
salt, pepper
3 tablespoons finely chopped
   parsley
1 1-lb.-13 oz. can whole hominy,
   drained
2 cups diced cooked ham or
   chicken

The whole hominy that can be bought in cans is best in this dish. *Serve with a salad of thin orange and onion slices with oil-and-lemon dressing and finely chopped chives; rum chiffon pie.*

Sauté mushrooms in butter until they look cooked but not browned. Remove with slotted spoon. Sprinkle flour in the same pan and cook over low heat until almost dry. Add milk, a little at a time, stirring constantly until smooth and thickened. Add mustard, grated cheese, salt, pepper, and parsley, and mix well. Put drained hominy in a casserole. Strew ham over it and pour in cheese sauce. Bake in 350° oven 40 to 50 minutes. Serves 4. Time: 1¼ hours.

Ham and Noodle Casserole

½ lb. egg noodles
4 tablespoons melted butter
1 lb. cooked ham, diced
3 eggs
1 cup milk
½ teaspoon salt

Noodles are one of the staples of the Middle European countries. Usually they are made fresh each time from the superb flour found there. Our flour is of slightly different texture; it makes a good noodle, better than the grocery-store ones, but this does take time. *Serve with cucumber salad; poppy-seed rolls; cherry turnovers.*

Cook noodles in a large amount of boiling salted water until barely tender and not mushy. Drain and transfer to 1-quart buttered casserole. Dribble melted butter over the noodles and strew ham on top. Buzz eggs, milk, and salt in a blender (or beat together) and pour over noodle-and-ham mixture. Bake in preheated 350° oven 35 to 50 minutes, or until the top is crusty and lightly browned. Serves 4. Time: 1½ hours.

Ham and Asparagus with Cheese Sauce

1½ lbs. fresh, or 2 10-oz. packages frozen, asparagus, cooked until tender
8 thin slices boiled ham
3 tablespoons butter
3 tablespoons flour
salt and pepper
1½ cups milk
1 cup grated Parmesan cheese

This is a good dish for luncheon or Sunday-night supper, and special enough for a guest. *Serve with salad of sliced raw red onion rings, soaked for an hour in diluted vinegar, drained, and dressed with olive oil, salt, and lots of freshly ground black pepper; macaroon soufflé (see index).*

Roll two stalks of cooked asparagus in each slice of boiled ham. Put two rolls in each of four individual casseroles. Make a sauce by melting butter, blending in flour, salt, and pepper, adding milk slowly, and cooking and stirring until smooth and thick. Add cheese and stir until it is melted and blended. Pour sauce over ham rolls and bake in 350° oven until piping hot and delicately browned, about 20 minutes. Serves 4. Time: 45 minutes.

Green Beans and Ham Baked in Cheese Sauce

2 lbs. fresh, or 2 9-oz. packages
  frozen, green beans, frenched
3 tablespoons butter
3 tablespoons flour
1 cup milk
½ teaspoon nutmeg
salt and pepper
1 cup grated Cheddar cheese
⅔ cup coarsely cubed ham, or 6
  slices diced cooked bacon

Serve with salad of tomato aspic with hearts of artichokes embedded in it, lettuce, French dressing, or mayonnaise; French bread; chocolate pudding made with slivered almonds and a jigger of rum.

Cook beans until tender. Make a sauce by melting butter and blending in flour until a smooth paste is formed, and then adding milk slowly. Cook until thickened. Add seasoning and cheese. Stir over low heat until cheese is melted. Drain beans and mix with cheese sauce. Pour into a buttered casserole and top with ham or bacon. Bake in 350° oven 20 to 25 minutes or until brown or bubbling. Serves 4. Time: 45 minutes.

Italian Potato Pie with Prosciutto

2 cups hot mashed potatoes
½ teaspoon salt
¼ teaspoon white pepper
pinch of nutmeg
milk
⅓ cup butter
¼ cup dry breadcrumbs (seasoned Italian ones work well
  in this)
¼ lb. Bel Paese or Swiss cheese,
  cut julienne
½ lb. prosciutto or baked ham,
  cut julienne
4 hard-cooked eggs, quartered

On a night when pressed for time, you can use instant mashed potatoes. They can be very good if you are watchful and wary. Sometimes, even in a busy supermarket, they acquire shelf age, which gives them an unpleasant off-flavor. Otherwise, cooked with milk instead of water and with a sizable lump of butter, they are good. *Serve with raw spinach salad with oil-and-vinegar dressing; fresh strawberries and heavy cream.*

Add to mashed potatoes seasonings and enough milk to make fluffy. Stir in 1 or 2 tablespoons butter. Butter a 9-inch ceramic pie or quiche plate or shallow casserole. Sprinkle with some of the breadcrumbs. Spread with half the potatoes, arrange cheese, ham, and eggs on these, then cover with the rest of the potatoes. Sprinkle with breadcrumbs and dot with small pieces of the rest of the butter. Bake at 400° 25 minutes or until lightly browned. Cut in wedges to serve. Serves 4 to 6. Time: 1 hour.

Black Beans with Ham in Sour Cream

1 lb. black beans, soaked and simmered until tender
1 lb. raw ham, diced, or ½ lb. bacon, diced
1 pt. sour cream
⅓ cup orange juice
1 teaspoon crumbled dry mint
½ teaspoon cinnamon
salt, pepper

Black beans now may be bought in cans in areas where people from the south of us live, but they are apt to be a little mushy and not as satisfactory as the canned kidney beans or dried limas. *Serve with hot rolls; fruit salad.*

Put drained beans in a casserole. Scald ham or sauté the bacon. Mix ham with beans. If bacon is used, add later. Mix sour cream with orange juice, mint, cinnamon, salt, and freshly ground black pepper. Add to beans and ham and mix. Sprinkle the top with bacon if that is used. Bake in a preheated 350° oven 30 to 40 minutes. Serves 4 to 6. Time: 1 hour.

Ham Baked with Endive

8 medium heads Belgian endive
3 tablespoons butter
1 tablespoon lemon juice
salt
8 thickish slices baked ham
½ cup freshly grated Parmesan cheese
freshly ground black pepper
1 cup heavy cream
half-and-half

At its best, and simplest, this dish induces a special kind of bliss. The best I believe to be when the endive is wrapped in ham cut from a baked country-cured one and cooked in heavy cream with no egg or flour-and-butter thickening. Even with adjustments to reality often necessary—i.e., delicatessen ham and cheese sauce—the dish is good. *Serve with plain boiled new potatoes; French bread; baked pears with a nut crust.*

Cook the well-washed heads of Belgian endive in butter over low heat, moving them around until they are slightly colored. Add lemon juice and some water, ¼ to ½ cup, depending upon size of pan. Cover tightly and cook 20 to 30 minutes or until tender. Remove, drain, and wrap each head in a slice of ham. Lay side by side in a shallow casserole where they fit closely. Sprinkle with Parmesan cheese and freshly ground black pepper. Add heavy cream. It should come almost to the top of the rolls; add more heavy cream or half-and-half, if necessary. Bake in preheated 350° oven 15 minutes. Just before serving put under the broiler so the top browns and blisters. Serves 4. Time: 50 minutes.

Argentine Ham and Cheese Pie (Torta de Queso y Jamon)

CRUST

2½ cups sifted all-purpose flour
1 teaspoon baking powder
salt, pepper
¼ lb. butter
1 egg
½ cup milk

FILLING

1½ lbs. mozzarella, sliced
5 or 6 slices cooked ham
1 egg, beaten
1½ tablespoons sesame seeds, toasted

The sesame seeds give a Mediterranean touch, and why not? The father of the Argentine doctor who gave me this recipe was from Syria. The crust is somewhat like an unsweetened cooky dough. A regular piecrust, with 2 tablespoons butter added for flavor, could be used. *Serve with a green salad with oil-and-vinegar dressing; follow with fresh diced fruit chilled in crème de cacao.*

For the crust, sift flour, baking powder, salt, and pepper. Cut in the cold butter, using a pastry blender or your fingers, and mix until somewhat like coarse corn meal. Add the egg and beat well. Add the milk, a little at a time. Make a large, soft ball. Let the dough rest about ½ hour at room temperature or overnight in the refrigerator. When ready to use, return to room temperature, divide in two, and pat out one half to fit a 9-inch ceramic or pottery pan.

Arrange half the mozzarella slices in pie shell. Add ham in overlapping slices. Arrange the rest of the mozzarella on ham. Roll or pat the rest of the dough in a circle to fit the top, and crimp the edges together. Paint top of crust with beaten egg. Sprinkle with sesame seeds. Bake in preheated 350° oven 45 to 55 minutes or until done. Serve as hot hors d'oeuvre or main dish. Cut in wedges, as with pizza. Serves 4 as a main dish. Time: 1½ hours.

Ham and Succotash

1 lb. raw ham, diced
1 10-oz. package frozen cut corn
1 10-oz. package frozen lima beans
1 9-oz. package frozen green beans
1 can condensed cream of Cheddar soup, undiluted
2 tablespoons finely chopped parsley

Streamlined Americana that may be as unstreamlined as you wish. *Serve with sliced tomatoes and lettuce with French dressing, garnished with small cubes of rattrap cheese; corn bread.*

Simmer the ham for 10 minutes. Place corn, lima beans, and green beans in a low buttered casserole. Add soup and drained ham. Sprinkle with parsley and bake in 325° oven about 45 to 50 minutes. Serves 4. Time: 1 hour or more.

Ham and Celery

2 bunches celery
1½ lbs. raw baking ham, diced
3 tablespoons butter
3 tablespoons flour
1½ cups milk
½ teaspoon dried basil
pinch of dry mustard
salt and pepper
8 to 10 tiny new potatoes, fresh
   or frozen
¼ cup coarsely chopped salted
   almonds

The almonds are a slightly unusual addition to this dish that give your guests something to mutter about. *Serve with asparagus and lettuce salad (canned tips with mayonnaise); fresh pears and* creme Chantilly.

Cut celery stalks in 1-inch pieces and simmer with ham and potatoes in water on top of stove for 15 minutes. Drain. Make a cream sauce, melting butter, blending in flour, and adding milk and seasonings gradually. Cook until well thickened, then add ham, celery, and potatoes. Pour into a low buttered casserole and top with chopped almonds. If the cream sauce is not thick enough, the almonds will sink in. Bake in 375° oven 25 minutes. Serves 4. Time: 50 minutes.

Ham Jambalaya

3 slices bacon, chopped
3 spring onions, tops and bulbs
   chopped
½ green pepper chopped, without seeds
1½ cups uncooked rice
2 cups beef broth or canned beef
   bouillon
2½ cups (1-lb. 4 oz. can)˅ tomatoes
¼ teaspoon paprika
¼ teaspoon thyme
a little salt
¾ lb. diced cooked ham
1 tablespoon chopped fresh
   herbs (parsley, chives, or
   basil)

One of the best-known New Orleans dishes, which has infinite variations. *Serve with endive and diced cucumbers with French dressing; Italian bread (sliced almost through, buttered, and browned in the oven); caramel pudding.*

Sauté bacon, onions, and pepper together until light brown. Place uncooked rice in bottom of casserole, add broth, tomatoes, paprika, thyme, salt, and meat. Cover and cook at 375° until rice is done—about 45 minutes. Sprinkle chopped fresh herbs (parsley is always obtainable, but the others are good) over the top and serve. Serves 4. Time: 1 hour.

Ham and Oranges

2 ¾-inch slices baking ham, cut in 2-inch pieces
7 or 8 cloves
small piece ginger root, or 1 teaspoon ground ginger
3 or 4 medium-sized boiled sweet potatoes, or 1 1-lb. can sweet potatoes
2 large oranges and peel of another
½ teaspoon powdered cinnamon

Fruit is a pleasing change from vegetables, too frequently forgotten when one is concocting casseroles. *Serve with chicory with lots of French dressing (2 parts olive oil, 1 part grapefruit juice, salt and pepper, dash of nutmeg); hot drop biscuits; coffee gelatin.*

Simmer ham 15 minutes, place in bottom of casserole, spike with cloves. Shave ginger root over ham, slice sweet potatoes and place over ham. Slice 2 of the oranges, unpeeled, and put on top, shake powdered cinnamon over them, grate the peel of the other orange and scatter it on top, add ½ cup water and bake in 350° oven 20 to 25 minutes. Serves 4. Time: 45 minutes.

Ham and Oyster Pie

1 lb. baking ham, diced
2 tablespoons butter
2 tablespoons flour
½ cup milk
½ cup white wine
oyster liquor
salt and pepper
1 pt. fresh, or 2 packages frozen, oysters
1½ lbs. fresh peas, shelled, or 1 10-oz. package frozen peas
2 cups prepared biscuit mix and 1 cup milk, or pastry for 1 crust

A delicate, festive, and yet hearty dish that appeals to the men. *Serve with romaine salad with French dressing; hot buttermilk biscuits.*

Simmer ham for 15 minutes while you make the cream sauce. Make sauce by melting butter, blending in flour, adding the liquids, including the juices from the oysters (there should be 1½ cups in all), and seasonings. Cook until smooth and thick. Drain ham, add to oysters and peas, and stir into cream sauce. Pour into a low buttered casserole. Mix lightly 2 cups prepared biscuit flour with 1 cup milk, or use any basic biscuit recipe, and pour dough on top of the casserole. For a more delicate version, use pastry for the top; crimp the edges and cut slits for the steam. Bake 30 minutes in 350° oven. Serves 4. Time: 1 hour.

Ham Baked with Onions and Cream

4 large onions, boiled until tender
2 tablespoons butter
4 slices bacon, diced and cooked
1 cup diced cooked ham
1 tablespoon melted bacon fat
2 eggs
1½ cups medium cream
salt and freshly ground black pepper

Some old friends in an unusual combination. *Serve with Italian eggplant relish (available in tiny cans in supermarkets); hot rolls; fresh peaches, peeled, chilled, and served in red wine.*

Quarter the onions and arrange in a shallow casserole with the butter. Bake in 350° oven until golden, about 15 to 20 minutes. Add bacon and the ham and melted bacon drippings. Beat eggs with cream, salt, and freshly ground black pepper. Pour over onions and bake in 350° oven until a pretty brown — about 30 to 35 minutes. Serves 4. Time: 1¼ hours.

Garnish the Pig

2 cups chopped raw spinach
2 cups chopped raw mustard greens
2 cups chopped watercress
¼ cup chopped parsley
1 lb. raw ham, cubed
1 onion, peeled and minced
1 cup concentrated chicken broth
pinch of marjoram
salt and pepper

This title is somewhat of a misnomer — after all, it's the pig that is garnishing the greens. *Serve with cottage cheese with chopped black olives and thinly sliced radishes; corn bread.*

Wash the greens thoroughly and shake off excess water. Chop and measure. Sauté ham and onion 10 minutes in some of the ham fat. Put greens, onion, ham, broth, and seasonings in a buttered shallow casserole, cover and bake 15 minutes in 350° oven. Serves 3 to 4. Time: 35 minutes.

Ham and Tomato Okra Pilau

3 slices bacon, diced
1 small onion, chopped
1 cup uncooked rice
2 cups thinly sliced okra or 1 10-oz. package frozen okra
2½ cups (1-lb.-4 oz. can) tomatoes
1 cup tomato juice
salt and pepper
1 cup diced cooked ham

Simple, succulent, and Southern. *Serve with hot poppy-seed rolls; honeydew melon.*

Sauté bacon. Remove and drain on paper towels. Cook onion and rice in the bacon fat until rice is translucent. Put onion, rice, bacon fat in a deep casserole with okra, tomatoes, tomato juice, salt, and pepper. Cover and cook in 350° oven 30 minutes or until liquid is absorbed. Remove from oven, fluff with a fork, and add cooked bacon and ham. Serves 4. Time: 50 minutes.

Ham Rolls with Cottage Cheese in Sour Cream

1 8-oz. carton cottage cheese

3 spring onions, tops and bottoms chopped fine

½ teaspoon dry mustard

salt

½ bunch watercress, stripped from the stems and finely chopped

12 thin slices home-baked ham

1 pt. sour cream

This is one of the good dishes to make with that ham you baked. It is not very good made with the rather flavorless boiled ham bought sliced at the delicatessen, but some of the spicier cold cuts might be an interesting variation. *Serve with potato puffs (frozen); escarole with tomato aspic; pumpernickel.*

Mix cottage cheese with spring onions, dry mustard, salt, and watercress. Divide into twelve parts and put one part on each piece of ham. Roll ham up, tucking in edges neatly so that each roll is a tidy package. (Skewer them with toothpicks if you are the very tidy type.) Arrange side by side in a shallow casserole. Pour in sour cream. Bake in 350° oven about 20 minutes. The cream will separate slightly when heated, but that does not affect the flavor. Serves 4. Time: 30 minutes.

Erik Lyhne's One Dish

4 medium-sized onions, sliced

2 tablespoons butter

1 cup diced cooked ham, sausage, or other meat

4 hard-cooked eggs, sliced

4 medium-sized boiled potatoes, sliced thin

Erik's soubise sauce

2 large onions, finely minced

3 tablespoons butter

2 tablespoons flour

1 cup veal or chicken broth

1 teaspoon sugar

salt

2 tablespoons cream

4 tablespoons butter

Erik Lyhne, a Danish dress designer, cooks very well, but only one dish—and this is it. *Serve with mixed greens with French dressing; pumpernickel; fresh plums.*

Sauté sliced onions in 2 tablespoons butter for 10 minutes. Put onions, ham, eggs, and potatoes in a casserole in layers. To make the sauce, sauté minced onions in 3 tablespoons butter until pale yellow. Blend in flour. Add broth slowly, sugar and salt, and cook over a very low flame about 20 minutes. Put through a sieve and add cream and 4 tablespoons butter. Stir and pour into casserole. Bake in 350° oven ½ hour and put under the broiler for a few minutes to brown the top. Serves 4. Time: 1¼ hours.

Ham Soufflé

6 tablespoons quick-cooking
  tapioca
salt and pepper
2 teaspoons grated onion
¾ cup milk
¾ cup ham stock or chicken
  broth
1 cup ground or finely diced
  ham
¼ cup finely chopped parsley
3 eggs, separated

To keep egg yolks, cover with cold water and refrigerate.

A soufflé with an interesting and slightly un-usual texture. It's also a way to keep you from being bored with the last of the ham. *Serve with romaine and sliced avocado sprinkled with finely minced onion, lime juice, and salt; English muffins, split and sprinkled with grated Swiss cheese, then put under the broiler until brown and bubbly; fresh raspberries with cream.*

Combine tapioca, salt, pepper, onion, milk, and stock or broth in pan and cook over medium heat, stirring constantly. Remove from heat when the mixture comes to a full boil. Add ham and parsley. Allow to cool slightly while beating egg whites until stiff. Add the egg yolks to the tapioca, mix well, and gently fold in the egg whites. Put into a greased deep baking dish with straight sides. Bake in 350° oven 45 to 50 minutes, or until soufflé springs back when lightly touched. Serves 4. Time: 1¼ hours.

Schinken Kartoffeln

6 raw potatoes, scraped and
  sliced thin
3 Bermuda onions, sliced thin
4 green peppers, sliced thin and
  seeds removed
1½ lbs. cooked ham, cut in
  chunks
salt
2 cups milk
2 eggs
freshly grated Parmesan cheese

This German dish is one of the best of all ways of combining ham with other foods, according to our prejudiced way of thinking. *Serve with salad of chicory, grapefruit segments with French dressing (2 parts olive oil, 1 part grapefruit juice, salt and pepper); hot rolls.*

Butter a deep casserole. Put a layer of raw potatoes on the bottom, a layer of onions, of green peppers, and finally of ham. Sprinkle with a little salt, depending upon how salty ham is. Repeat until all ingredients are used. Beat eggs and milk together and pour in casse-role. Cover tightly and bake in 350° oven 45 minutes, or until vegetables are tender and the egg and milk custardy. Just before serving, sprinkle grated Parmesan cheese on top. Serves 4 or more. Time: 1 hour.

Ham and Pea Soufflé

1 can frozen concentrated cream of pea soup, thawed but undiluted
4 tablespoons flour
1 teaspoon dry English mustard
⅔ cup ground ham or 6 slices cooked bacon, crumbled
3 eggs, separated

Serve with Caesar salad; hot poppy-seed rolls (brown-and-serve); lemon chiffon pie.

Mix soup, flour, mustard, ham, and egg yolks together. Whip the whites until stiff; fold in gently. Pile into a buttered casserole with straight sides. Bake in 350° oven 50 to 60 minutes or until the top springs back when lightly touched. Serves 4. Time: 1 hour.

Ham and Spinach Soufflé

3 tablespoons butter
3 tablespoons flour
1 cup milk
½ teaspoon marjoram
salt and pepper
4 eggs, separated
1 cup ground cooked ham
2 cups chopped fresh spinach, or 1 10-oz. package frozen chopped spinach, slightly thawed

Serve with tiny new potatoes boiled and served in their skins; salad of lettuce, cucumbers, tomatoes, a few thin slices of onion, with plain fresh sour cream, sprinkled with minced chives; corn muffins; canned pears with chocolate sauce.

Make cream sauce, melting butter, blending in flour, and adding milk, marjoram, salt, and pepper. Remove from stove and stir in yolks of eggs. When smooth, add ham and spinach. Beat egg whites until stiff, fold in gently, and transfer mixture to a low buttered casserole. Bake in 350° oven 40 to 45 minutes, or until the top springs back when lightly touched. Serves 4. Time: 1 hour.

Sausages in Wine

1 lb. link sausages
3 medium-sized potatoes, boiled, peeled, and diced
¼ lb. fresh, or 1 6-oz. package frozen, mushrooms, sliced
½ cup white wine
¼ cup cream
2 tablespoons butter
a little salt and pepper

Serve with grapefruit segments and fresh orange segments dressed with sour cream zipped up with brandy; Italian bread, cut in hunks.

Fry sausages and potatoes in a dry skillet long enough to brown the potatoes and get some of the grease out of the sausages. Drain carefully. Place in a low buttered casserole with mushrooms, wine, cream, butter, and seasoning. Cover and bake in 325° oven 25 minutes. Serves 4. Time: 40 minutes.

Flageolets and Sausages with Aioli

1 lb. flageolets, soaked and simmered until tender.
1 10½-oz. can beef gravy
¼ cup red wine
salt, pepper
½ lb. Italian sweet sausages, sautéed briefly
aioli

Flageolets are tender dried green French beans—alas, not too well known here. Lentils could be used. Aioli is mayonnaise made with garlic. A good brand of mayonnaise, *not* salad dressing, with the juice of 2 cloves of garlic stirred in, could be used, but it will not be as good as that made in a blender or by hand. *Serve with sweet red peppers; poppy-seed rolls; cream puffs with coffee-flavored whipped cream.*

Put drained cooked flageolets in casserole. Mix beef gravy with wine, salt, and pepper and add to beans. Top with sausages. Bake in 350° oven 30 minutes. Serve with aioli in separate bowl. Serves 4. Time: 35 minutes.

Sausages, Oranges, and Sweet Potatoes

1 lb. good link sausages (Jones or Deerfoot)
3 medium-sized sweet potatoes, boiled and sliced, or 1 1-lb. can sweet potatoes, sliced
salt and pepper
2 medium-sized onions, sliced thin
2 oranges, sliced, rind and all, with seeds removed
1 teaspoon dried mint, or 1 tablespoon chopped fresh mint
⅓ cup bouillon

Sausages are all very fine for breakfast, but much more versatile than that. They are, for instance, a dominant part of a quickly assembled casserole such as this. *Serve with romaine with hearts of artichokes and French dressing; corn bread.*

Sauté sausages to remove excess fat. Drain on paper towels. Arrange slices of sweet potato in the bottom of a medium-sized casserole. Salt and pepper them and add onions. Add orange slices and sprinkle with mint. Place sausages symmetrically on top. Add bouillon. Bake in 350° oven 45 to 50 minutes. Serves 4. Time: 1 hour.

Baked Peppers with Macaroni and Sausage

8 large green peppers
½ lb. country sausage
3 cups cooked macaroni,
   drained
⅓ cup chili sauce
grated Parmesan cheese
1 tablespoon chopped chives

To fill in the budget gap made by a fancy meal. Good (very) and cheap (very). *Serve with cottage cheese in individual wooden bowls, mixed with sour cream and horseradish, and garnished with watercress; Italian bread sticks.*

Cut away tops of peppers and remove seeds and fibers. Parboil 5 minutes, drain, and cover with cold water. Sauté sausage, crumbling it as it cooks, pour off excess fat, mix with drained macaroni and chili sauce. Drain peppers, fill with mixture, place in casserole, and cover with grated cheese and chopped chives. Pour ½ cup water around peppers and bake in 350° oven until well heated and as brown on top as you like—about 15 to 20 minutes. Serves 4. Time: 30 minutes.

1 tablespoon butter or oil in water for boiling pasta helps to prevent it from sticking together.

Canadian Bacon with Lima Beans

4 medium-sized sweet potatoes,
   peeled and sliced thin, or 1
   1-lb. can sweet potatoes, sliced
1 tablespoon chopped parsley
½ teaspoon thyme
very little salt, pepper
1 pt. fresh, or 1 10-oz. package
   frozen, lima beans
½ lb. Canadian bacon, sliced
   thin
1½ cups chicken broth

Canadian bacon isn't really bacon; it's a very nice smoked pork tenderloin that comes in small, neat, round slices. It's very salty, so don't put much salt with this dish. *Serve with Italian salad (cooked green peas, diced beets, carrots, and celery) with French dressing; poppy-seed bread cut in hunks.*

Place sweet potatoes at the bottom of low buttered casserole. Sprinkle with parsley, thyme, salt, and pepper. Add lima beans and top with overlapping slices of Canadian bacon. Pour chicken broth over top. Bake in 350° oven 45 minutes, or until sweet potatoes and lima beans are tender. Serves 4. Time: 1 hour.

Canadian Bacon with Cranberries

4 medium-sized sweet potatoes,
boiled and sliced, or 1 1-lb.
can sweet potatoes, sliced
1 lb. raw cranberries plus 1 cup
honey, or 1 1-lb. jar whole-
cranberry sauce plus ⅓ cup
honey
1 teaspoon allspice
a little salt and a dash of freshly
ground pepper
½ cup chicken broth
1 lb. Canadian bacon, cut in
thick slices

*Serve with escarole with raisins and pignolias sprin-
kled between the leaves and then steamed for about
five minutes; corn sticks; toasted angel-food cake
slices, spread with frozen fruit.*

Arrange sweet potatoes on the bottom of a
medium-sized casserole that has a lid. Next
add raw cranberries and larger amount of
honey or whole-cranberry sauce with a smaller
amount of honey. Sprinkle with allspice (it
gives an unusual emphasis), add chicken broth
and salt and pepper. Arrange slices of Canadian bacon on top. Cover and bake in 350°
oven 30 minutes. Serves 4. Time: 45 minutes.

Canadian Bacon with Apples and Red Wine

4 medium-sized sweet potatoes,
boiled and sliced, or 1 1-lb.
can sweet potatoes, sliced
4 large cooking apples, peeled,
cored, and sliced, or 1 1-lb.
can sliced pie apples
2 tablespoons brown sugar
pinch of cinnamon
grated peel of ½ lemon
salt and pepper
½ lb. Canadian bacon, sliced
thin
1 cup red wine, preferably
claret

Any light red wine — say a cabernet or claret —
will do. Drink the same wine with the meal.
*Serve with mixed greens (watercress, chicory, endive,
and a little chopped parsley, for instance) with
French dressing; hot buttermilk biscuits.*

Place sweet potatoes on bottom of low buttered
casserole. Arrange apple slices in layer over
them. Sprinkle with sugar, cinnamon, grated
lemon peel, salt, and pepper — and go easy on
the salt because the bacon is quite salty. Top
with a neatly arranged circle of bacon slices
and pour in wine. Bake in 350° oven 30 minutes. Serves 4. Time: 45 minutes.

Canadian Bacon with Oyster Plant

2 bunches oyster plant, scraped
and sliced thin
3 medium-sized potatoes, or 8 to
10 frozen new potatoes boiled,
peeled, and diced
4 tablespoons butter
2 tablespoons flour
1 cup milk
salt and pepper
1 tablespoon chopped chives
1 tablespoon chopped parsley
1 lb. Canadian bacon, sliced
thin

Serve with salad of tomatoes, cucumber, and a little onion, cubed, with salt, freshly ground black pepper, and sour cream; Italian bread, cut in hunks.

Soak oyster plant in cold water with a little vinegar to keep it white. Drain and parboil in fresh water for 15 minutes. Brown potatoes in 2 tablespoons butter. Melt 2 more tablespoons butter, blend in flour, and add milk and seasoning slowly, stirring until smooth and thickened. Add drained oyster plant and browned potatoes. Stir in chives and parsley. Remove to a low buttered casserole. Arrange Canadian bacon on top and bake in 350° oven 50 minutes. Serves 4. Time: 1½ hours.

Sliced Veal Hearts Baked in Sour Cream and Madeira

4 veal hearts (or 2 beef hearts),
sliced thin, with veins and fat
removed
¼ lb. fresh mushrooms, sliced
thin (or 1 tablespoon dried
mushrooms soaked in ¼ cup
water)
3 tablespoons butter
1 pt. sour cream
3 medium-sized potatoes, or 8
to 10 frozen new potatoes,
boiled and diced
1 jigger Madeira wine
salt and freshly ground pepper

Veal and beef hearts are among the most neglected of the variety meats—and among the most delicious. *Serve with watercress with orange and grapefruit segments and Roquefort cheese dressing; hot rolls.*

Sauté slices of heart and mushrooms (if fresh are used) in butter. Transfer to a shallow casserole that has a lid. Add sour cream and potatoes, then Madeira and salt and pepper. (If dried mushrooms are used, add, with the water in which they soaked.) Cover and cook in preheated 325° oven 50 to 60 minutes, or until the hearts are tender. The cream will clot a bit, but that does not affect the flavor. Serves 4. Time: 1¼ hours.

Baked Sliced Veal Hearts with Lima Beans

2 veal hearts, veins and fat removed, sliced
3 tablespoons oil
1 10-oz. package frozen Fordhook lima beans
1 9-oz. package frozen artichoke hearts, thawed and quartered
1 tablespoon finely chopped onion
3 tablespoons butter
3 tablespoons flour
1½ cups chicken broth
2 tablespoons lemon juice
1 teaspoon grated lemon peel
salt, white pepper

A refreshingly different combination of flavors and textures. *Serve with cherry tomatoes; hot corn bread; pineapple sherbet sprinkled with shaved chocolate.*

Sauté slices of heart in oil. Transfer to a casserole. Parboil lima beans for 10 minutes. Drain and add to casserole with thawed artichoke hearts. Sauté onion in butter until pale yellow. Sprinkle with flour and cook 2 or 3 minutes over low heat. Add chicken broth, a little at a time, stirring constantly until smooth and thickened. Add lemon juice, grated peel, salt, and white pepper. Pour over hearts, lima beans, and artichoke hearts. Bake in 350° oven 1 hour or more until hearts, lima beans, and artichoke hearts are tender. Serves 4. Time: 1½ hours.

Stuffed Veal Hearts in Claret with Apples

2 veal hearts—tubes, fat, membranes, and central partitions removed
3 tablespoons bacon fat
2 cups dry crumbled bread
4 tablespoons melted butter
1 medium-sized onion, chopped
½ celery stalk, chopped fine
1 tablespoon leaf sage
salt and pepper
6 baking apples, peeled and cored
1 cup claret or any good red wine

Serve with tiny new potatoes in warm sour cream with freshly ground black pepper; raw spinach salad with chopped hard-boiled egg and French dressing; hard rolls.

Sear the hearts in fat. Make a stuffing with dry bread, melted butter, onion, celery, sage, and salt and pepper. Stuff hearts, place in a casserole, and pack surplus stuffing (if any) in centers of apples. Encircle the hearts with the apples. Pour claret over everything. Bake in 350° oven 1¼ hours, or until fork-tender. Slice the hearts before serving. Serves 4. Time: 2 hours.

Parsley Hearts with New Potatoes

2 beef hearts or 4 veal hearts
1 bunch parsley, chopped
¼ lb. butter
8 tiny new potatoes, or 8 to 10
   frozen new potatoes, boiled
salt and pepper
2 tablespoons flour
½ cup cream
3 tablespoons currant jelly

Serve with young leaf lettuce with sour-cream and garlic dressing (½ cup sour cream mixed with 1 teaspoon lemon juice in which a garlic clove has been resting, salt, and lots of freshly ground black pepper); hot poppy-seed rolls.

Cut veins and fat from hearts and slit openings to make slightly larger pockets. Put parsley in the pockets. Take half the butter and divide into two or four parts, depending upon how many hearts are being used. Put one part in each heart, on top of parsley, and partly close the openings with poultry skewers. Sauté hearts and potatoes in the rest of the butter. Put in a casserole with a lid, adding salt and pepper and all the butter and juices from the skillet. Cover tightly and bake in 350° oven 1 to 1½ hours, or until tender. Mix flour with cream and currant jelly and add. Stir until jelly is melted and all is mixed into the gravy. Slice hearts before serving. Serves 4. Time: 1¾ hours.

Kidney, Heart, and Liver in Soubise Sauce

1 veal kidney, cut in pieces, the
   white removed
1 veal heart, fat and veins removed, sliced thin
2 slices calf's liver, cut in small
   pieces
¼ cup butter or bacon fat
2 very large onions or 4 medium-
   sized onions, minced fine
2 tablespoons flour
1 cup chicken stock
1 jigger Madeira
salt and pepper

Serve with baked potatoes and salad of celery cabbage with hot bacon dressing (2 pieces diced cooked bacon sprinkled on the torn-up greens with a tablespoon of the hot fat and a tablespoon of hot fresh lemon juice).

Sauté kidney, heart, and liver briefly in fat. Transfer to a shallow casserole. Sauté onions in the same fat. When onions are pale yellow, sprinkle flour on top. Blend and then add chicken stock, Madeira, and seasonings slowly, cooking until smooth and thickened. The sauce can be cooled slightly and put in a blender or through a food mill for a smoother texture, or left as is. Pour into casserole with the meat. Bake in 350° oven about 45 to 50 minutes. Serves 4. Time: 1¼ hours.

Sweetbreads, Scallops, and Almonds

1 pair sweetbreads
1 teaspoon lemon juice
½ cup sliced mushrooms
¾ lb. scallops, quartered
4 tablespoons butter
4 tablespoons flour
1½ cups milk
¼ cup dry white wine
salt and pepper
¼ cup blanched almonds,
  coarsely slivered

The most delicate of all variety meats, both in flavor and texture, fittingly embellished by almonds and wine. *Serve with baked tomatoes (cut off tops and slash crosses in them, sprinkle with salt, pepper, and marjoram, push in a lump of butter, and bake); hard French rolls; macaroon soufflé (see index).*

Soak the sweetbreads in ice water for 20 minutes. Then simmer them for 20 minutes in salted water to which a teaspoon of lemon juice has been added. Plunge them in ice water, drain, remove the membranes, and cut in pieces. Sauté mushrooms and scallops in butter. Add milk gradually, stirring constantly. When the sauce is slightly thickened add wine and seasoning. Add sweetbreads and mushrooms to the sauce. Pour into 4 individual casseroles, sprinkle with almonds, and bake at 350° for 20 minutes. Serves 4. Time: 1 hour.

½ pound fresh mushrooms equals 2½ cups sliced. ☕ 2½

Kidney Stew

8 lamb kidneys
½ lb. fresh, or 1 6-oz. package
  frozen, mushrooms, sliced
1 small bunch spring onions,
  tops and bottoms chopped, or
  2 medium-sized onions, sliced
  thin
4 tablespoons butter
3 medium-sized potatoes,
  peeled and diced, or 8 to 10
  frozen new potatoes, diced
2 tablespoons flour
½ cup beef bouillon
½ cup red wine
salt and pepper

Serve with sliced cucumbers and sliced radishes dressed with French dressing; hot French bread (brown-and-serve).

Have the butcher split and skin the kidneys. Cut out white part; slice them thin. Sauté kidneys, mushrooms, and onions in butter for 10 minutes. Remove to a buttered casserole. Brown potatoes in the same butter and add to casserole. Make gravy by blending flour with the juices in the pan and then thinning with bouillon and wine. Add salt and pepper and add to casserole. Cover and simmer in 325° oven about 30 to 40 minutes. Serves 4. Time: 1 hour.

Liver and Rice

1 cup uncooked rice
2 onions, minced
1 lb. beef liver, cut in 2-inch squares
3 tablespoons butter or bacon fat
3 cups bouillon
½ teaspoon thyme
salt and pepper
1 pt. fresh, or 1 10-oz. package frozen, lima beans

Serve with squares of Cheddar cheese, nuts, raisins, quarters of apples dipped in lemon juice—all in salad bowl; Ry-Krisp.

Brown the rice in a dry skillet. Transfer to a deep buttered casserole. Sauté onions and liver in fat. Add to casserole with lima beans and pour in bouillon mixed with seasonings. Cover and bake in 350° oven 45 to 55 minutes. Fluff the rice mixture with a fork before serving. Serves 4. Time: 1¼ hours.

Liver Loaf with Potato Top

1 lb. yearling beef liver
2 tablespoons minced onion
2 tablespoons butter
1 cup breadcrumbs
salt and pepper
2 eggs, slightly beaten
3 potatoes, cooked and sliced
2 medium-sized onions, sliced thin
4 slices bacon, cut into small pieces

Liver with its tried companions, but presented differently. *Serve with lettuce, Swiss chard, watercress, and French dressing; pumpernickel and sweet butter.*

Remove skin and membrane from liver. Put through the meat grinder. Sauté minced onion in butter and add ½ cup hot water. Pour over breadcrumbs, add seasoning and then liver, then eggs, and put mixture in a buttered casserole. Cover with sliced potatoes and sliced onions, and top with bacon pieces. Cook 1 hour at 350°. Serves 4. Time: 1½ hours.

Liver Soufflé

3 tablespoons butter
3 tablespoons flour
¼ teaspoon marjoram
salt and pepper
½ cup milk
½ cup white wine
3 eggs, separated
1 8-oz. can liver pâté

Serve with romaine and orange salad with French dressing (2 parts olive oil, 1 part lemon juice, pinch of chopped fresh mint, salt and pepper); biscuits; Italian cheesecake (see index).

Make a cream sauce by melting butter, blending in flour and seasonings, and adding the liquids slowly, stirring until smooth. Cook for 2 to 3 minutes until thick, remove from stove, stir in egg yolks and liver pâté. Beat whites until stiff, fold into sauce, and pour into a low buttered casserole. Bake 45 to 50 minutes at 350°, or until the top springs back when lightly touched. Serves 4. Time: 1¼ hours.

Sweetbread and White Grape Soufflé

1 pair sweetbreads
1 tablespoon lemon juice
2 tablespoons butter
3 tablespoons flour
1 cup milk
salt and pepper
4 eggs, separated
½ cup seedless grapes, pulled
  from the stems
¼ cup coarsely chopped unsalted almonds

This is one of those recipes we hope will impress you. Besides, it's good. *Serve with risi pisi (rice cooked first in butter, then in chicken broth, with fresh cooked peas added); watercress with sliced water chestnuts and French dressing; hot biscuits;* crème Chantilly.

Soak sweetbreads in ice water for 20 minutes. Parboil for 20 minutes in salted water with lemon juice. Then plunge them again in ice water, drain, and cut in ½-inch cubes. Make a cream sauce, melting butter, blending flour, adding milk and seasoning slowly, stirring until smooth and thick. Remove from the fire and stir in egg yolks. Add diced sweetbreads, white grapes, and almonds. Fold in the stiffly beaten egg whites and pour into a low buttered casserole. Bake in 350° oven 40 minutes. Serves 4 lightly. Time: 2 hours.

Creamed Tripe with Onions

1½ lbs. honeycomb tripe, cut in
  1½-inch squares
3 medium-sized onions, sliced
½ teaspoon pepper
4 tablespoons butter
4 tablespoons flour
1 cup milk
salt

Tripe looks unbelievably bleak and unpalatable at the butcher's but, with long, gentle cooking and imaginative seasoning, is subtle and delectable. Most recipes for tripe come from France, but this dish is of Scottish origin. It makes a good Sunday-morning breakfast dish. The Scots call it "poor man's oysters." *Serve with rhubarb cooked with strawberries; corn muffins.*

I stick of butter
equals ¼ pound
or ½ cup.

Simmer tripe and onions in water for 3 to 4 hours, or cook in a pressure cooker with 2 cups water for 1 hour at 15 pounds pressure, with the pepper but no salt. Let stand in the water overnight. Next morning make a heavy cream sauce by melting butter, stirring in flour until there is a smooth paste, adding milk, salt, and stirring until blended. Cook slowly until thick. Drain tripe and onions. Add to the cream sauce and pour into a shallow buttered casserole. Bake in 350° oven until hot and browned on top. Serves 4. Time: 12 hours.

Brussels Sprouts and Tongue in Cheese Sauce

2 1-pt. boxes, or 2 10-oz. packages frozen, Brussels sprouts
3 tablespoons butter
3 tablespoons flour
salt and pepper
1½ cups milk
1 cup grated sharp cheese
1 cup diced cooked or canned tongue

A simple and sturdy dish. *Serve with thin rings of sweet red onion marinated in diluted vinegar, then drained and dressed with olive oil, salt, and freshly ground black pepper; French bread; white grapes.*

Cook Brussels sprouts until barely tender. Drain. Put in a shallow casserole. Sprinkle with diced cooked tongue. Melt butter, stir in flour, cook for a minute or two. Add salt and pepper, then milk slowly, stirring until smooth and thick. Remove from heat. Add cheese and stir until that is melted. Pour over Brussels sprouts and tongue. Bake in a 350° oven until brown and bubbling, about 20 minutes. Serves 4. Time: 45 minutes.

Baked Tongue in Mushroom Sauce

½ lb. fresh, or 1 6-oz. package frozen, mushrooms, sliced
3 tablespoons butter
3 tablespoons flour
1½ cups half-and-half
salt, freshly ground black pepper
1 teaspoon grated lemon rind
pinch of nutmeg
2 cups diced cooked tongue, either fresh or smoked
2 tablespoons finely chopped chives or parsley

A cooked tongue, either fresh or smoked, is a handy thing to have around for many dishes. *Serve with mashed potatoes; salad of chicory and grapefruit segments with oil-and-lemon dressing; cherry tarts.*

Sauté mushrooms in butter until limp. Sprinkle with flour. Add half-and-half, a little at a time, stirring until smooth. Season with salt and pepper, lemon rind, and nutmeg. Add tongue and put into a small buttered casserole. Sprinkle with chives or parsley. Bake in a preheated 350° oven about 30 minutes. Serves 4. Time: 1 hour.

Tongue Casserole

1 medium-sized onion, chopped
3 medium-sized potatoes, boiled
and diced, or 2 cups quartered
frozen new potatoes
2 tablespoons olive oil
4 thick slices cooked tongue, cut
in 2-inch pieces
1½ cups canned tomatoes
¼ teaspoon rosemary
1 tablespoon finely chopped
parsley
1 pinch curry powder
salt and pepper
1 cup chicken broth

This is good for a summer day that is unexpectedly cool—one on which you expected to have cold tongue but decided a hot dinner would be best. *Serve with salad of diced cucumber, chopped watercress, sweet red pepper, with sour cream, in individual bowls; rye bread; fresh pears and cheese.*

Brown onion and potatoes in olive oil. Place in the bottom of a low casserole with the tongue. Add tomatoes. Sprinkle herbs and seasonings on top and pour in chicken broth. Simmer 1 hour in a 350° oven. Serves 4. Time: 1½ hours.

Venison Stew

3 to 4 lbs. venison, cut in 2-inch
chunks
1½ cups red-wine vinegar
1 onion, sliced thin
6 peppercorns
1 bay leaf
¼ teaspoon thyme
2 whole cloves
¼ lb. salt pork, diced
3 tablespoons flour seasoned
with salt and pepper
1 cup red wine
1 cup beef bouillon
1 cup chopped fresh mush-
rooms
1 tablespoon grated lemon rind
½ cup sour cream

In these days of affluent leisure there is more venison available to more people, either from one's own hunting or from hunter friends. *Serve with egg noodles; orange-and-onion salad with French dressing; apricot soufflé (see index).*

Marinate venison for 24 hours in mixture of vinegar, 3 cups water, onion, peppercorns, bay leaf, thyme, and cloves. Drain venison when ready. Fry diced salt pork in flameproof casserole that can be covered. Roll venison in seasoned flour and brown. Add red wine, beef bouillon, mushrooms, and lemon rind, and stir in sour cream. Cover, and bake in a 350° oven 1 hour or more, until venison is tender. Serves 6. Time, aside from marinating: 1½ hours.

Poultry
and
Game

Poultry and Game

Poulet Marengo

½ cup flour
1 teaspoon salt
freshly ground black pepper
1 teaspoon dried basil
1 2½-lb. chicken, cut in pieces
¼ cup olive oil
¼ cup butter
1 jigger brandy (if you wish)
1 cup dry white wine
½ lb. mushrooms, sliced
1 clove garlic, minced
2½ cups (1-lb.-4 oz. can)
  tomatoes
parsley

When Napoleon's chef first whipped up this dish for him after he had won the Battle of Marengo, they were far ahead of their supply train. What was available at nearby farms included crayfish and eggs, and these were used. However, crayfish and fried eggs sound unappetizing with the dish. Here is a contemporary version, much like chicken *chasseur,* and it assumes your supply train is close at hand. *Serve with noodles; Belgian endive salad; wine sherbet strewn with fresh sliced strawberries.*

Mix flour with salt, pepper, and basil. Flour the pieces of chicken and save the rest of the flour. Sauté chicken in olive oil and butter. Transfer to a heavy casserole. Add flour to the oil-and-butter mixture. Stir until well blended. Add brandy and wine, a little at a time, stirring with a wire whip until smooth and thickened. Add mushrooms, garlic, and tomatoes. Stir and pour over the chicken. Cover and bake in preheated 350° oven until the chicken is tender, 40 to 50 minutes. Before serving, sprinkle with finely chopped parsley. Serves 4. Time: 1¼ hours.

Chicken in Sour Cream with Dumplings

1 3½-lb. chicken, cut up for frying, or 2 lbs. chicken breasts
flour
salt and pepper
½ teaspoon powdered ginger
3 tablespoons olive oil
1 lb. small onions, boiled 15 minutes, or 1 1-lb. can small onions
1 pt. sour cream
1 cup prepared biscuit flour
½ cup milk
1 egg, beaten

Serve with lettuce, cranberry, and orange (put raw cranberries and raw orange through the meat chopper) with French dressing; hot biscuits.

Dredge chicken with flour, salt, pepper, and ginger. Sauté in olive oil until brown on all sides. Place in deep buttered casserole. Add onions. Dilute sour cream with 1 cup water, pour it over all, and cover tightly. Bake 45 minutes or until tender, in 350° oven. Make dumplings by mixing prepared biscuit flour with milk and beaten egg. Drop in casserole in separate spoonfuls. Replace cover and bake 20 minutes more. Serves 4. Time: 2 hours.

Chicken with Green Noodles

½ lb. green noodles
6 tablespoons butter
6 tablespoons flour
2 cups chicken broth
salt, freshly ground black pepper
¼ cup sherry
½ cup heavy cream
½ lb. fresh, or 1 6-oz. package frozen, mushrooms, sliced and sautéed in butter
2½ cups diced cooked chicken
grated Parmesan cheese
butter

I cup uncooked noodles makes 1 3/4 cups cooked!

A fine meal for an evening when time is short but the desire to pamper strong. Pick up a roasted chicken from a food store that has a rotisserie. *Serve with grapefruit and mixed green salad; French bread; sliced pound cake with vanilla ice cream topped with puréed frozen raspberries.*

Cook noodles in a large pan of boiling salted water until just barely tender. Remove, drain, and put in a medium casserole with a lump of butter under the noodles to keep them from sticking. Make a sauce by melting 6 tablespoons butter and cooking with flour for 3 or 4 minutes. Add broth, a little at a time, beating with a wire whisk until smooth and thickened. Add salt, pepper, and sherry, stir, add cream, a little at a time. Remove from stove, add mushrooms and chicken. Spoon over noodles, sprinkle the top with the grated cheese, and dot with butter. Bake in preheated 350° oven 20 to 30 minutes or until the top is brown and bubbling. Serves 4 to 5. Time: 50 minutes.

Scott's Peanut and Chicken Dish

⅓ cup chopped green onions
2 tablespoons butter
2 cups diced cooked chicken
1 can condensed cream of
  chicken soup, undiluted
⅓ cup coarsely chopped peanuts
  and cashew nuts, mixed
2 cups cooked rice

A pleasurable concoction devised one idle evening by a friend who has eaten well all of his young life but is just beginning to cook for himself and others. *Serve with tossed green salad; French bread; cherry-topped cheesecake.*

Cook green onions in butter until slightly wilted. Add chicken and push around briefly until well mingled with the butter and onions. Add chicken soup. Spread cooked rice in a shallow buttered casserole. Cover with onion-butter-and-chicken mixture. Sprinkle with chopped nuts. Bake at 350° for 30 to 35 minutes. Serves 4. Time: 1 hour.

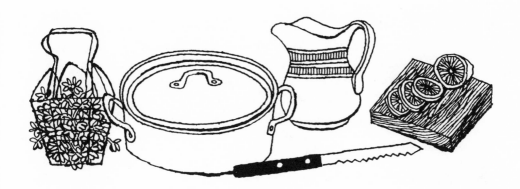

Chicken Italian Style

2 cloves garlic, minced
4 tablespoons olive oil
salt and pepper
1 2½ lb. chicken, cut up
1 bay leaf, crumbled
1 tablespoon chopped fresh
  basil
¼ cup wine vinegar

This dish is for those who know and love herbs. *Serve with pimiento rice (rice cooked first in butter, then in chicken broth, with 2 chopped pimientos added); tossed green salad with French dressing; Italian bread.*

Brown garlic in oil in heavy skillet, then remove. Rub salt and pepper on chicken and brown in oil; then transfer to shallow casserole uncovered. Add herbs and vinegar. Cook slowly, basting occasionally, at 350° for 35 to 40 minutes or until chicken is tender. Serves 4. Time: 50 minutes.

Chicken Baked with Smoked Oysters and Italian Green Beans

1 9-oz. package frozen Italian
    green beans
1 roast or barbecued chicken
1 3-⅔-oz. can smoked oysters
1 can condensed cream of celery
    soup
3 slices cooked bacon, crumbled

For a quick assembly job, the barbecued or roast chicken warm from the supermarket is best for last-minute cooking, juicier and more flavorful than that in cans. *Serve with hot buttermilk biscuits; poached pears with raspberry sauce (put 1 package slightly thawed raspberries in the electric blender).*

Cook the green beans according to directions until barely tender. Drain and arrange in casserole. Cut the warm chicken from the bone in bite-sized pieces. Arrange on green beans. Drain and sprinkle smoked oysters on top. Pour in undiluted cream of celery soup. Sprinkle crumbled bacon on top. Bake in 350° oven until brown and bubbly, about 35 to 45 minutes. Serves 4. Time: 1¼ hours.

Chicken Breasts in Cream with Ham and Mushrooms

¼ lb. uncooked ham, diced
salt and pepper
2 lbs. chicken breasts, split by
    butcher
6 tablespoons butter
3 tablespoons flour
2 cups heavy or medium cream
½ cup white wine
¼ lb. fresh, or 1 6-oz. package
    frozen, mushrooms, sliced

Bland but not boring. The ham and mushrooms add a subtle but positive note. *Serve with baked potatoes; lettuce and orange sections with French dressing, sprinkled with finely chopped mint leaves; hot buttermilk biscuits.*

Simmer ham in a little water for 15 minutes. Salt and pepper chicken breasts and sauté them in a skillet in 3 tablespoons butter. Transfer to a medium buttered casserole. Make a cream sauce in the skillet used for the chicken, melting 3 tablespoons butter, blending in flour, and slowly stirring in cream and wine. Add seasoning and cook until smooth and thickened. Add drained ham to the chicken in the casserole, sliced mushrooms, and more seasoning if necessary. Pour sauce over all. Bake in 350° oven 30 minutes. Serves 4. Time: 50 minutes.

Chicken Baked in Buttered Corn

1 2½-lb. chicken, cut up
3 tablespoons olive oil
½ lb. butter
8 ears fresh corn, cut from the cob, or 2 10-oz. packages frozen cut corn
salt and pepper

A south-of-the-Mason-Dixon-line dish with Yankee appeal and lots of lovely calories. *Serve with cucumber and red sweet onions sliced thin with rings of green pepper with French dressing; hot biscuits.*

Sauté chicken in olive oil until lightly browned on all sides and tender. Place in a casserole, dot with part of the butter, and sprinkle the corn over it. Break the rest of the butter into pieces on top and add salt with lots of freshly ground black pepper. Bake in 350° oven until lightly browned — about 30 minutes. Add more butter if it starts to get too dry. Serves 4. Time: 1 hour.

Brandied Chicken

1 2½-lb. chicken, cut up
2 cloves garlic, minced
¼ cup butter
1 cup heavy cream
2 jiggers brandy or rum
1 tablespoon good curry powder
salt and pepper

One of the simpler and better ways of cooking and serving chicken. *Serve with baked rice pilaf (see index); green pepper rings with French dressing; hot rolls.*

Sauté chicken and garlic in butter and transfer to a casserole with the juices from the pan. Add cream, brandy, curry powder, salt, and pepper. Cover and bake in 350° oven 35 to 40 minutes or until tender. Serves 4. Time: 1 hour.

Chicken Baked with Soy Sauce and Butter

1 2½-lb. chicken, cut up
2 tablespoons soy sauce
salt, pepper
1 tablespoon lemon juice
1 tablespoon crumbled dried hot red pepper pods
¼ lb. (1 stick) butter

From the Far East. *Serve with rice; leaf lettuce with lemon and cream dressing; French bread; fresh blueberries with cream; sponge cake.*

Arrange pieces of chicken in a shallow casserole. Put the rest of the ingredients in a small saucepan with ½ cup water and boil for 10 minutes. Pour over chicken and bake in preheated 400° oven 30 to 40 minutes or until the chicken is browned and tender, basting occasionally with the juices in the pan. Serves 4. Time: 1¼ hours.

Chicken Baked in Tomato and Olive Sauce

2 cloves garlic, mashed or minced

2 anchovy fillets, or 1 tablespoon anchovy paste

4 large tomatoes, skinned, seeded, and chopped

¼ cup wine, preferably white

¼ teaspoon thyme

¼ teaspoon marjoram

1 teaspoon basil

salt, pepper

1 chicken, about 2 to 2½ lbs., quartered

slivers of garlic

sprigs of thyme or basil

lemon juice

flour

¼ cup olive oil

½ 4½-oz. can chopped black olives.

More robustly flavored than most chicken dishes. *Serve with Belgian endive salad; sesame-seed rolls; spumoni.*

Cook garlic, anchovy, chopped tomato, wine, and seasonings together over low heat until thickened. Insert slivers of garlic and a sprig of thyme or basil under the skin of each quarter of chicken. Brush skin with lemon juice and dust with flour seasoned with salt and pepper. Brown on both sides in olive oil. Arrange chicken quarters in bottom of shallow casserole, overlapping if necessary. Put tomato sauce over them. Sprinkle drained olives on top. This much may be prepared ahead of time. Bake in 350° oven 40 to 50 minutes. Serves 4. Time: 1½ hours.

Viennese Chicken

1 2½-lb. chicken, cut up

flour

salt, pepper

3 tablespoons butter

1 cup finely chopped onions

1 cup finely chopped mushrooms

⅔ cup finely chopped fresh parsley

¾ cup dry white wine

4 slices bacon, cut in pieces

juice of ½ lemon

1 cup sour cream

Another recipe that has been changed somewhat to suit our ways of cooking and eating. *Serve with poppy-seed rolls; fresh peach shortcake.*

Dust the pieces of chicken with flour mixed with salt and pepper. Brown on all sides in butter. Put half the onions, mushrooms, and parsley in a medium casserole with a tightly fitting lid. Arrange chicken over them and top with the rest of the onions, mushrooms, and parsley. Pour in white wine. Sprinkle with salt and pepper. Cook bacon very briefly, just long enough to remove a little of the fat. Drain bacon, strew on top of the dish, cover and bake in preheated 350° oven about 1 hour. Just before serving, mix a ladleful of juices from the chicken with sour cream and lemon juice and stir in to the casserole. Serves 4. Time: 1¾ hours.

Chicken Breasts with String Beans and Ginger

⅓ cup flour
½ teaspoon thyme
¼ teaspoon leaf sage
2 lbs. chicken breasts, split by butcher
3 tablespoons butter
1 small onion, sliced thin
3 medium-sized potatoes, peeled and diced, or 2 cups quartered frozen new potatoes
1 lb. fresh, or 1 package frozen, green beans, frenched
1 small piece green ginger root, shaved

The ginger root is most likely to be found in Chinese food stores. *Serve with endive with French dressing with crumbled blue cheese; Melba toast.*

Mix thyme and sage with flour. Dredge the chicken breasts with this. Sauté in butter in a skillet until brown on both sides and tender. Place the chicken breasts in a shallow buttered casserole. Brown onion and potatoes in skillet and transfer to casserole. Thicken juices in skillet with rest of seasoned flour and thin with 1½ cups water. Add green beans to casserole, sprinkle with shaved ginger, and pour gravy over all. Bake in 350° oven 35 minutes. Serves 4. Time: 1¼ hours.

Chicken Olla

1 clove garlic
⅓ cup fat, preferably bacon drippings
1 2½-lb. chicken, cut up
1 cup uncooked brown rice
2 large onions, sliced thin
2½ cups tomato juice
salt and pepper
paprika
6 to 8 cherry stone clams, still in their well-scrubbed shells

Chicken cooked with clams or other seafood is usually of Spanish derivation. This recipe comes directly from Madrid. *Serve with chicory with a dressing of half mayonnaise and half sour cream mixed with ½ teaspoon anchovy paste; French bread, cut in thick slices ⅞ through, spread with softened butter mixed with chopped salad herbs, and browned in a hot oven.*

Sauté garlic in fat. Remove garlic and brown chicken in the same fat. Transfer the pieces of chicken to a deep casserole that has a tightly fitting lid. Cook rice in the fat with onions until the rice changes color, but do not brown. Add rice and onions to the chicken. Pour tomato juice over the chicken, and add seasoning and clams still in their shells. Cover and steam gently in preheated 350° oven, 35 to 40 minutes, or until chicken is tender. The clams will open during cooking, and the juices will permeate the rest of the dish. Serves 4. Time: 1¼ hours.

Chicken with Hearts of Artichokes and Shrimp

½ lb. fresh or frozen shrimp, peeled and deveined, or 1 5½-oz. can shrimp
1 3½- to 4-lb. chicken, cut up
1 green pepper, seeded and chopped
1 clove garlic, minced
1 small onion, chopped
¼ cup olive oil
1 cup uncooked rice
1 8-oz. can hearts of artichokes, drained and sliced
2½ cups (1-lb.-4-oz. can) tomatoes
2 cups chicken broth
salt and pepper

Serve with escarole with French dressing; French bread.

If canned shrimp are used, rinse them in cold water and drain. Sauté chicken, green pepper, garlic, and onion in olive oil. Transfer to a deep buttered casserole. Add uncooked rice to oil in skillet. Stir and cook until rice is translucent. Transfer to casserole, add shrimp, artichoke hearts, tomatoes, chicken broth, and seasoning. Cover and bake in 350° oven for 1 hour, or until chicken is tender. Serves 4 to 6. Time: 1¼ hours.

Chicken and Green Beans Baked in Mustard Sauce

1 cup plus 2 tablespoons milk or half-and-half
½ cup sugar
1 tablespoon dry English mustard
pinch of salt
1 tablespoon cornstarch
1 egg yolk, beaten
¼ cup diluted tarragon vinegar (2 tablespoons vinegar, 2 of water)
3 tablespoons fat
1 2½-lb. chicken, cut up
1 lb. green beans, frenched, or 1 9-oz. package frozen frenched green beans, slightly thawed

This mustard sauce, with its almost Pennsylvania Dutch sweet-sour taste, gives the chicken and beans an unusual flavor. *Serve with tomato slices, sprinkled with salt, pepper, chopped basil, and a little olive oil; cheesecake.*

Put 1 cup milk in a double boiler and let come to a boil. Mix dry ingredients together and blend with 2 tablespoons cold milk. Add gradually to the boiled milk, stirring constantly. Turn the heat down and add beaten egg yolk. Add diluted vinegar and cook 2 minutes, until slightly thickened. Sauté chicken briefly in the fat until it is a delicate brown, and transfer to a shallow casserole with a lid. Arrange beans on top, pour mustard sauce over all, and cover. Bake in 350° oven about 45 minutes, or until chicken and beans are tender. Serves 4. Time: 1¼ hours.

Lemon Chicken

flour
salt and pepper
1 2½- to 3-lb. chicken, cut up
2 tablespoons salad oil
2 eggs
juice of 1½ lemons
1 tablespoon grated lemon peel
1 cup chicken broth, warm, but
   not boiling

The simple lemon-and-egg thickening used in Greek cookery was the beginning of both mayonnaise dressing and Hollandaise sauce, and appears in a still different guise in this dish. *Serve with asparagus; butterflake rolls; cream puffs.*

Flour and season chicken lightly. Sauté in oil until golden brown on both sides and partially cooked. Place chicken in a shallow casserole. Beat eggs and add lemon juice and grated peel. Beat some more. Add chicken broth slowly, beating after each addition. Pour the mixture over the chicken. Bake in 350° oven 20 to 25 minutes, or until chicken is just tender. The lemon sauce, which is almost a custard, is better if not cooked too long. Sometimes some broth will settle at the bottom of the custard, but that is all right. Serves 4. Time: 1 hour.

Chicken Stewed in Sherry

1 3½-lb. chicken, cut up
2 cloves garlic, chopped fine
2 medium-sized onions,
   chopped
2 small bay leaves or 1 large one
1 tablespoon chili powder
1 teaspoon orégano
2 4½ oz. cans pitted ripe olives,
   chopped
1 pt. sherry
salt
2 tablespoons flour (optional)

Richly flavored, this Mexican dish is a surprise to those who think all south-of-the-border dishes hot and harsh, and to others who think all sherry dishes very bland. *Serve with baked rice pilaf (see index); salted cucumber sticks; French bread; peaches chilled in rosé wine (put a whole peeled peach for each person in a large clear glass pitcher; fill with rosé wine; chill. Put the pitcher on the table and serve the wine during dinner, and the peaches at the end).*

Put chicken in a deep casserole with garlic, onion, bay leaf, chili powder, and orégano, and add 3 cups boiling water. Cover and bake in 350° oven 45 minutes. Remove cover and add olives, sherry, and salt. Bake 15 minutes longer, or until chicken is tender. If a thick gravy is desired, mix flour with enough water to make a thin paste, add the flour thickening to the boiling liquid, and cook 5 minutes longer. I prefer the natural juices reduced somewhat as they are by this cooking. Serves 4. Time: 1½ hours.

Chicken Creole Maybe

1 3- or 3½-lb. chicken, cut up
salt and pepper
flour
3 spring onions, tops and bottoms chopped
3 tablespoons olive oil
½ lb. raw ham, diced
1 pt. okra, sliced, or 1 10-oz. package frozen
3½ cups (1-lb.-14-oz. can) Italian plum tomatoes
1 8-oz. can water chestnuts, drained and cut in ½-inch slices
2 tablespoons soy sauce
1 bay leaf
½ teaspoon thyme
½ teaspoon marjoram

Serve with endive and watercress with French dressing mixed with crumbled Roquefort cheese; hot biscuits.

Dredge chicken in salt, pepper, and flour. Brown chicken and onions in olive oil and transfer to deep buttered casserole. Brown ham in the same skillet and place in the casserole. Add okra, tomatoes, water chestnuts, soy sauce, 2 cups water, and seasoning. Cover tightly and simmer in 350° oven about 1 hour, or until chicken is tender. Serves 4 or more. Time: 1¼ hours.

Hot Baked Chicken Salad

2 cups cooked chicken, cut in large dice
2 cups diced celery
1 teaspoon curry powder
½ cup mayonnaise
toasted slivered almonds
finely chopped chives

The mayonnaise and the partly cooked celery give this dish its name. *Serve with tossed green salad; hot rolls; macaroon soufflé.*

Mix cooked chicken and raw celery with curry powder and mayonnaise. Toss well and put into four individual baking dishes or one shallow one. Sprinkle almonds and chives on top. Bake 30 to 40 minutes at 350°. The celery will still be rather crisp, giving it the salad-like flavor. Serves 4. Time: 50 minutes.

Crêpes with Chicken Filling and Cheese Sauce

CRÊPES

4 eggs
1 cup milk
¼ teaspoon salt
2 cups flour
¼ cup melted butter
butter for frying

FILLING

3 tablespoons butter
2 onions, chopped
½ green pepper, seeded and
** chopped**
½ lb. fresh, or 1 6-oz. package
** frozen, mushrooms, sliced**
2 cups diced cooked chicken
1 cup sour cream
salt, pepper

SAUCE

1 tablespoon butter
1 tablespoon flour
1½ cups milk
salt, pepper
1 cup grated cheese

Unsweetened crêpes with a meat, seafood, or cheese filling make a fine entree. The batter may be made in the blender and any left over kept in the refrigerator for several days before using. *Serve with braised endive; hot biscuits; lemon mousse sprinkled with finely chopped pistachios.*

For the crêpes, put eggs, 1 cup water, milk, and salt in an electric blender. Blend, then add flour and melted butter. Blend some more, scraping down the flour from the sides with a small wooden or rubber scraper. Let the batter stand in the refrigerator for at least 2 hours to ripen. This will make about 12 to 16 crêpes. Cook the crêpes, one at a time, in a 6-inch skillet in butter. They should be very thin. If necessary, thin the batter with a little water; flours vary as to brand and as to the moisture in the atmosphere. Put a spoonful of batter into the hot butter and quickly tilt the pan around. Cook lightly on both sides and keep warm.

For the filling, melt butter and sauté onion, green pepper, and mushrooms until limp. Mix with diced chicken, sour cream, and seasonings and put some of the filling on each crêpe. Roll crêpes up and put side by side in a shallow rectangular casserole. For the sauce, melt butter, add flour, and cook for 3 to 4 minutes until dry. Add milk, a little at a time, and beat well with a wire whip; add salt, pepper, and cheese. Stir until cheese is melted. Pour over crêpes and bake at 350° for 35 to 45 minutes or until brown and bubbling. If you wish, put under the broiler for about 5 minutes to brown and blister. Serves 4 to 6. Time: 1¼ hours, aside from chilling crêpe batter.

To avoid trouble with weevils, keep flour or corn meal in glass jar or plastic bag in Refrigerator.

Chicken au Gratin

3 tablespoons butter
3 tablespoons flour
1 cup milk
½ cup heavy cream
2 teaspoons French prepared mustard
1 teaspoon dried tarragon, or 1 tablespoon chopped fresh tarragon
salt, freshly ground black pepper
2 cups cooked chicken, cut in thin strips
3 tablespoons grated Swiss cheese
breadcrumbs
butter

Somehow the word "leftover" connotes something very dreary rather than an interesting take-off for many dishes requiring, say, cooked chicken. *Serve with spoon bread; beet and endive salad with vinaigrette dressing; blueberry tarts.*

Make a sauce by cooking butter and flour together until dry and well mingled. Add milk, half at a time, and beat vigorously with a wooden spoon or a wire whip. Add cream, mustard, tarragon, salt, and pepper. Stir until smooth and thickened. Add chicken strips and put in a small buttered casserole. Sprinkle the top with the cheese and breadcrumbs. Dot with small pieces of butter. Bake in a 400° oven 15 to 20 minutes. Serves 4. Time: 45 minutes.

Chicken More or Less Tetrazzini

1 8-oz. package spaghetti, or one of the many pretty shapes of pasta
4 slices bacon
½ lb. fresh, or 1 6-oz. package frozen, mushrooms, sliced
3 spring onions, tops and bulbs chopped
1 green pepper, chopped, without seeds
3½ cups tomatoes (1-lb.-14-oz. can, drained, but save the juice)
2 cups diced cooked chicken
salt and pepper
grated Parmesan cheese

A dish that is plain enough for every day, but fancy enough for a buffet dinner. *Serve with mixed greens with French dressing; Vienna rolls.*

Break spaghetti into 2-inch pieces. Put into a large kettle of salted boiling water and boil about 9 to 10 minutes, or until tender but still firm when pinched with the fingers. The time will vary according to the shape. Drain. Fry bacon. Remove, and sauté mushrooms, onions, and green pepper in the same skillet until onions are golden brown. Add tomatoes, chicken, salt, and pepper. Butter a low casserole and put ⅓ the cooked spaghetti on the bottom, then ⅓ the chicken mixture, and repeat until there are three alternating layers of spaghetti and chicken mixture. Pour 1 cup tomato juice over all, and sprinkle the top with Parmesan cheese. Bake in 350° oven 25 to 30 minutes. Serves 4. Time: 1 hour.

Chicken Coolie

6 large potatoes, peeled and halved
1 fat hen, 3½ to 5 lbs., cut up
2½ cups (1-lb.-4-oz. can) tomatoes
4 medium-sized onions, peeled and cut in thick slices
1 lb. bacon, cut in pieces
salt and pepper

This is a good substantial dish — it is practically a meal — to cook and serve for a number of people. It can burble merrily on in the oven while you babble equally merrily on in the living room with your guests. *Serve with very, very young greens — tender beet tops, turnip tops, and dandelion greens — with sour cream and a dash of tarragon vinegar, sprinkled with chopped hard-cooked egg; French bread.*

In a deep casserole place a layer of potatoes, one of chicken, a layer each of tomatoes, onions, and bacon, salt and pepper. Repeat until all ingredients are used. Cover and cook in 300° oven 1½ to 2 hours. Serves 4 to 6. Time: 2½ hours.

Chicken George Murphy

1 2½-lb. chicken, cut up
flour
salt and pepper
paprika
3 tablespoons fat
2 strips bacon, cut in pieces
1 lb. fresh shelled, or 1 10-oz. package frozen, peas
1 lb. fresh, or 1 9-oz. package frozen, green beans, frenched
¼ lb. fresh mushrooms, sliced thin lengthwise
1 medium-sized green pepper, sliced thin and seeds removed
1 medium-sized onion, sliced thin
1 clove garlic, minced

This recipe is from George Murphy, an alumnus of the early days of vaudeville, later a very spry young-old bartender at the Newspaper Guild in New York. *Serve with French bread; lemon sherbert.*

Sprinkle chicken with flour, salt, pepper, and paprika, sauté in fat, and put in the bottom of a large deep casserole. Add pieces of bacon. Mix peas, green beans, mushrooms, green pepper, onion, and garlic together and put in the casserole on top of the bacon and chicken. Sprinkle with more salt, pepper, and paprika. Cover tightly and bake in 350° oven for 45 minutes, or until chicken is tender. Add ½ cup chicken broth or white wine if it starts to dry out. The "juices from the vegetation" will season and should provide enough moisture for this dish. Do not thicken. Serves 4. Time: 1¼ hours.

Hungarian Chicken

¼ lb. butter
3 onions, chopped
2 2½-lb. chickens, cut up
salt
cayenne pepper
2 tablespoons flour
1 pt. sour cream

This is even better the second day, hence the two chickens. *Serve with baked pilaf (see index); orange, grapefruit, and tangerine segments on a bed of greens with a tart dressing (2 parts olive oil, 1 part grapefruit juice, 1 teaspoon grated lemon peel, salt, pepper); Vienna bread.*

Sauté onions in butter. Transfer both to the bottom of a deep casserole that has a tightly fitting lid. Lightly sprinkle the uncooked pieces of chicken with salt and lots of cayenne. Arrange in the casserole on bed of onions with the heavier pieces of chicken on the bottom, smallest and lightest pieces on the top. Cover tightly and let chickens stew in their own juices 45 to 60 minutes in a 350° oven. Baste occasionally with a baster, being careful to replace the lid. Sprinkle flour over the chicken and add sour cream. Put in oven for 10 minutes more and serve. Serves 4 for 2 days. Time: 1½ hours.

Creamed Chicken with Cranberry Rice

1 cup uncooked rice
2 cups cranberry juice
2 tablespoons butter
2 tablespoons flour
1 cup milk or chicken broth
salt and pepper
2 cups diced cooked chicken, duck, or turkey
2 tablespoons slivered almonds, toasted

This is probably the simplest and prettiest way of serving leftover chicken or duck. *Serve with romaine with tangerine (or orange) segments with Roquefort cheese dressing; hot biscuits.*

Cook the rice Chinese fashion: put in a heavy pan with a tightly fitting lid, add cranberry juice. Bring to a boil. Cover and cook over low heat 14 minutes. Remove from heat, take off lid, and fluff with a fork.

Make a sauce by melting butter, stirring in flour until well blended, adding milk slowly, and then the seasoning. Stir until smooth and thick. Put the cranberry rice in a low buttered casserole. Add diced chicken or duck to the sauce and pour over the rice. Sprinkle the top with slivered almonds. Bake in 350° oven about 20 minutes, or until the flavors have had time to get acquainted. Serves 4. Time: 45 minutes.

Chicken Baked with Green Peppers

1 fat clove garlic, minced
1 medium-sized onion, chopped fine
4 large green peppers, cut in thin strips, seeds removed
4 tablespoons olive oil
1 2½-lb. chicken, cut up
1 cup chicken broth
1 lemon, sliced thin, seeds removed
salt and pepper

Serve with spoon bread (see index); tiny cherry tomatoes; pineapple sherbet.

Sauté garlic, onion, and green peppers in olive oil until slightly tender but not brown. Remove from fat. Brown chicken in the same fat. Transfer chicken to a casserole and sprinkle garlic, onion, and green pepper on top. Add chicken broth, lemon, salt, and pepper. Cover and bake at 350° 45 to 50 minutes, or until tender. Serves 4. Time: 1¼ hours.

An Extemporaneous Chicken Pot Pie

1 2½-lb. chicken, cut up
2 tablespoons fat, preferably bacon drippings
1 10-oz. package frozen lima beans
2 cups (1-lb. can) small boiled onions
1 can condensed cream of mushroom soup
2 cups prepared biscuit flour
milk
a little salt (the soup has lots)

This is a streamlined version that can be made easily even after the third martini. *Serve with mixed greens with French dressing; drop biscuits; pineapple chunks and raspberries.*

Sauté chicken in fat. Transfer to a casserole and add lima beans, onions and juice, and undiluted cream of mushroom soup. Mix biscuit dough according to directions on the box. Do not roll it, but drop it by spoonfuls on the casserole. Bake in a 400° oven 35 to 40 minutes. Serves 4 generously. Time: 1 hour.

Canned Chicken with Artichokes and White Wine

2 cups cooked rice
1 can whole chicken, fricassee style, with gravy
1 9-oz. can hearts of artichokes, drained
½ cup chopped onions, fresh or frozen
1 lemon, sliced thin, seeds removed
1 cup white wine
salt and pepper, if needed

Important enough to please a guest. *Serve with romaine with French dressing; hot biscuits; fresh or frozen strawberries or cherries with* crème Chantilly *(the delicate Swedish dessert cheese).*

Mix all the ingredients together in a deep casserole. Cover and bake in a preheated 350° oven for 20 minutes. Add chicken broth if the dish starts to dry out. Serves 4. Time: 30 minutes.

Coq au Vin

2 broilers, 2-3 lbs. each, quartered
salt and pepper
¼ lb. butter, melted
2 tablespoons bacon fat
12 white onions, peeled
½ lb. large mushrooms, caps only
½ cup flour
3 cups Burgundy wine
½ cup chicken broth
bay leaf, crumbled
¼ teaspoon leaf thyme
4 tablespoons chopped parsley

This version of the world-famous French dish has something extra-French about it in flavor; maybe it's the tiny touch of bacon that isn't even detectable as such by the time the cooking is finished. *Serve with watercress and Boston lettuce tossed with oil-and-vinegar dressing; hot rolls; raspberry sherbet.*

Salt and pepper chicken pieces, brown all over in melted butter and bacon fat in large heavy skillet over moderate heat. Arrange browned chicken in large casserole that can be covered. Glaze the onions in skillet, adding more butter if necessary, and add to casserole; do the same with the mushroom caps. Add flour and a little of the wine to the skillet and stir until smooth. Add remainder of wine and the broth, and heat while stirring for about 5 minutes. Pour wine sauce over chicken and sprinkle in bay leaf, thyme, and 1 tablespoon chopped parsley. Cover and bake at 350° for 45 minutes or until chicken is tender. Sprinkle with 3 tablespoons chopped parsley before serving. Serves 8. Time: 1½ hours.

Chicken Oregon

1 cup cooked chicken or turkey, diced
1 10½-oz. can condensed cream of mushroom soup
1 cup sour cream
½ cup chopped celery
½ cup chopped onions
½ lb. fresh mushrooms, sliced
1 tablespoon lemon juice
1 4½-oz. can chopped ripe olives
½ cup grated Parmesan cheese
½ cup slivered almonds
3 canned whole pimientos, diced
1 3-oz. can Chinese noodles

Named for an Oregon friend who once lived in Hawaii and invented this delicious, slightly chow-meinish dish. *Serve with Bibb lettuce with oil-and-vinegar dressing; hot biscuits; lemon pudding (see index).*

Preheat oven to 350°. Mix together chicken or turkey, mushroom soup, sour cream, celery, onions, mushrooms, and lemon juice. Pour into shallow buttered casserole. Top with olives and Parmesan cheese. Sprinkle almonds over all and garnish with pimientos. Bake for about 40 minutes or until piping hot. Warm noodles in oven 3 or 4 minutes (watch that they don't burn) and serve these separately as a base for each helping. Serves 4. Time: 1 hour.

Chicken Kooma

1 2½-lb. chicken, cut up
1 clove garlic, minced
1 teaspoon turmeric
1 cup yogurt
2 tablespoons butter
2 tablespoons oil
1 small onion, chopped
4 cardamom seeds
¼ teaspoon cloves
½ teaspoon cinnamon
2 tablespoons grated coconut
salt
juice of ½ lemon

Chicken in India is scarce and expensive, so much care and pride goes into the cooking. Our chickens do not need to be marinated to make them more tender, but marinating will improve the flavor. *Serve with Boston lettuce; French bread; watermelon.*

Marinate the pieces of chicken in the garlic, turmeric (which gives it a lovely color besides flavor), and yogurt for about 1 hour. Melt the butter with the oil and sauté onion with the cardamom seeds, cloves, and cinnamon until nice and aromatic. Drain the pieces from the marinade, add, and cook briefly. Put in a casserole with the contents of the browning pan, add the marinade, and sprinkle with coconut. Salt lightly. Dribble lemon juice over all. Bake until tender in oven preheated to 350° for about 45 minutes. Serves 4. Time, aside from marinating: 1¼ hours.

Duck with Oranges, White Grapes, and Sauerkraut

1 4-5 lb. duck, quartered
½ cup flour for dredging
salt and pepper
3 tablespoons bacon fat or cooking oil
1 small onion, chopped
2 lbs. sauerkraut, rinsed and squeezed
1 cup canned mandarin oranges, drained
1 cup fresh or canned seedless white grapes
½ cup white wine
1 cup chicken broth

It is a taste-expanding delight to learn some of the exciting ways sauerkraut is cooked in other countries. This is an adaptation of a German dish. *Serve with hot poppy-seed rolls; brownie pudding (see index).*

Dredge duck pieces in flour well seasoned with salt and pepper. Brown on all sides in bacon fat or cooking oil in heavy skillet. Sprinkle onion in large casserole, add sauerkraut, arrange duck on top, and add oranges, grapes, wine, and broth. Cook in 350° oven, uncovered, 1 hour or more, until duck is tender. Serves 4. Time: 1½ hours.

Chicken Ripperger

3 tablespoons butter
2 tablespoons flour
1 cup chicken broth
3 cups diced cooked chicken (roasted tastes best)
salt and pepper
1 cup Hollandaise sauce
2 medium-sized hot boiled potatoes
1 egg
8 large mushroom caps

This is chicken hash in its most exalted form. *Serve with halves of avocado with fresh lime juice and salt; hot biscuits with sweet butter; spice cake.*

Make a white sauce by melting 2 tablespoons butter, blending in flour, adding chicken broth, and cooking until slightly thickened. Season chicken with salt and pepper and add it to the cream sauce. Pour into a buttered pottery loaf-shaped casserole handsome enough to bring to the table. Spread generously with Hollandaise sauce. Mash the boiled potatoes with hot milk, butter, and salt and pepper. Stir the egg into the mashed potatoes and, using a pastry tube, put an edging of potatoes around the dish. Sauté the mushroom caps in 1 tablespoon butter, place them down the middle of the dish. Put in a 350° oven until potatoes are browned, or brown under a broiler. Serves 4. Time: 45 minutes.

Chicken and Mushroom Hash

¼ lb. fresh, or 1 6-oz. package frozen, mushrooms, sliced
3 tablespoons butter
4 medium-sized potatoes, boiled, peeled, and diced, or 8 to 10 frozen new potatoes, diced
2 cups diced cooked chicken
2 cups medium cream
2 eggs
¼ cup brandy or sherry
¼ teaspoon tarragon
salt and pepper

This is a pleasing departure from the usual concept of hash. *Serve with watercress with tomato aspic and mayonnaise; hot poppy-seed rolls (brown-and-serve); baked pears with shaved chocolate (see index).*

Sauté mushrooms in butter. Add potatoes and brown slightly, and then brown the chicken. Transfer to shallow casserole. Beat cream slightly with eggs, brandy, tarragon, salt, and pepper. Pour over the hash and bake in a 350° oven 30 to 40 minutes. There should be a slight custardy look about the dish. Serves 4. Time: 1 hour.

Diced Turkey with Onions and Apricots

1 bunch green onions, chopped
3 tablespoons butter
2 cups diced cooked turkey or chicken
½ cup quartered dried apricots
⅓ cup chopped parsley
1 teaspoon dried mint
½ teaspoon cinnamon
salt, pepper
½ cup dry white wine
½ cup chicken broth

A nice way of using cooked turkey, either from a roast or from a cooked turkey roll. *Serve with mixed green salad; sesame-seed rolls; honeydew melon sprinkled with powdered ginger.*

Sauté onions in butter until slightly wilted. Put them and their butter into a shallow casserole with the other ingredients and stir together. Bake in preheated 350° oven for 30 to 40 minutes to 1 hour. Serves 4. Time: 1¼ hours.

Swedish Chicken Livers with Rice

1½ lbs. chicken livers, cut in pieces
flour
salt, pepper
5 tablespoons butter
2 cups cooked rice
4 hard-cooked eggs, sliced

SAUCE
½ cup blanched slivered almonds
2 cups chicken broth
4 tablespoons butter
5 tablespoons flour
1 cup half-and-half
1 teaspoon salt
dash of cayenne pepper
2 tablespoons sherry or Madeira

Simmering the almonds for a half-hour in the chicken broth gives a delicate, definite almond flavor, more so than if they are just sprinkled on top. *Serve with cucumber salad; hot biscuits; poached pears with chocolate sauce.*

Dust chicken livers with lightly seasoned flour. Sauté in butter. Spread cooked rice on the bottom of a shallow casserole and arrange chicken livers and hard-cooked eggs over it. Meanwhile, for the sauce, simmer almonds in chicken broth for 30 minutes. Melt butter and add flour, stirring with a wire whisk or wooden spoon until well blended, for 3 to 4 minutes, then add half-and-half, a little at a time, stirring constantly, until smooth. Add broth and almonds the same way. Stir in salt, cayenne, and sherry, and simmer for about 10 minutes. Check seasoning. Add more if necessary, but do not overwhelm the delicate flavor of the almonds. Pour sauce over livers and rice. Bake in preheated 375° oven 35 to 45 minutes or until the top is lightly brown and bubbling. Serves 4. Time: 1¼ hours.

Chicken Livers in White Wine Sauce with Wild Rice

1 cup wild rice or wild-rice mixture

2 cups chicken broth, or more

SAUCE

1 lb. chicken livers, each cut in 3 or 4 pieces

2 tablespoons bacon fat

2 tablespoons flour

salt and pepper

½ cup white wine

1 cup chicken broth

A good recipe even though the inflated price of wild rice makes it rather unrealistic. There is a mixture of wild rice and long-grain rice in the markets which has an interesting flavor and texture and costs much less. *Serve with tomato slices spread with mayonnaise mixed with finely minced raw onion, then placed under the broiler until brown and puffy; French bread cut in hunks, with sweet butter; chocolate soufflé (see index).*

Cook the rice in 2 cups chicken broth. (There should be enough broth to cover rice; add more if rice starts to dry out.) Bring to a boil, cover, and turn flame down low for 50 to 60 minutes or until rice is tender and liquid is absorbed. Fluff with a fork. For the sauce, sauté chicken livers in fat until brown. Remove livers from pan, blend flour and seasonings into the fat, and slowly add wine and broth. When the sauce is smooth, return the chicken livers to the pan. Put rice on the bottom of a medium-sized shallow casserole and pour chicken livers and sauce over the top. Bake in 350° oven 20 minutes. Serves 4. Time: 1½ hours.

Creamed Turkey with Sausage

½ lb. sausage, either link or bulk

4 tablespoons butter

4 tablespoons flour

2½ cups milk

salt, pepper

1 tablespoon Hungarian sweet rose paprika

3 cups diced cooked turkey

breadcrumbs

more butter

There are lots of turkeys these days, but, as usual, they are seldom finished at one meal. *Serve with spiced pears; yellow plum tomatoes; hot poppy-seed rolls; and lime pie.*

Sauté sausage until brown and crisp. Cut in small pieces. Melt butter, add flour, and cook for 3 to 4 minutes until dry and well blended; then add milk, ½ cup at a time, beating vigorously until smooth and thickened. Add seasonings and turkey. Put a layer of creamed turkey in a medium baking dish, then a layer of sausage, and repeat until all ingredients are used, ending up with a layer of turkey on top. Sprinkle with breadcrumbs and top with small pieces of butter. Bake in preheated 400° oven 30 minutes. Serves 6. Time: 50 minutes.

Chicken Livers and Spaghetti Aldo

¾ lb. round steak, ground
1 clove garlic, minced
2 medium onions, chopped
3 tablespoons olive oil
2½ cups (1 lb.-4 oz.-can) tomatoes, put through a sieve
1 6-oz. can Italian tomato paste
1 teaspoon dried basil
salt and cayenne pepper
½ lb. spaghetti
1 lb. chicken livers, quartered
flour
2 tablespoons butter

Never underestimate the power of a woman. When this recipe was first published in the first casserole book, we gave it the name of the café we loved and where we ate it, though not, of course, in a casserole. Now, years later, when Aldo's has flourished, expanded, and splintered splendidly, if somewhat uncozily, it is called on the menu "Chicken Livers Maria." Maria was indeed the wife and cook way back when. *Serve with sour-cream slaw with green grapes; Italian bread; watermelon sherbet.*

Sauté round steak, garlic, and onions in olive oil. Add tomatoes, tomato paste, and seasoning. Let cook slowly, stirring once in a while with a wooden spoon, and adding a little water if necessary for a smooth, thick consistency. Aldo said it should cook for 2 hours, but 30 minutes will make a good sauce. Cook spaghetti in a large pot of boiling salted water about 7 minutes. It should be barely tender. Drain and put in a casserole. Lightly flour chicken livers, sauté in butter, and add to sauce. Pour over spaghetti and bake in preheated 350° oven 25 to 30 minutes. Serves 4 to 6. Time: 1¼ hours.

Turkey and Apple Casserole

6 tart apples, peeled, cored, and sliced
¼ cup melted butter
2 cups diced cooked turkey or chicken
salt
½ cup heavy cream

A tart and pleasing way to serve cooked turkey, say a half of a frozen turkey roll. *Serve with baked sweet potatoes; Boston lettuce salad with a lemon dressing; cherry strudel (frozen).*

Arrange half the apple slices in a shallow casserole. Dribble over them half the melted butter. Add diced turkey or chicken, then the rest of the apples and butter. Lightly salt, and then pour in cream. Bake in preheated 350° oven about 30 to 40 minutes. Serves 4. Time: 1 hour.

Chicken Giblet Risotto with Sweet Red Pepper and White Grapes

1½ cups diced chicken giblets
¼ lb. butter
½ cup chopped green onions
1 cup uncooked rice
3½ cups chicken broth
1½ teaspoons grated orange rind
salt, pepper
½ cup seedless white grapes
½ cup diced sweet red (or green) pepper

Since the enchanted day when I was six and food shopping with my mother and the butcher gave me *six* chicken hearts with one chicken, giblets have gotten easier to come by. Now one can buy them in packages at the supermarket or accumulate them from a multiple buy of chickens for the freezer or a party. *Serve with mixed green salad; hot rolls; lemon-curd tarts.*

Cook giblets, onion, and rice in butter for 10 to 15 minutes. Put in a small deep casserole that can take top-of-the-stove heat. Add 2 cups chicken broth, orange rind, and seasonings, bring to a boil, cover, and put in preheated 350° oven. After about 25 to 30 minutes, look at the dish and add more chicken broth if it appears to be drying out. This is, in effect, a baked pilaf, and that means the liquid needed is somewhat variable and must be added as absorbed. About 5 minutes before serving, stir in the white grapes and diced raw peppers. They should be barely heated and slightly wilted but not too much. Fluff with a fork. Serves 4. Time: 1¼ hours.

1 slice of bread makes ¾ cup soft crumbs.

Duck Baked in Applesauce

1 5-lb. Long Island duckling, cut up
flour
salt, pepper
2 tablespoons butter
1 onion, chopped
⅓ cup finely chopped parsley
1 tablespoon flour
1 1-lb. can applesauce

A dish with a Polish influence. *Serve with mashed potatoes; vanilla ice cream and chocolate brownies.*

Dust the duck with flour mixed with salt and pepper. Brown pieces of duck in 1 tablespoon butter and remove. Drain most of the fat that comes off the duck; brown onion in remaining fat. Remove onion with a slotted spoon. Mix parsley, 1 tablespoon of butter, 1 tablespoon flour, and the applesauce. Put half this mixture in a medium casserole. Add browned duck and sautéed onion. Add the rest of the applesauce. Bake in 350° oven until duck is tender and flavors well intermingled, about 1½ hours. Serves 4. Time: 2 hours.

Scalloped Turkey and Oysters

5 tablespoons butter
6 tablespoons flour
2 cups half-and-half
1 teaspoon salt
freshly ground black pepper
1 pint oysters
12 slices cooked turkey
½ cup soft breadcrumbs
½ cup grated cheese
2 tablespoons finely chopped
   parsley

This is an elegant and traditional way of serving turkey several days after the feast. *Serve with asparagus vinaigrette; hot butterflake rolls; meringues with raspberry purée.*

Make a sauce: melt butter and cook with flour for 3 or 4 minutes; add half-and-half, a little at a time, beating vigorously with a wire whip, until smooth and thickened. Add salt and pepper and ½ cup water. When blended, add oysters and their juice and stir until well amalgamated. Put a layer of the oyster sauce in a shallow buttered casserole and add a layer of turkey slices. Repeat until these ingredients are all used. Mix breadcrumbs, cheese, and parsley and sprinkle thickly on top. Bake in a 350° oven for 35 to 40 minutes. Serves 4 to 6. Time: 1 hour.

Turkey Loaf Michel

2 tablespoons finely chopped
   green onion
½ lb. fresh, or 1 6-oz. package
   frozen, mushrooms, sliced
4 tablespoons butter
1 teaspoon grated lemon rind
2 cups diced cooked turkey
1 egg
1 cup milk or cream
½ cup Italian seasoned breadcrumbs
¼ teaspoon thyme
½ cup pistachio nuts
salt, pepper
finely chopped chives
pimiento cut in hearts (if you
   wish)

A frivolous and festive way of using cooked turkey, whether it be from a whole roasted turkey or half of a baked frozen turkey roll. *Serve with tiny new potatoes cooked in their skins; fresh peas; green salad; vanilla ice cream topped with sliced fresh strawberries.*

Sauté onion and mushrooms in butter. Add lemon rind. Blend diced turkey with egg and milk or cream in an electric blender or put the turkey through a meat grinder and mix with egg and milk. Add to onion-and-mushroom mixture along with breadcrumbs, thyme, pistachio nuts, salt, and freshly ground black pepper. Pat into a buttered pottery loaf pan. Sprinkle the top with chives and arrange the pimiento cut in hearts or, of course, in any other design you wish. The round cans of vegetable cutters available in most fancy food-equipment stores give a choice of shapes, or you may cut them free hand. Bake in pre-heated 350° oven 50 minutes to an hour. Serves 4 to 6. Time: 1¼ hours.

Turkey and Cranberry Roll

1 batch dough for drop biscuits
2 cups sliced or coarsely diced cooked or canned turkey
1 can whole-cranberry sauce, slightly broken up

A new twist on the turkey-and-cranberry theme. Now that both are around-the-year foods, it's good to know this simple and savory dish. Duck, guinea hen, or chicken could be used. *Serve with watercress with finely chopped kumquats (the ones preserved in rum); drop biscuits; Roquefort cheese and toasted crackers.*

Pat—don't roll—the biscuit dough into an oval or loaf-shaped casserole so that it forms a lining, letting some hang over the sides. It should be rather thick, say ½ to ¾ of an inch. Put turkey and broken-up cranberry sauce in the dough, fold dough over the top, and pinch together. Bake in a 400° oven 25 to 30 minutes, or until dough is cooked through and lightly browned. Test with a fork. Serves 4. Time: 45 minutes.

Duck Divan

1 large bunch broccoli, stems trimmed, or 1 10-oz. package frozen broccoli
roast duck, chicken, or turkey slices
3 tablespoons butter
3 tablespoons flour
2 cups milk
1 teaspoon dry mustard
salt, pepper
⅓ cup grated Parmesan cheese
½ cup Hollandaise sauce
2 tablespoons sherry
⅓ cup sour cream

Turkey or chicken may be used interchangeably in this dish. A less voluptuous and simpler version omits the Hollandaise and cream. *Serve with French bread; strawberry soufflé.*

Cook broccoli in salted boiling water until barely tender. Drain and arrange in casserole with slices of duck on top. Make a sauce by melting butter and cooking with flour over low heat until almost dry. Add milk a little at a time, stirring constantly until smooth and thickened. Add mustard, salt, and pepper. Stir in grated cheese. Fold in Hollandaise, sherry, and sour cream. (Traditionally, whipped sweet cream is added, but the sour cream is good and convenient). Put in a 350° oven and bake until brown and bubbly, about 30 to 45 minutes. Serves 4. Time: 1 hour.

Pepperidge Farm Turkey Pudding

about 12 slices roast turkey (or
  duck or chicken)
12½-oz. jar preserved kumquats,
  drained, sliced, and juice
  saved
1 8-oz. can small boiled onions
  and juice
1 package Pepperidge Farm
  herb-seasoned stuffing
4 eggs
1 cup milk

Naturally the very best way to eat cold roast
turkey is in the kitchen, pulling it greedily
from the bones with your fingers, but for just
slightly more formal people this is good. The
kumquats give the same acid emphasis as cranberries, but they add a sharp and different
aroma. *Serve with salad of chicory and escarole
with a dressing of mashed hard-cooked egg yolk
mixed with a little oil, tarragon vinegar, salt, and
pepper; rhubarb custard with meringue (see index).*

Place slices of turkey in four deep individual
greased casseroles or one large one. Divide
kumquats and onions into four parts and place
on turkey slices. Mix the stuffing with the
whole raw eggs, half the juice from the kumquats, the juice from the onions, and milk.
No extra seasoning is needed. Pour the stuffing
batter on top of each casserole and bake in
350° oven 35 minutes, or until firm. Serves 4.
Time: 45 minutes.

Polenta with Turkey

1 tablespoon salt
1 cup yellow corn meal
4 tablespoons butter
3 slices bacon, diced
½ lb. mushrooms, sliced
  through the caps and stems
½ cup white wine
1 pt. sour cream
2 cups thin slices roast turkey
  (or chicken or duck)
⅔ cup grated Parmesan cheese
salt and lots of freshly ground
  black pepper

A different and unleftoverish dish to make
with the rest of the roast turkey. *Serve with
cucumbers sliced thin and chilled in French dressing;
cold watermelon.*

Bring 1 quart water to a boil with the salt and
add corn meal slowly. (Turn heat down before
each addition or it will go *plop* in your face.)
Stir with a wooden spoon until smooth and
thick. You will need a large, heavy pan for
this. Melt butter and cook bacon and mushrooms in it at the same time over very low heat
until both are partially done. Add white wine
and sour cream and mix somewhat. Put ⅓ of
the corn meal mixture in a deep casserole;
spread with ⅓ of the slices of turkey. Pour on
⅓ of the bacon-mushrooms-sour-cream-and-
wine mixture. Add another third of the corn
meal mixture. Add more turkey, and so on
until all the ingredients are used. Sprinkle the
top with the Parmesan cheese and bake in 350°
oven 30 minutes. Serves 4. Time: 1 hour.

Roast Duck with Yorkshire Pudding

1 5- or 6-lb. Long Island duckling, cut up
½ lemon
1 package popover mix
2 eggs
2 cups milk
2 cups cranberries, chopped
½ cup sugar

This provocative combination is astoundingly good. Any basic Yorkshire pudding recipe may be used instead of popover mix. *Serve with mixed greens with French dressing (2 parts olive oil, 1 part fresh lime juice, pinch of grated lime peel, pinch of mixed herb blend, salt and pepper).*

Rub the duck with half a lemon. Place, skin side up, on a rack in a shallow roasting pan. Roast, uncovered, in a slow oven until most of the fat has cooked out of the skin. This should take about 1 hour. Meanwhile prepare popover mix according to directions on the box, adding eggs and milk. Remove duck from oven. Pour ⅓ cup duck fat into a deep casserole that has been heated, and arrange the pieces of duck on the bottom. Sprinkle cranberries and sugar over duck and pour in prepared popover mix. Place in a preheated 425° oven for 15 minutes. Then lower heat to 350° and continue cooking until pudding is browned and done, about 45 minutes. Cut pudding in squares, cutting around the pieces of duck, before serving. Serves 4 generously. Time: 2 hours.

Duck with Orange Rice

2 cups roast duck, turkey, or
  chicken, cut julienne fashion
2 tablespoons, plus ¼ cup, butter
¼ cup diced onion
¼ cup finely diced celery
¼ lb. fresh or frozen mushrooms, sliced
2 cups cooked rice
2½ cups orange juice
1 teaspoon salt
dash of pepper

Almost any kind of cold roast fowl blends with this pleasurable mélange of flavors. *Serve with watercress and thinly sliced water chestnuts with sour-cream dressing (⅓ cup sour cream, 1 teaspoon horseradish); hot rolls.*

Sauté duck in 2 tablespoons butter. Melt ¼ cup butter in a saucepan. Add onion, celery, and mushrooms and cook over moderate heat about 5 minutes. Add rice, stirring until it is coated with butter. Transfer the rice combination to a shallow buttered casserole and add duck and orange juice, salt and pepper. Stir once. Cover tightly and bake in 350° oven about 40 minutes, or until liquid is absorbed. Serves 4 amply. Time: 1 hour 15 minutes.

Duck Cooked in Red Wine

1 5-lb. duck, cut up
2 teaspoons powdered ginger
3 tablespoons butter
1 spring onion, top and bulb
  chopped
½ lb. fresh, or 1 6-oz. package
  frozen, mushrooms sliced
1 cup uncooked rice
½ teaspoon chervil
¼ teaspoon marjoram
¼ teaspoon rosemary
salt and pepper
2 cups red wine (preferably
  claret)

Serve with salad of endive, grapefruit segments, white grapes, chopped almonds, with plain fresh sour cream; hot rolls, sweet butter.

Skin the pieces so that the duck will not be too fatty. Season, sprinkle with ginger, and brown the pieces in butter with onion and mushrooms. Spread uncooked rice on the bottom of a deep buttered casserole. Put duck and juice from the pan, mushrooms, and herbs in the casserole and pour in red wine and 1 cup water. Cover casserole tightly and simmer in 350° oven until the duck is tender, about 1 hour. Serves 4. Time: 1¼ hours.

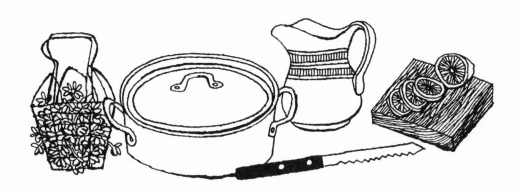

Rock Cornish Hens in Madeira

1 cup uncooked rice
4 Rock Cornish hens
salt and pepper
½ lb. fresh, or 1 6-oz. package
  frozen, mushrooms, sliced
8 to 10 small onions, peeled, or
  1 1-lb. can small boiled onions
1 cup chicken broth
1 cup Madeira

One to be served with a flourish to some very special guests. *Serve with hearts of artichoke marinated in French dressing; hard finger rolls.*

Brown uncooked rice in a dry skillet. Place in bottom of a deep casserole. Season hens well inside, and put in casserole. Surround with mushrooms and onions. Pour broth and wine over hens. Cover tightly and simmer in 350° oven about 30 to 40 minutes, or until tender. Don't thicken the juices, which should be partly absorbed by the rice. Serves 4. Time: 1¼ hours.

Duck in Tangerine Gravy on Parched Rice

1 cup rice
1 duck, about 5 lbs., cut up
4 tablespoons fat from the duck
4 tablespoons flour
2 cups duck broth
1 teaspoon Kitchen Bouquet
salt
2 tablespoons undiluted concentrated tangerine juice

Serve with cucumber mayonnaise (1 cup diced cucumber, 1/2 cup real mayonnaise, preferably homemade); hot biscuits.

Toast the dry rice in a dry skillet over a low flame, shaking it constantly until rice is an even light brown. Put into a saucepan, cover with 1 inch water. Bring to a boil, turn heat low, and steam, tightly covered, about 20 to 25 minutes without looking at it. Remove lid and fluff with a fork. Meanwhile, sauté pieces of duck in their own fat until brown and almost tender. Place rice in a deep buttered casserole with duck on top. Measure 4 tablespoons fat into another pan, add flour, blend, and then add duck broth, Kitchen Bouquet, salt, and tangerine concentrate. Cook the sauce until smooth and thickened. Pour over the duck and rice. Bake in 350° oven 20 to 25 minutes to allow the flavors to become well intermingled. Serves 4. Time: 1½ hours.

Brunswick Stew

1 3½-lb. chicken, cut up
4 tablespoons bacon fat or
  butter
½ cup chopped onion
1½ cups fresh corn cut from
  cob, or 1 12-oz. can cut corn or
  1 10-oz. package frozen cut
  corn
1 cup fresh shelled lima beans,
  or 1 10-oz. package frozen lima
  beans
2½ cups diced fresh, or 1-lb.-4
  oz. can, tomatoes
2 cups bouillon
⅓ cup finely chopped parsley
1 bay leaf
½ teaspoon thyme
1 teaspoon Worcestershire
  sauce
salt, peppercorns
4 slices cooked bacon, crumbled

Some Southern cooks always make this with squirrel and others with rabbit. Both are plentiful in some regions. People in Maryland and Virginia prefer to use chicken. Some stews are cooked to a highly seasoned mush; others, like this, retain the identity of the different ingredients. *Serve with corn bread; lemon chiffon pie.*

Brown the pieces of chicken in bacon fat or butter. Add onion and cook until pale yellow. Put chicken, onion, corn, lima beans, tomatoes, bouillon, and seasonings in a casserole. Bake, covered, in preheated 350° oven for 35 minutes or until chicken is tender and lima beans are cooked. Add bacon and cook 5 or 10 minutes more. This will wait gracefully. Serves 4 to 6. Time: 1¼ hours.

Hasenpfeffer

1 rabbit, fresh or frozen, cut in small pieces
1 cup claret
1 onion, chopped
½ teaspoon thyme
pinch of leaf sage
8 whole peppercorns
¼ lb. butter
½ lb. salt pork, diced
1 bunch small carrots, scraped and cut in 1-inch pieces
8 small white onions or 1 cup frozen chopped onions
8 small potatoes, scraped, or 8 frozen new potatoes
¼ lb. fresh, or 1 6-oz. package frozen, mushrooms
2 tablespoons flour

Serve with mixed greens with French dressing; Italian bread; fresh cherries.

If you are forehanded enough, the rabbit should stand for 2½ hours in the claret, mixed with 1 cup water and 1 chopped onion, and all the seasoning. If you aren't, just call it rabbit stew. Melt butter. Brown rabbit and salt pork in this. Place in a deep buttered casserole. Brown carrots, onions, potatoes, mushrooms in the butter, and then put into the casserole. Mix the butter gravy from skillet with the flour and marinade (or the claret mixed with 1 cup water and seasoning), and pour over rabbit. Cover tightly and simmer about 1 hour in 375° oven until everything is tender (a frozen rabbit takes less time). Serves 4 or more. Time: 4 hours if you marinate the rabbit; if not, just 1½ hours.

Sweet Potatoes Stuffed with Birds

4 very large smooth red sweet potatoes
4 tiny birds (quail or dove), or 4 boned chicken breasts
4 slices bacon
salt and pepper
butter

If you never thought of stuffing sweet potatoes, now is the time to begin. They make an impressive meal, whether you use tiny tender birds or less exotic (and more available) but equally tender chicken breasts. *Serve with tangerine slaw (shredded cabbage and chopped tangerine segments, with a dressing of sour cream mixed with a good squirt of lemon juice and a dash of grated lemon peel); hot butterflake rolls.*

Scrub potato skins well and cut in half lengthwise. Scoop out centers with a melon-ball scoop or a grapefruit knife so that the center is like that of a scooped-out cantaloupe. Wrap a piece of bacon around each bird or chicken breast and put one inside one-half of each potato. Sprinkle with salt and pepper. Put the potato halves back together and skewer closed with toothpicks. Butter the potato skins. Place potatoes in a shallow casserole side by side. Bake in 325° oven until potatoes are done—about an hour. It is almost impossible to overcook; the potatoes get a better flavor the longer they bake. Serves 4. Time: 1½ hours.

Baked Rabbit with Artichokes

2 large artichokes, cut in half
and parboiled 10 minutes
1 rabbit, about 2½ to 3 lbs., cut
in pieces
2 cloves garlic, minced
½ cup olive oil
½ teaspoon thyme
¼ teaspoon rosemary
⅓ to ½ cup finely chopped
parsley
salt
lots of freshly ground black
pepper

Serve with hearts of celery, radishes, wrinkled black olives (the Greek kind); corn sticks.

Cut hard tips off the artichoke leaves. Pull choke from center by the long hairs and throw away. Arrange artichoke halves in bottom of a deep casserole with a lid. Saute pieces of rabbit and garlic in a little olive oil. Transfer to casserole and arrange on top of artichokes. Add the rest of the olive oil and the other ingredients. Cover and bake in a 400° oven for about 1½ hours, adding more olive oil if it starts to dry out. Serves 4. Time: 1¾ hours.

Fish
and
Shellfish

Fish and Shellfish

Fish Fillets with Cheese Sauce and White Grapes

1 cup uncooked rice
2 cups chicken broth
¼ lb. butter
1 lb. fresh or frozen fish fillets
⅓ lb. white grapes, peeled, or 1
   8-oz. can white grapes,
   drained

CHEESE SAUCE

3 tablespoons butter
3 tablespoons flour
1 cup chicken broth
⅔ cup grated Cheddar cheese
½ cup cream
salt and paprika

¼ pound of Cheddar cheese makes 1 cup grated.

This is an English dish which does not fit in with the unkind things that people say about English food. The grapes are really best peeled. *Serve with tossed green salad with French dressing; hot biscuits; fresh raspberries and cream.*

Put rice in a pan with 2 cups chicken broth, bring to a fast rolling boil, cover, and steam over a very low flame for 15 minutes without peeking. Meanwhile make the sauce. Melt butter, add flour, blend, and add 1 cup chicken broth and cook until smooth and thick. Add cheese and stir until it is melted. Add cream and salt and paprika. Cook over low heat, stirring occasionally, until sauce is smooth. Put cooked rice in the bottom of a casserole or deep earthenware platter. Cut butter into as many pieces as there are fish fillets, roll each fillet around a lump of butter, and arrange them on top of rice. If frozen fillets are not thawed completely, arrange them in serving-size chunks with lumps of butter between them on top of the rice. Cover with cheese sauce, sprinkle white grapes on top, and bake in 350° oven about 15 minutes. Serves 4. Time: 45 minutes.

Zuppa da Pesce

½ cup olive oil
2 cloves garlic, halved
1 large solid fish, sea bass or striped bass, about 2 to 2½ lbs.
18 Little Neck clams, well scrubbed
12 mussels, well scrubbed
½ to ¾ lb. raw shrimp, shelled and cleaned
salt and pepper
⅓ to ½ cup chopped parsley

It doesn't matter whether you call it bouillabaisse, cioppino, zuppa da pesce, or just fish stew; whether it has lots of liquid, or, like this, is simmered in its own richly aromatic juices. It's not just good, it's wonderful. To put it in the oven is somewhat illegitimate, but you are much less apt to overcook it. *Serve with rice (for the hearty ones); tossed green salad; French or Italian bread to sop up the juices.*

Put olive oil and garlic in a warm deep casserole and heat. Place the fish on the bottom, then the clams, mussels, shrimp. Season and sprinkle parsley over all. Cover tightly and bake in 350° oven about 25 minutes, or until fish is opaque and flakes when poked with a fork, the shrimp and mussels are open. Baste from time to time with the juices, using an oversized eyedropper called a baster. Serve in deep hot plates. Serves 6 generously. Time: 45 minutes.

Poached Fish Fillets and Fish Balls in Shrimp Sauce

1 lb. fresh or frozen fish fillets
1 cup clam juice or broth from fish balls
2 10-oz. packages frozen chopped spinach (thawed)
1 15-oz. can Danish or Norwegian fish balls, cut in half
2 cans frozen condensed cream of shrimp soup (thawed)

Some of the Danish and Norwegian fish balls come canned in bouillon or broth, others in water. If using the former, poach the fillets in the broth. *Serve with cucumber salad; hot corn sticks; cherry cheesecake.*

Poach fish fillets briefly in clam juice or broth until opaque. Arrange thawed spinach in casserole. Arrange fish fillets on top and fish balls on top of the fillets. Pour in the thawed but undiluted shrimp soup. Bake in 350° oven 35 to 45 minutes. Serves 4. Time: 1¼ hours.

Paprika Fish

4 medium potatoes, cooked, peeled, and cut in ½-inch slices
2 large green peppers, parboiled, seeded, and sliced
salt, pepper
2 large tomatoes, skinned, seeded, and diced
2 lbs. fillet of flounder or haddock, cut in pieces
3 slices bacon, diced and cooked briefly to remove excess fat but not until done
1 cup clam juice
1 tablespoon Hungarian sweet rose paprika
1 tablespoon flour
1 cup sour cream

Hungarians in their dishes use fish that are not found here. Theirs are all fresh-water fish, as is natural in a landlocked country. Their methods of cooking, however, are applicable to other varieties. *Serve with noodles; Boston lettuce with white grapes, oil-and-lemon dressing; hard rolls; glazed oranges.*

Arrange cooked potato slices in bottom of a shallow casserole greased with bacon drippings. Cover with green pepper slices. Add some salt and pepper, then a layer of diced tomatoes. Season again lightly. Arrange fish on top and sprinkle with half-cooked pieces of bacon. Pour in clam juice. Mix paprika and flour and sprinkle on top. Bake in preheated 400° oven 15 to 20 minutes, or until fish looks opaque and can be flaked with a fork. Remove casserole from oven and spread sour cream on top. Bake 5 minutes more. Serves 4. Time: 50 minutes.

Fish Stuffed with Parsley and Onion

1 bunch parsley, chopped coarsley, without stems
1 small onion, minced
½ cup salad oil
1 2-lb. sea bass or mackerel, cleaned and boned, with head and tail left on
salt and pepper

Serve with new potatoes, a salad of very young tender beet, mustard, and turnip greens with sour-cream dressing; cloverleaf rolls; lemon chiffon pie.

Mix parsley and onion with just enough salad oil to bind them together loosely. Season, and stuff the fish with the mixture and sew together, or skewer together with toothpicks or poultry nails. Curl the fish and fit it into a large shallow casserole. Bake in preheated 400° oven 35 minutes, or until the flesh is tender and flaky when poked with a fork, basting with the rest of the oil from time to time. Before serving pour off any surplus oil. Serves 4. Time: 50 minutes.

Fish Baked in Cream and Horseradish

1½ lbs. fish fillets
1 cup bottled clam juice
1 small onion, chopped
3 tablespoons butter
3 tablespoons flour
1 cup heavy cream or sour cream
salt and pepper
2 tablespoons freshly grated horseradish, or 4 tablespoons bottled grated horseradish
2 tablespoons chopped chives

Any fish fillet, fresh or frozen, may be used in this dish. *Serve with baked potatoes; mixed green salad; French bread; fresh raspberries with heavy cream and chocolate shavings.*

Simmer fillets in clam juice with onion until fish is opaque. Drain fish, strain the liquid, and save for sauce. Cook butter and flour together 3 or 4 minutes until dry and blended, add strained clam juice, beating vigorously with a wire whip. Add cream, half at a time, and beat to blend. Season and cook until smooth and thickened. Stir in horseradish and chives. Arrange the fillets on a shallow buttered baking dish and cover with sauce. Bake in preheated 350° oven about 20 minutes. Put under the broiler about 5 minutes to brown and blister. Serves 4. Time: 1 hour.

Fish Fillets in Sour Cream and Wine Sauce

3 medium potatoes, peeled and sliced thin
2 tablespoons butter
salt, pepper
1 cup sour cream
½ lb. fresh, or 1 6-oz. package frozen, mushrooms, sliced
⅔ cup dry white wine
2 lbs. fish fillets, cut in small squares

Serve with romaine salad; hot flaky rolls; cherry pie.

Line a shallow buttered casserole with potato slices, overlapping a bit. Dot with butter and sprinkle with salt and pepper. Add half the sour cream. Simmer mushrooms for 5 minutes in wine. Pour wine and mushrooms into the casserole. Arrange pieces of fish on top. Sprinkle with more salt and pepper. Spread the rest of the sour cream on top. Bake in 350° oven 40 to 50 minutes or until potatoes are tender and fish flaky. Serves 4. Time: 1¼ hours.

Fillets of Flounder with Asparagus and Cream of Shrimp Soup

1 lb. fresh, or 1 10-oz. package frozen, asparagus
1 lb. fillets of flounder or haddock, fresh or frozen
1 cup dry white wine
salt, pepper
1 can frozen condensed cream of shrimp soup, undiluted, partially thawed
breadcrumbs
butter

A pleasant dish, easily assembled. *Serve with spoon bread; sliced cucumbers with chopped parsley; warm cherry strudel (frozen).*

Wash and break off the tough ends of the asparagus, if fresh. Cook in boiling salted water until almost tender. Drain. Arrange in a shallow buttered casserole with fish fillets on top. Add white wine, salt, pepper, and cream of shrimp soup. Sprinkle the top with breadcrumbs and dot with small pieces of butter. Bake in preheated 350° oven 45 to 55 minutes or until fish is opaque and flakes when poked with a fork, and the top is crusty and brown. Serves 4. Time: 1¼ hours.

Fish Fillets with Mussel or Oyster Sauce

COURT BOUILLON

1 small onion, chopped
1 carrot, scraped and chopped
2 cups white wine
salt and pepper
1 lb. fish fillets

SAUCE

3 tablespoons butter
3 tablespoons flour
court bouillon
½ cup heavy cream
salt
paprika
1 lb. fresh mussels or oysters, or 1 9-oz. can mussels, drained
⅓ cup white grapes

This will impress your friends out of all proportion to the slight fuss of preparation. *Serve with baked potatoes; sliced cucumbers, chilled in diluted tarragon vinegar; French bread; fresh raspberries mixed with equal amounts of cold cooked rice and whipped cream.*

Make a court bouillon by simmering onion, carrot, and white wine and seasoning for about 15 minutes. Poach fish fillets in this until they are white and opaque, about 5 to 10 minutes. Remove fillets, drain, and put in a warm shallow casserole. Strain the court bouillon. Melt butter, blend in flour, and add the court bouillon slowly. Add heavy cream, salt, and paprika. Stir and cook until the sauce is smooth and thick. Remove from stove. If fresh mussels are used, scrub, and steam them until the shells open. Add mussels or raw oysters to the sauce and pour over the fish fillets in the casserole. Sprinkle white grapes on top and bake briefly in 350° oven, about 20 minutes. Serves 4. Time: 1 hour.

Corinne's Fish Tuesday

4 small onions, sliced
1 clove garlic, sliced
2 tablespoons olive oil
1 6-oz. can Italian tomato paste
2 bay leaves, crumbled
1 teaspoon cinnamon
salt and pepper
2 lbs. fresh or frozen fish fillets

It's the seasoning that makes this sauce on the fillets different and delicious, shocking as it may sound to a conventional cook. *Serve with hashed potatoes; lettuce with lemon dressing (3 parts heavy cream, 1 part lemon juice, dash of grated lemon peel, pinch of salt); muffins.*

Sauté onions and garlic in oil until soft. Add tomato paste, bay leaves, cinnamon, salt, pepper, and 1 cup water. Simmer until you have a thick, smooth, and fragrant sauce, about 20 to 25 minutes. Arrange the fillets in a shallow casserole. Pour sauce over them. Bake in 350° oven 20 minutes or until the fish is white and flaky. Serves 4. Time: 45 minutes.

Baked Fish Fillets in Mustard Sauce

3 medium-sized potatoes, boiled
  and sliced
2 tablespoons butter
1 lb. fresh or frozen fish fillets
½ cup dry white wine
1 tablespoon prepared mustard
a little salt
1 tablespoon capers

Serve with quartered or sliced Japanese persimmons with chicory and a dressing of 2 parts salad oil (not olive), 1 part fresh lime juice, grated lime peel; French bread; custard pie with chocolate meringue (see index).

Brown potatoes in butter. Put them in a shallow casserole and arrange the fillets on top. Dilute the wine with ⅓ cup water, mix with mustard little by little, and pour over fillets. Add salt. Sprinkle the top with capers. Bake in 350° oven until the fillets are white and flaky—about 20 minutes. Serves 3 to 4. Time: 40 minutes.

Fillets of Sole East Indian

6 fillets of sole or flounder
(about 1½ lbs.)
about 5 tablespoons butter
1 spring onion, top and bulb
chopped
salt and pepper
1 teaspoon curry powder
¾ cup white wine
¼ lb. fresh mushrooms, sliced
2 tablespoons flour
½ cup milk
2 pimientos, diced

Serve with baked potatoes; salad of lettuce, cooked green beans, French dressing; cornbread.

Put fillets and onion in buttered skillet (to keep from breaking fillets). Season with salt, pepper, and curry powder. Add white wine and poach over very low heat until fish is white (about 10 minutes). Remove fillets to a casserole. Strain the liquid in which fish cooked. Sauté mushrooms in about 2 tablespoons butter. Melt 2 more tablespoons butter, blend with the flour, add milk and the wine liquid plus ¼ cup water slowly, stirring until smooth and thickened. Pour over fish in casserole and garnish with mushrooms and pimientos dotted with 1 tablespoon butter. Bake at 350° 15 to 20 minutes, or until brown and bubbly. Serves 4 or more. Time: 50 minutes.

Halibut Steak with Olive and Almond Sauce

¼ lb. butter
¼ cup almonds, blanched and
slivered
2 teaspoons dry mustard
2 tablespoons tarragon vinegar,
diluted with 2 tablespoons
water
¼ cup chopped or sliced ripe
olives
2 lbs. halibut steak, fresh or
frozen

With a couple of good sauces in your culinary repertoire, it is easy to get a reputation for being a good cook. This one, with sharp contrasts in texture, flavor, and color, is good with either fish or chicken. *Serve with rice cooked in chicken broth; salad of quartered tomatoes, sliced leeks (the white part only) in individual bowls, with French dressing; French bread; rhubarb custard pie (see index).*

Melt butter, sauté almonds lightly, and add mustard, vinegar, and olives. Arrange fish steaks in a shallow buttered casserole. Pour the sauce over the top and bake at 350° until the fish is opaque, about 25 to 35 minutes. Serves 4. Time: 40 minutes.

Halibut Steak in Lemon Sauce

2 cups mashed potatoes, or 3
   medium-sized potatoes, boiled
   and diced
1½ lbs. fresh or frozen halibut
   steak
2 tablespoons butter
2 tablespoons flour
2 tablespoons lemon juice
1 cup chicken broth
salt and pepper
1 tablespoon chopped chives
1 teaspoon grated lemon rind

Nothing revolutionary, but we like the flavor added by chives and chicken broth. *Serve with salad of marinated cooked string beans with dressing of 2 parts olive oil, 1 part vinegar, salt and pepper, pinch of sugar, chopped black walnuts; cornbread.*

Put potatoes in the bottom of a low buttered casserole. Place halibut on top. Make sauce by melting the butter, blending in the flour, and adding lemon juice, chicken broth, salt, and pepper. Pour over the fish and potatoes. Sprinkle top with chives and lemon peel. Bake in 350° oven 20 to 25 minutes. Serves 4. Time: 30 minutes.

Baked Codfish

4 large potatoes, sliced very thin
4 cups canned codfish flakes, or
   1½ lbs. fresh codfish steaks or
   fillets
5 onions, sliced very thin
2 cups (1-lb. can) tomatoes
2 tablespoons olive oil
1 cup chicken broth (or water)
salt and pepper
1 green pepper, chopped (without seeds)
breadcrumbs
2 tablespoons butter

A Boston dish with Portuguese overtones. *Serve with cole slaw with Pennsylvania sweet cream dressing (toss 1 small head cabbage, shredded fine, with ½ cup heavy cream, ¼ cup vinegar, ½ cup sugar); corn bread.*

Butter a deep casserole. Place half the potatoes on the bottom, then half the fish, half the onions, and half the tomatoes. Add olive oil, salt and pepper, and repeat the layers in the same order. Pour in 1 cup liquid, water or broth. Sprinkle the top with minced green pepper and breadcrumbs and dot with butter. Bake in 350° oven 35 to 45 minutes or until potatoes are tender. Serves 4. Time: 50 minutes.

Halibut Steak with Onions

1½ lbs. fresh or frozen halibut
  steak
salt and pepper
1 onion, cut in thin slices
melted butter
⅓ cup heavy cream

Simple and soothing, to cook and to eat, after a hard, hard day. *Serve with potato salad with dressing made with 1 part vinegar and 1 part hot bacon drippings, topped with crumbled cooked bacon; hot rolls.*

Put the fish in a buttered baking dish, sprinkle with salt and pepper, and cover with slices of onion pulled into rings. Dribble melted butter over the onion and fish. Add cream. Bake in 350° oven 20 to 25 minutes or until the fish is tender. The onion should be slightly crisp and underdone. Serves 4. Time: 30 minutes.

Codfish with Wine and Egg Sauce

2 tablespoons butter
2 tablespoons flour
1 tablespoon chopped chives
salt and pepper
½ cup cream
½ cup white wine
1 lb. fresh codfish, or ½ lb.
  dried codfish, soaked and
  flaked, or 2 cups canned
  codfish
2 eggs, hard-cooked

Cape Cod on the loose. *Serve with salad of romaine, slivered cooked string beans, chopped pimiento, sliced cooked beets, and French dressing; biscuits.*

Make cream sauce by melting butter, blending in flour, adding chives and seasonings, and then the liquids slowly. Pull the fish apart. Peel and chop hard-cooked eggs and add to sauce with the codfish. Put in a shallow baking dish and bake in 350° oven 30 minutes or until brown and bubbly. Serves 4. Time: 45 minutes.

New Brunswick Haddock Hash

1 lb. haddock fillets
2 slices lemon
1 bay leaf
¼ lb. salt pork, blanched and
  diced, or 4 slices bacon,
  cooked and crumbled
3 cups diced cooked potatoes
½ cup heavy cream
1 cup diced cooked beets
salt, freshly ground black pepper

A Canadian piscatorial version of red flannel hash. *Serve with sweet pickles; hot corn bread; lemon chiffon pie.*

Simmer haddock in water to cover, with lemon and bay leaf, until tender. Drain and flake. Mix with blanched salt pork or cooked and crumbled bacon, potatoes, heavy cream, and beets. Season with salt and pepper and put into a baking dish. Bake in preheated 400° oven 15 to 20 minutes. Serves 4. Time: 45 minutes.

Mackerel in Wine Sauce

2 tablespoons butter
2 tablespoons flour
½ teaspoon basil
salt and pepper
½ cup cream
½ cup white wine
2 lbs. frozen or fresh mackerel, cleaned, boned, and split (salt mackerel won't do)
3 tomatoes, sliced

Mackerel in a patrician guise. *Serve with salad of sliced avocado and grapefruit segments with French dressing and topped with ⅓ cup finely chopped parsley; spoon bread (see index); sliced or canned pears topped with mashed raspberries, fresh or frozen.*

Make a wine sauce, melting butter, blending in flour and seasonings, and adding the liquids —first cream and then wine—slowly, stirring constantly until smooth and thickened. Season fish with salt and pepper and lay it on the bottom of a casserole. Place tomato slices on top and pour in the wine sauce. Bake in 350° oven, 30 minutes or until fish is opaque and flaky. Serves 4. Time: 50 minutes.

> To peel a tomato, hold it for a minute in boiling water or gas flame, then pull off skin with a knife.

Baked Ocean Perch with Rice

1 cup raw rice
1 lb. fresh or frozen ocean perch fillets, or any other fillets
1 spring onion, top and bulb chopped
2 tablespoons butter
juice of ½ lemon
1 bay leaf
½ teaspoon sugar
salt and pepper
2 cups (1-lb. can) tomatoes
pinch of gumbo filé

One of the easiest, and one of the best. A delicious fish that lends itself extremely well to casserole treatment. *Serve with green beans and almonds; stuffed celery (stuff 4-inch pieces of celery with ½ Roquefort, blended well and slightly thinned with cream, ½ cream cheese); Italian bread; sour-cream mousse.*

Put uncooked rice in the bottom of a low buttered casserole and place perch fillets on top. Sauté onion gently in butter, add lemon juice, sugar, seasoning (except filé powder), and tomatoes. Cook for 10 minutes and pour over the fish and rice. Add 1 cup water, cover, and bake at 350° for 35 to 40 minutes, or until rice is cooked and the liquid absorbed. Just before serving, add the gumbo filé powder—it toughens if cooked. Serves 4. Time: 1 hour.

Swordfish Casserole

extra-long tops only of 2
  bunches scallions or leeks
2 lbs. fresh or frozen swordfish
  steak
1 cup clam broth
8 tiny new potatoes, boiled and
  peeled, or 8 frozen new potatoes
8 tiny beets, boiled and peeled,
  or 1 8-oz. can tiny whole beets,
  drained
salt and pepper

*Serve with mixed green salad with French dressing;
hot corn bread; fresh or frozen pineapple chunks
marinated in rum.*

Line a low buttered casserole with tops of
scallions or leeks. Place swordfish on the leeks,
add ½ cup clam broth, and bake in a 450°
oven 10 minutes. Remove from oven, reduce
heat to 350°, place potatoes and beets in a ring
around the swordfish, add remaining clam
broth, and return to the oven. Bake 30 minutes more, or until the swordfish is opaque and
flakes easily with a fork. Serves 4. Time:
1¼ hours.

Swordfish or Halibut Steaks with Anchovy Sauce

1½ lbs. swordfish or halibut
  steaks
½ cup olive oil
½ 2-oz. can anchovies, each cut
  in three pieces
pepper

*Serve with baked potatoes; watercress with sliced
pickled mushrooms; French bread; fresh cherries.*

Arrange the swordfish in a shallow casserole,
anoint with the olive oil, and sprinkle the
anchovies on top. Be lavish with freshly ground
black pepper. Bake in 350° oven until the fish
is opaque, about 20 to 30 minutes. Serves 4.
Time: 30 minutes.

Salmon Steaks with Lima Beans

1½ lbs. fresh or frozen salmon
  steaks
2 tablespoons olive oil
3 medium-sized potatoes, boiled
  and diced
1 10-oz. package frozen lima
  beans or 1 pt. fresh lima beans,
  shelled
½ teaspoon dry mustard
1 tablespoon lemon juice and a
  bit of grated lemon peel
salt and pepper
2 cups sour cream

*Serve with salad of sliced cucumber and lettuce with
French dressing; French bread cut in hunks.*

Sauté salmon briefly in olive oil and transfer to
a low buttered casserole. Brown potatoes in
the same skillet. Place in casserole with lima
beans. Stir mustard, lemon juice and grated
lemon peel, salt, and pepper into sour cream,
add to the casserole, and bake in 350° oven 50
to 60 minutes. Serves 4. Time: 1¼ hours.

Swordfish Steak Baked in Sweet Cream

1½ lbs. swordfish steak
½ lime
1 lb. fresh peas, or 1 10-oz. package frozen peas parboiled
½ pt. (1 cup) heavy cream
1 tablespoon grated lime peel (no juice)
salt and pepper

Swordfish steak is one of the most delicate and adaptable foods to come from the sea. These days it is available almost everywhere. *Serve with potato soufflé (see index); tomato aspic, watercress, and mayonnaise mixed with capers; hot butterflake rolls; fresh raspberries and cream.*

Rub both sides of swordfish steak with half a lime. Place fish in a shallow casserole that has a lid. Add peas, then cream, and top with grated lime peel, salt, and pepper. Cover and bake in a 350° oven until the meat is white and flaky, about 25 to 30 minutes. Serve in the cream — which will have cooked down and thickened by this time. Serves 4. Time: 45 minutes.

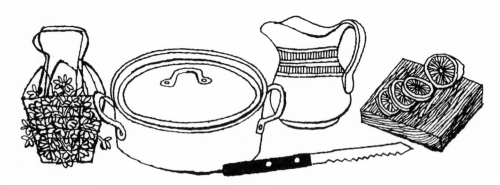

Salmon Steaks in Wine and Egg Sauce

2 tablespoons butter
2 tablespoons flour
½ cup milk — or, better, cream
½ cup white wine
¼ teaspoon basil
salt and pepper
2 eggs, hard-cooked
1 tablespoon capers
1½ lbs. fresh or frozen salmon steaks
1 10-oz. package frozen peas, or 1½ lbs. fresh peas, shelled

According to best gastronomic customs, the same wine is used at the table as is used in the dish. *Serve with tiny new potatoes boiled and served in their skins; salad of mixed greens with French dressing; French bread.*

Make a cream sauce by melting butter, blending in flour, adding the liquids and seasonings slowly, and stirring over low heat until smooth and thickened. Peel and chop the eggs. Add, with the capers, to the sauce. Place salmon in the bottom of a shallow buttered casserole. Place uncooked peas over it, and pour the sauce over all. Bake in 350° oven 25 to 35 minutes, or until the salmon is tender and opaque. Serves 4. Time: 50 minutes.

Salmon Baked with Belgian Endive

1 lb. Belgian endive
1 tablespoon butter
½ cup beef bouillon
1 1-lb. can red salmon, drained
    and flaked
2 eggs
1 cup milk
1 teaspoon grated lemon rind
salt, pepper
butter

The name endive means different greens to different people — to some, chicory; but here it means the slim, elegantly formed, subtly colored, and differently flavored green, served both raw and cooked, that we call Belgian endive and others, witloof. It is expensive when compared to everyday greens like spinach and such, but worth it for special occasions. *Serve with grapefruit and avocado salad with oil-and-vinegar dressing; hot poppyseed rolls; lemon meringue pie.*

3 ounces dried mushrooms equal 1 pound fresh.

Cook endive in 1 tablespoon butter and the bouillon for 20 to 30 minutes. Drain and put in a shallow casserole. Arrange salmon flakes over the endive. Buzz eggs, milk, lemon rind, salt, and pepper in the blender. Pour over salmon and endive. Dot with small pieces of butter. Bake in preheated 325° oven 30 minutes or until the custard is set. Serves 4. Time: 1¼ hours.

Baked Salmon with Mushrooms

1 small onion, chopped fine
½ lb. fresh, or 1 6-oz. package
    frozen, mushrooms, sliced
2 tablespoons butter
3 tablespoons flour
3 tablespoons heavy cream
salt
2 1-lb. cans salmon, drained and
    flaked
2 eggs, beaten with a fork
3 tablespoons chopped parsley
1 teaspoon dried dill
salt, pepper
1 pt. sour cream
3 tablespoons tarragon vinegar
4 tablespoons Italian seasoned
    breadcrumbs
butter

A somewhat varied approach to usual ingredients. *Serve with watercress, cucumber, and radish with oil-and-vinegar dressing; hot sesame rolls; cream puff filled with lemon curd.*

Cook onion and mushrooms in butter until limp. Sprinkle with flour. Stir and add heavy cream. Salt to taste. Mix flaked salmon with eggs, parsley, dill, and salt and pepper to taste. Put half the salmon mixture in a shallow buttered casserole. Spread over it onion-and-mushroom mixture and top with the rest of the salmon mixture. Thin sour cream with tarragon vinegar and pour over the top of the casserole. Sprinkle with breadcrumbs and dot with small pieces of butter. Bake in preheated 350° oven 30 minutes or until crusty and golden. Serves 4 to 6. Time: 50 minutes.

Salmon Soufflé

3 tablespoons butter
3 tablespoons flour
1 cup milk
¼ teaspoon thyme
½ teaspoon dry English mustard
salt and pepper
3 eggs, separated
1 7¾-oz. can salmon, flaked

For that unexpected guest. *Serve with salad of lettuce, radishes, and sliced cucumber, with French dressing; drop biscuits.*

Make cream sauce by melting butter, blending in flour, and adding milk slowly, stirring until smooth and thickened. Add thyme, mustard, salt, and pepper. Remove from stove, let cool slightly, add yolks of eggs and salmon, and stir well. Beat egg whites until stiff and fold into sauce. Put in a buttered casserole with straight sides and bake in 375° oven 40 to 45 minutes, or until the top springs back when lightly touched. Serves 4. Time: 1¼ hours.

Salmon Loaf with Cucumber Sauce

1 1-lb. can salmon
2 medium-sized onions,
  chopped fine
4 celery stalks, chopped
12 saltines, mashed fine
salt and pepper
2 eggs
1 cup milk

CUCUMBER SAUCE

1 cucumber, peeled and diced
2 tablespoons butter
2 tablespoons flour
1 cup boiling water
½ teaspoon salt
½ lemon, juice and grated peel
2 egg yolks

Serve with green pepper and onion rings marinated in French dressing, romaine; Ry-Krisp; apricot upside-down cake.

Mix the loaf ingredients together in the order given and put them in a greased pottery loaf pan. Bake in 350° oven until firm, about 40 to 45 minutes. To make sauce, simmer cucumber in water until it is transparent. Melt butter in a double boiler. Blend in flour. Add boiling water and salt and cook until thick. Add lemon juice and peel and the drained cooked cucumber, and mix thoroughly. Remove from the fire. Beat egg yolks and stir them into the sauce. Serve with the loaf. Serves 4. Time: 1 hour.

Baked Tuna Niçoise

2 7-oz. cans solid-packed tuna
3 green onions, chopped
⅓ cup chopped parsley
1 10-oz. package frozen green
  beans, cooked
2 whole canned pimientos, cut
  in pieces
3 small new potatoes, cooked,
  peeled, and diced
6 to 8 black olives, pitted
4 to 6 anchovies, cut in pieces
1 8-oz. can tomato sauce (or
  more)
salt, pepper
1 tablespoon capers

This is obviously much the same as a *salade niçoise* but served hot on a cold day. Ingredients may be added and omitted according to whim. *Serve with French bread; orange chiffon pie.*

Mix together everything except capers and place in shallow casserole. Add another can of tomato sauce if needed, according to bulk. Sprinkle top with capers. Bake in 350° oven about 25 to 35 minutes. Serves 4 or more. Time: 50 minutes.

Leftover pimientos won't spoil if covered with cooking oil and kept in refrigerator.

Laks Pudding

4 thick slices smoked salt
  salmon (6 x 2 inches)
milk
4 medium-sized boiled potatoes,
  sliced
2 eggs
1½ cups light cream
2 sprigs fresh dill, chopped, or
  ½ teaspoon dried dill

This laks (or salmon) pudding, delicate in color, flavor, and texture, is a specialty of Rolf Svensson, chef of the Swedish-American Line's *Stockholm. Serve with a pale green cucumber salad that complements the pale pink of the pudding; hot French bread; fruit and cheese.*

Soak salmon several hours, or overnight, in milk. Drain and stand slices on end in buttered casserole, alternating with slices of potatoes. Beat eggs and add cream to them. Stir until well blended. Sprinkle dill on the salmon and potatoes. Pour in the egg mixture. Bake in preheated 350° oven 20 to 25 minutes. Serves 4. Time: 4 hours (including minimum soaking time).

Tuna Fish in Mushroom Sauce

2 tablespoons butter
2 tablespoons flour
½ teaspoon marjoram
salt and pepper
1 cup milk
½ lb. fresh, or 1 6-oz. package frozen, mushrooms, sliced
2 7-oz. cans tuna fish
breadcrumbs
2 tablespoons grated Cheddar cheese

Keep this in reserve for a lazy Sunday evening. *Serve with Chinese fried noodles; salad of watercress, romaine, cucumbers, and white grapes, with French dressing; hot drop biscuits.*

Make a cream sauce, melting butter, blending in flour and seasonings, and adding milk slowly, stirring until smooth and thickened. Stir in mushrooms and tuna fish and pour into a shallow buttered casserole. Sprinkle breadcrumbs mixed with cheese over the top and bake in 350° oven 20 minutes. Serves 4. Time: 30 minutes.

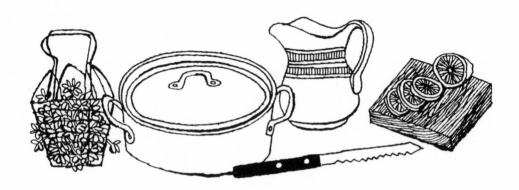

Tuna Fish and Spinach in Lemon Sauce

¼ cup butter
¼ cup flour
2 cups chicken broth
1 egg yolk, beaten
juice of 1 lemon, strained
salt and pepper
1 10-oz. package frozen, or 1 lb. fresh, chopped spinach, cooked and drained
2 7-oz. cans white tuna, drained and separated with a fork
buttered breadcrumbs

Two sometimes mundane foods given the glamour treatment. *Serve with Chinese fried noodles; cherry tomatoes; butterflake rolls.*

Make the sauce by melting butter, rubbing in flour until smooth, and gradually adding broth. Cook, stirring constantly, until slightly thickened. Remove from fire, stir in beaten egg yolk, strained lemon juice, salt, and pepper. Mix half the sauce with the chopped spinach and transfer to a shallow buttered casserole. Arrange flaked tuna on top, and pour over it the balance of the sauce. Sprinkle with buttered breadcrumbs and bake in 350° oven 15 to 20 minutes. Serves 4. Time: 40 minutes.

Sardine Tarts

1 large onion, chopped fine
2 cans large, plump sardines in oil or tomato sauce, or 8 fresh smelts, cleaned, plus 2 tablespoons olive oil
½ cup Durkee's dressing
pie dough for 1 crust

Sardines can be more than a quick snack. The big fat ones canned in oil are best for this recipe, although the ones in tomato sauce might combine with the mustard sauce in an interesting way. *Serve with French-fried potatoes; salad of young greens, radishes, and spring onions with French dressing; hot toast.*

Take four individual casseroles and sprinkle ¼ the chopped onion in each. Arrange sardines on the beds of onion, and pour Durkee's dressing on top. Top each casserole with a circle of pie dough. Bake in preheated 400° oven about 15 minutes, or until piecrust is browned. The onions will be pleasantly underdone and crisp. Serves 4. Time: 30 minutes.

Baked Creamed Finnan Haddie

1½ lbs. finnan haddie
milk
3 tablespoons butter
3 tablespoons flour
2 tablespoons lemon juice
a little salt
1½ cups milk (not that the fish was cooked in)
⅓ cup grated Parmesan cheese
⅓ cup finely chopped parsley

An old-fashioned dish that suits our new-fashioned ways of cooking and eating. *Serve with baked potatoes; salad of sliced cucumbers with thin strips of green pepper, chilled in French dressing; hot toast circles; lemon sherbet.*

Soak finnan haddie in milk 1 hour. Simmer in the same milk until white and opaque, about 20 minutes. Drain, discard milk, and flake. Melt butter, blend in flour, and add lemon juice and a small amount of salt — the fish has some. Add milk slowly, stirring until smooth and thick. Mix with the flaked fish, sprinkle the top with grated cheese and parsley and bake in 350° oven 20 minutes, or until the cheese is melted and slightly browned. Serves 4. Time: 2 hours.

Clam Batter Pudding and Salt-Pork Gravy

¼ lb. salt pork, sliced crosswise
   ¼ inch thick
1 12-oz. can minced clams and
   juice
1 egg
1 package corn-bread mix
1½ tablespoons flour, plus flour
   for salt pork
salt and pepper
1 cup milk

This is for those with lusty appetites who like seafood but don't think it sufficiently filling. *Serve with raw spinach salad with onion rings and cucumber slices, and French dressing; orange sherbet.*

Soak pork in warm water for 10 minutes. Mix clams, clam juice, and egg with the corn-bread mix. Bake in a deep greased quart casserole about 15 minutes in a 350° oven. The pudding must be somewhat the consistency of spoon bread and should be served with a spoon. Meanwhile drain water from salt-pork slices, flour lightly, and sauté in an iron skillet until golden and crunchy. Pour out all the fat except for about 2 tablespoons. Add flour, salt, and pepper and stir over low heat until browned and blended. Add milk slowly and cook until thickened. Serve the gravy in a pitcher, and put the salt-pork slices around the pudding. Serves 4. Time: 30 minutes.

Clam and Eggplant Casserole

1 large eggplant, cubed but *not*
   peeled
1 medium onion, chopped
3 tablespoons butter
2 7-oz. cans minced clams
2 cups dry breadcrumbs
⅓ cup finely chopped parsley
salt
freshly ground black pepper
¼ cup milk
more butter

A subtle and enticing combination of flavors, simple and frugal to make and not very fattening — what more could one ask of a dish? *Serve with cherry tomatoes; onion rolls; pear and custard pie.*

Cook eggplant in boiling salted water to cover for about 10 minutes, then drain. Sauté onion in 3 tablespoons butter until limp and golden. Drain clams and save the juice. Mix clams with onion and butter in which onion was cooked. Mix the crumbs with the parsley. Sprinkle a thin layer of crumbs in a shallow buttered casserole, then a layer of eggplant, then a layer of clams. Season each layer with salt and pepper and repeat until all ingredients are used, ending with a layer of crumbs. Pour clam juice and milk over all. Dot with small pieces of butter. Bake in preheated 350° oven 45 to 50 minutes or until the top is brown and crusty. Serves 4. Time: 1½ hours.

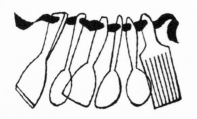

Clam Stew

3 large onions, sliced
6 potatoes, cubed
6 slices lean bacon, cut in 1-inch
  pieces
2 cups milk or half-and-half
3 tablespoons butter
1 pt. freshly shucked clams,
  chopped, or 2 7-oz. cans
  minced clams
pinch of nutmeg
salt and pepper

If you use canned clams, you can whip this up easily for an impromptu late supper. *Serve with salad of lettuce, grapefruit segments, and French dressing (2 parts olive oil, 1 part grapefruit or lemon juice, salt and pepper); apricot nut pudding (see index); sea biscuit.*

Cook onions and potatoes in just enough water to cover for 15 minutes. Fry bacon until brown. Put bacon, onions, potatoes, milk, butter, clams and juice, and seasoning in a deep buttered casserole. Cover and simmer in 350° oven 15 to 20 minutes. Serves 4. Time: 45 minutes.

Yellow Squash with Clams, Parsley, and Bacon

8 small or 4 large yellow
  squashes or zucchini, sliced
  thin but not peeled
1 12-oz. can minced clams
6 strips cooked crumbled bacon
1/3 cup finely chopped parsley,
  or 4 green onions, tops and
  bottoms finely chopped
salt and pepper

Serve with tomatoes scooped out and filled with diced cucumber and mayonnaise; salt-sticks (brown-and-serve); Italian cheesecake (see index).

Make a layer of half the squash slices in a shallow casserole, and add half the minced clams and juice. Sprinkle with salt and pepper and half the bacon and parsley or onion. Repeat. Bake in 350° oven 20 to 25 minutes or until the squash is tender. Serves 4. Time: 40 minutes.

Clam and Spinach Soufflé

1 lb. fresh washed spinach, or 1
  10-oz. package frozen chopped
  spinach
1 12-oz. can minced clams, well
  drained
3 tablespoons butter
3 tablespoons flour
1 tablespoon grated lemon peel
1/8 teaspoon nutmeg
salt and pepper
2/3 cup heavy cream
3 eggs, separated

Serve with codfish balls; French bread; Roquefort cheese and crackers.

Cover and cook spinach in its own moisture until barely tender. Drain thoroughly and put through a food mill or purée in the blender. Mix with clams. While spinach is cooking make a heavy cream sauce by melting butter, blending in flour, lemon peel, nutmeg, salt and pepper; add cream slowly, cooking until smooth and very thick. Remove from heat, stir in egg yolks, blend, and add the spinach-and-clam mixture. Beat whites until stiff and fold in gently. Pile into a buttered casserole with straight sides. Bake in 350° oven 40 to 50 minutes, or until the top springs back when lightly touched. Serves 4. Time: 1¼ hours.

Oysters and Parched Rice

1 cup raw rice
½ lb. fresh, or 1 9-oz. package frozen, green beans
salt and pepper
½ green pepper, chopped, without seeds
1 pt. fresh oysters and their liquor, or 2 7-oz. cans frozen oysters
1 teaspoon gumbo filé

Parched rice is a simple, Oriental way of giving rice a delicately nutty flavor and an appetizing tan. *Serve with salad of cole slaw with sour-cream dressing (1 cup sour cream, 2 tablespoons vinegar, 1 teaspoon salt, ½ teaspoon celery seed, 1 tablespoon sugar, ½ teaspoon dry mustard, 1 teaspoon paprika); hot biscuits; lemon sherbet sprinkled with fresh blueberries.*

Toast uncooked rice in a dry skillet. Place in a low buttered casserole with beans. Add seasonings (except the filé) and 2 cups water. Sprinkle green pepper on top, cover, and bake in 350° oven 40 minutes, or until rice is tender and liquid is absorbed. Add oysters and oyster liquor, cover, and cook 5 to 10 minutes, or until the liquid is absorbed and the oysters are ruffled. Remove from oven and add gumbo filé. Fluff rice with a fork before serving. Serves 4. Time: 1 hour.

Clam and Potato Soufflé

1 can frozen condensed cream of potato soup, thawed but not diluted
4 tablespoons flour
1 12-oz. can minced clams, well drained
⅓ cup finely chopped chives or parsley
3 egg yolks
4 egg whites

This has one of the frozen and condensed soups as a base. Making the cream sauce which is the basis for most soufflés is a simple business, but boiling, peeling, and mashing potatoes can be arduous. *Serve with broiled Canadian bacon; salad of watercress and thin slices of water chestnuts with French dressing; hot biscuits; brownies.*

Mix soup with flour, then add the thoroughly drained clams, chives or parsley, and egg yolks. Beat whites until stiff and fold in gently. Pour into buttered casserole with straight sides. Place in 350° oven and bake 50 to 60 minutes or until the top springs back when lightly touched. Serves 4. Time: 1¼ hours (not counting thawing time for the soup).

Bermuda Mussel Pie

¼ lb. salt pork, diced and
   scalded
1 large onion, minced fine
1 unbaked pie shell, with salt
   and pepper in the dough
¼ quart mussels, well scrubbed,
   or use 1 9-oz. can, drained
salt and pepper

The mussel is one of the most beautiful of
shellfish, and in this country one of the most
neglected, although even inlanders may buy
them now in cans. *Serve with diced cucumbers,
sliced radishes, and finely chopped green onions,
blanketed with sour cream; hot biscuits; lemon pudding (see index).*

Sauté pork and onion together and spread
some of the fat at the bottom of the pie shell.
Steam fresh mussels open—about 5 minutes
in ¼ cup water—and remove shells. Arrange
mussels and drained pork and onion in pie
shell. Sprinkle with salt and pepper. Bake in
400° oven 20 to 25 minutes, or until the crust
is brown and tender. Serves 4. Time: 45 minutes.

Mushrooms and Mussels in a Wine Sauce

1 lb. fresh mushroom caps (save
   the stems for soup another
   day)
4 tablespoons butter
salt and pepper
2 lbs. fresh mussels, well
   scrubbed, or 2 9-oz. cans,
   drained
1 small onion, chopped fine
2 tablespoons flour
⅔ cup chicken broth
⅔ cup white wine
1 egg
breadcrumbs

Fresh mussels are best; the pretty black shells
are often cooked and served in the dish, and
sometimes even used as spoons. *Serve with
baked rice pilaf (see index); salad of cooked fresh
asparagus tips, green peas, and green beans marinated at least 1 hour in French dressing; French
bread.*

Sauté mushroom caps in 2 tablespoons butter
with salt and pepper. Steam fresh mussels
open—about 5 minutes in about ½ cup water—
and remove the shells. Sauté onion in 2 tablespoons more butter, sprinkle with flour, and
blend. Add broth and wine slowly, stirring
until smooth and thick. Remove from heat and
add egg. Return to the stove and cook slowly
until slightly thickened. Put mushrooms and
the mussels in shallow individual casseroles.
Pour the sauce on top and sprinkle with breadcrumbs. Bake 20 minutes in 350° oven. Serves
4. Time: 45 minutes.

Oysters with Anchovy Sauce

3 tablespoons butter
3 tablespoons flour
½ cup cream
½ cup white wine
2 teaspoons anchovy paste
½ teaspoon grated lemon rind
salt, pepper, paprika
1 pt. oysters, drained, or 2 7-oz.
  cans frozen oysters
cracker crumbs
more butter

Serve with pimiento rice (rice cooked first in butter, then in chicken broth, with 2 coarsely diced pimientos added); broccoli marinated in French dressing; hot poppy-seed rolls (brown-and-serve).

Make cream sauce by melting 3 tablespoons butter, blending in flour, and adding cream and wine, anchovy paste, lemon rind, seasoning, and oysters. Place in a buttered shallow casserole. Sprinkle top with cracker crumbs, dot with butter, and bake in 400° oven about 15 mintues. Serves 3 to 4. Time: 45 minutes.

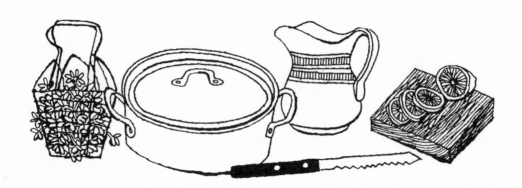

Crabmeat and Eggplant Casserole

1 large eggplant, peeled and
  diced
juice of 1 lemon
1 lb. crabmeat, flaked, membranes removed
4 medium-sized ripe tomatoes,
  diced, seeded, juice discarded,
  or 2 8-oz. cans tomato sauce
salt, pepper
½ cup breadcrumbs
2 tablespoons finely chopped
  parsley
3 tablespoons butter

In this dish shrimp, crabmeat, and diced cooked lobster tails are interchangeable. *Serve with tomato aspic on lettuce; orange soufflé.*

Sprinkle eggplant with lemon juice, cover with water, and cook over medium heat until barely tender, about 10 minutes. Drain and put into a baking dish. Add crabmeat and pour over it tomatoes or tomato sauce. Add salt and pepper. Mix breadcrumbs and parsley, sprinkle on top, and dot with butter. Bake in 350° oven 20 to 25 minutes. Serves 4. Time: 1 hour.

Crab in the Basque Manner

1 tablespoon olive oil
1/4 lb. butter
1 clove garlic, minced
1 medium onion, finely chopped
2 leeks, chopped
1 tablespoon tomato paste
1/4 cup sherry
1/4 cup brandy
2 7-oz. cans crabmeat, membranes removed, finely chopped or mashed
2 or 3 tablespoons clam juice
salt, pepper
pinch of cayenne
breadcrumbs
1 tablespoon finely chopped parsley

A highly seasoned dish that works well with any good-quality canned crabmeat. *Serve with rice; grapefruit and avocado salad with watercress and oil-and-vinegar dressing; French bread; lemon sherbet with fresh blackberries.*

Heat oil and half the butter in a skillet. Brown garlic and discard. Add onion and leeks. When they begin to brown, add tomato paste and stir constantly while adding sherry, brandy, crabmeat, clam juice, salt, pepper, and cayenne. Put in a small buttered casserole or four individual ones. Mix breadcrumbs with parsley, sprinkle on top, and dot with the rest of the butter. Bake in preheated 400° oven about 15 minutes. Serve very hot. Serves 4. Time: 45 minutes.

Crabmeat Norfolk

2 lbs. fresh, fresh lump crabmeat
1/2 lb. (2 sticks) unsalted butter
1 tablespoon lemon juice
salt, pinch of cayenne

As far as I know, there is no better way of eating crabmeat than this, but to be at its best the crabmeat should be the lump kind, almost quivering from the shock of being snatched from the crabs, and that kind of crabmeat can be found only in the crab regions. *Serve with stuffed artichokes (see index); hot biscuits; macaroon soufflé (see index).*

Remove membranes from the crabmeat, being careful not to break it up too much. Take four individual shallow metal casseroles (I use copper; Washington restaurants use aluminum). Melt half a stick of butter in each casserole, add part of lemon juice, salt, and cayenne. Divide crabmeat into four parts and add to hot butter. Bake in preheated 400° oven just until bubbling. Sprinkle a little lemon juice, salt, and a pinch of cayenne on each dish. This should not be more than 5 to 10 minutes. Serves 4 lavishly and ambrosially. Time: 20 minutes.

Bachelor Crabmeat

1 lb. fresh, or 2 6½-oz. cans, crabmeat
1 can condensed cream of tomato soup, undiluted
1 can condensed pea soup, undiluted
1 cup cream (let your budget be your guide as to whether it's light or heavy)
1 jigger sherry
½ teaspoon curry powder
¼ teaspoon cayenne

This crabmeat recipe is surprisingly simple and surprisingly appealing both to those with varied tastes in food and those who dislike being startled by anything new. *Serve with baked potatoes and a salad of greens with diced raw cucumbers, diced cooked beets, hard-cooked eggs, and sour-cream dressing (⅔ sour cream, ⅙ olive oil, ⅙ garlic vinegar, salt, and freshly ground pepper); pilot biscuits; fresh or frozen pineapple chunks soaked in banana liqueur, Cointreau, or rum.*

Pick crabmeat over carefully and remove membranes. Mix all ingredients together and heat in a shallow casserole, or individual casseroles, in 350° oven 20 to 25 minutes. Serves 4. Time: 40 minutes.

Shellfish Mélange

3 tablespoons butter
3 tablespoons flour
1½ cups half-and-half
a little salt
pinch of nutmeg
4 tablespoons grated Parmesan cheese
1 tablespoon tomato paste
½ lb. lump crabmeat, membranes removed
½ lb. cooked shrimp, peeled and deveined
1 9-oz. package frozen artichoke hearts, cooked and quartered
breadcrumbs
more butter

Best, of course, with fresh lump crabmeat, but canned or frozen will do. *Serve with baked stuffed potatoes, asparagus, lemon pudding (see index).*

Make a cream sauce, melting butter and cooking with flour for 3 or 4 minutes before adding half-and-half, a little at a time, stirring with a wire whip until smooth and thickened. Salt lightly and add nutmeg, grated Parmesan cheese, and tomato paste. Arrange crabmeat, shrimp, and artichoke hearts in a shallow buttered casserole. Pour in sauce. Sprinkle lightly with breadcrumbs, dot with butter, and bake in preheated 350° oven 35 to 45 minutes or until the top is lightly browned and bubbling. Serves 4. Time: 1 hour.

Oysters and Scallops Louisiana

½ cup chopped onions
1 clove garlic
¼ cup chopped green pepper
4 tablespoons butter
2 tablespoons flour
2½ cups canned tomatoes
1½ teaspoons salt
dash of pepper
dash of cayenne
1 teaspoon chili powder
½ teaspoon sugar
¼ cup grated Parmesan cheese
1 pt. fresh oysters, drained, or 2
   7-oz. cans frozen oysters
1 lb. scallops, or 1 8-oz. package
   frozen scallops
3 cups hot cooked rice (1 cup
   raw)

Serve with salad: watercress and chilled grapefruit segments with French dressing (3 parts olive oil, 1 part garlic vinegar, celery seed, salt, pepper); hot biscuits.

Sauté onion, garlic, and green pepper in butter 5 minutes or until delicately browned. Add flour and blend well. Add tomatoes, salt, pepper, cayenne, chili powder, sugar, and cheese. Add oysters and scallops. Spread hot rice in a shallow casserole and pour sauce with oysters and scallops over it. Heat in 325° oven about 10 to 15 minutes, just until the edges of the oysters curl. Serves 4 in a civilized way. Time: 55 minutes.

Bacon and Oyster Soufflé

4 slices lean bacon, cut in pieces
3 tablespoons flour
1 cup milk
salt and pepper
3 eggs, separated
1 pt. fresh oysters, or 1 7-oz. can
   frozen oysters, chopped

Delicate treatment for a delicate food. *Serve with salad of romaine with egg dressing (mash one hard-boiled egg, add pinch of paprika, salt, pepper, ½ teaspoon mustard, ½ teaspoon chives, 2 tablespoons olive oil, 3 tablespoons tarragon vinegar); Italian bread, cut in hunks and browned briefly in the oven; cherry pudding (see index).*

Sauté bacon slowly until crisp. Remove from skillet and drain on paper towels. Pour off surplus fat, leaving about 3 tablespoons in skillet. Blend flour with this fat, and add milk and seasoning slowly, stirring until smooth and thickened. Remove from fire, cool slightly, and stir in egg yolks. Add oysters, their juice, and bacon pieces to sauce. Beat egg whites until stiff and fold gently into the mixture. Pour into a low buttered casserole and bake in 350° oven 40 to 45 minutes, or until top springs back when lightly touched. Serves 4. Time: 1 hour.

Cheese and Smoked-Oyster Soufflé

3 tablespoons butter
3 tablespoons flour
1½ cups milk
1 cup grated Cheddar cheese
3 eggs, separated
salt, but not much
1 3-oz. can smoked oysters, drained and cut in small pieces

Smoked oysters bear no resemblance to fresh ones except in shape and origin, having an elusive and intriguing flavor that adds a piquant touch to this dish. *Serve with salad of romaine with slices of avocado and a bland French dressing; hot biscuits; blueberry pie.*

Melt butter and blend in flour. Add milk slowly, stirring until quite thick. Add grated cheese and cook over a low flame until melted. Remove from heat and stir in egg yolks, salt, and pieces of smoked oysters. Beat egg whites until stiff, fold them into the mixture, and pour into a buttered casserole with straight sides. Bake in preheated 350° oven 45 to 50 minutes, or until the top springs back when lightly touched. Serves 4. Time: 1½ hours.

Deviled Crabmeat

⅓ cup (6 tablespoons) butter, plus butter for top
1 small onion, chopped
⅓ cup (6 tablespoons) flour
1 teaspoon Worcestershire sauce
1 teaspoon dry English mustard
salt
2 cups milk, or 1 cup cream and 1 cup chicken broth
2 egg yolks, slightly beaten
1 tablespoon chopped chives
1 lb. fresh crabmeat, or 1 1-lb. package frozen, or 2 6½-oz. cans, well picked, membranes removed
prepared mustard
breadcrumbs

Serve with Italian salad of ⅖ cooked green peas, ⅕ small diced cooked carrots, ⅕ diced cooked white turnip, ⅕ small cut cooked string beans, with French dressing flavored with chopped chervil, tarragon, and chives, garnished with sliced cooked beets; Italian bread, cut in hunks; lemon pudding (see index).

Melt butter and cook onion until pale yellow and soft. Blend in flour, Worcestershire sauce, dry mustard, and salt. Add the liquid slowly, stirring until thick and smooth. Remove from heat and add egg yolks, stirring until well blended. Add chives and crabmeat. Put the mixture into individual baking shells or one very shallow baking dish. Spread tops thinly with prepared mustard, sprinkle with breadcrumbs, and dot with bits of butter. Bake in 350° oven until brown and bubbly (about 15 to 20 minutes). Serves 4 to 6. Time: 40 minutes.

Crabmeat and Broccoli Casserole

1 bunch fresh, or 1 10-oz. package frozen, broccoli, cooked until barely tender
½ lb. fresh, or 1 6½-oz. package frozen, or 1 6½-oz. can, crabmeat, pulled apart and membranes removed
1 cup (½ pt.) sour cream
⅓ cup chili sauce
1 small onion, chopped fine
1 cup grated sharp Cheddar cheese
2 tablespoons fresh lemon juice
1 tablespoon grated lemon peel
salt and pepper

Serve with salad of watercress, tomato aspic with mayonnaise; hot poppy-seed rolls, or spoon bread (see index); orange sherbet; coffee.

Break broccoli into very small flowerets. Mix with crabmeat, sour cream, chili sauce, onion, cheese, lemon juice, lemon peel, salt, and pepper. Put into a small shallow buttered casserole. Bake in 350° oven about 20 minutes or until cheese is melted and top is browned. Serves 4. Time: 45 minutes.

Crabmeat and Mushrooms in Wine Sauce

1 lb. fresh, or 2 6-oz. packages frozen, or 2 6½-oz. cans, crabmeat
¼ lb. fresh, or 1 6-oz. package frozen, mushrooms
3 tablespoons butter, plus butter for top
2 tablespoons flour
½ teaspoon dry mustard
¼ teaspoon dry tarragon
salt and pepper
½ cup cream
½ cup white wine
breadcrumbs

Impressive to serve, easy to make. Don't let them in the kitchen, or this will be everybody's secret. *Serve with kasha (cooked buckwheat); salad of thin onion and pepper rings with French dressing; hot buttermilk biscuits (prepared ones that come in a tube).*

Pull crabmeat apart and remove stiff membranes. Slice and sauté mushrooms in 1 tablespoon butter. Make cream sauce by melting 2 tablespoons butter, blending in flour and seasonings, and adding liquids slowly, stirring until smooth and thick. Add crabmeat and mushrooms. Place in four individual casseroles. Sprinkle tops with breadcrumbs and dot with butter. Bake in 350° oven about 15 minutes, then put under broiler for 5 minutes to blister and brown. Serves 4. Time: 40 minutes.

Crabflake Soufflé

½ lb. fresh, or 1 6-oz. package
   frozen, or 1 6½-oz. can, crabmeat
3 tablespoons butter
3 tablespoons flour
¾ cup milk
¼ cup sherry
salt and pepper
3 eggs, separated
2 tablespoons capers

Excellent for luncheons, bridge and such, or for light eaters anytime. *Serve with tiny new potatoes, boiled in their skins; endive salad with French dressing mixed with crumbled Roquefort cheese; Italian bread; lemon pudding (see index).*

Pull crabmeat apart and remove stiff membranes. Make a cream sauce, melting butter, blending in flour, adding liquids and seasoning. Cook until smooth and thick. Remove from fire, cool slightly, and stir in egg yolks. Add crabmeat and capers. Beat egg whites until stiff, fold in gently, and pour into a low buttered casserole. Bake 40 to 45 minutes in 350° oven. Serves 4. Time: 1 hour.

Crabmeat Dietz

1 6½-oz. can crabmeat, pulled
   apart
2 cans Spanish rice
½ clove garlic, minced
1 shallot or 1 spring onion,
   minced
a little salt
pepper
½ cup diced Cheddar cheese
⅓ cup crumbled potato chips
1 tablespoon butter

Anyone with a little imagination and a kitchen shelf well stocked with seafood can cope with almost any emergency. *Serve with salad of escarole, slices of avocado, and grapefruit segments with a bland French dressing; butterflake rolls; cheesecake (frozen).*

Mix crabmeat, rice, garlic, shallot, salt, pepper, and half the cheese. Spoon into a shallow buttered casserole. Top with crumbled potato chips and strew around the other half of the cheese. Dot edges of the casserole with butter and put a few pieces on top. Bake in 350° oven 15 to 20 minutes, or until it bubbles around the edges and turns brown. Serves 4. Time: 40 minutes.

Scallops and Mushrooms

½ lb. fresh, or 1 6-oz. package
   frozen, mushrooms, sliced
3 tablespoons butter
2 tablespoons flour
1 cup cream
1 tablespoon dry vermouth
salt and pepper
1 lb. fresh scallops, or 2 8-oz.
   packages frozen scallops,
   either the tiny bay ones or
   larger sea ones, quartered
breadcrumbs
more butter

Don't hesitate to use more mushrooms if you really like them. *Serve with baked potatoes; salad of avocado, grapefruit sections, romaine with French dressing; hot drop biscuits; lemon pudding (see index).*

Cook mushrooms in butter until limp or about 5 minutes. Then blend in flour, add cream slowly, stirring until a thin sauce is made. Add vermouth and seasonings. Add scallops, put in a casserole. Cover with breadcrumbs and dot with butter. Cover and cook 10 to 15 minutes in 375° oven. Serves 4. Time: 30 minutes.

Baked Eggs with Crabmeat

½ lb. fresh, or 1 6½-oz. can, or 1
   6-oz. package frozen, crabmeat
8 eggs
½ cup milk
½ teaspoon tarragon
salt and pepper

A little tedious, this picking, but it pays dividends. *Serve with cucumbers, sliced radishes, and a few thin slices spring onions in individual wooden salad bowls with sour cream; Swedish bread.*

Pick over crabmeat and remove all the stiff membranes. Beat eggs slightly with a wire whisk, add milk and seasoning, and beat a little more. Stir in crabmeat and pour into individual buttered casseroles. Bake in 350° oven 25 to 30 minutes or until the eggs have a custard-like consistency. Serves 4. Time: 45 minutes.

Lobster and Mushrooms

½ lb. fresh mushrooms, sliced
   through caps and stems
¼ lb. butter
3 tablespoons flour
1½ cups heavy cream
½ cup white wine
salt and pepper
1 tablespoon grated lemon peel
1 lb. fresh, or 2 8-oz. packages
   frozen, or 2 8-oz. cans, lobster
   meat

Serve with wild rice or wild-rice mixture; salad of watercress and cubed avocado with French dressing (1 part pineapple juice, 2 parts olive oil, salt and pepper); hot rolls; coffee; Bavarian cream.

Sauté mushrooms in butter. Add flour. Stir in cream first, and then wine, gradually. Add salt and pepper and lemon peel. Remove from heat and add the lobster. Pour into a low buttered casserole and bake in 350° oven 15 to 20 minutes. Serves 4. Time: 40 minutes.

Farmyard Lobster

3 tablespoons butter
3 tablespoons flour
1 cup milk
salt and pepper
3 eggs, separated
1 cup lobster meat, fresh or canned, pulled apart
4 eggs, lightly poached

Four golden ducats lie buried in the heart of this delicate pink soufflé. *Serve with tiny new potatoes, boiled and served in their skins; salad of chicory and sliced water chestnuts with a tarragon dressing (3 parts olive oil, 1 part tarragon vinegar, salt, freshly ground black pepper, and maybe a sprig of chopped tarragon for emphasis); toasted English muffins.*

Melt butter and blend in flour. Stir and cook until the floury taste is gone. Add milk slowly, stirring over low heat until sauce is smooth and thick. Add seasoning. Remove from heat, add the 3 egg yolks, stir, and add lobster meat. Beat egg whites until stiff and fold in. Turn half the mixture into a greased casserole with straight sides. Arrange the four poached eggs on this half of the mixture. Pour the rest of the soufflé mixture over the eggs. Bake in 350° oven about 50 minutes, or until the top springs back when lightly touched with a finger. It is best to make some mark in the top to indicate the position of the eggs so as not to cut them in half when serving. Serves 4. Time: 1¼ hours.

Shrimp Topped with Clam and Wine Soufflé

½ lb. cooked shrimp, peeled and deveined
⅔ cup seedless white grapes
2 tablespoons butter
2 tablespoons flour
¾ cup clam juice
¼ cup dry vermouth or dry sherry
2 tablespoons chopped fresh dill, or 1 teaspoon dried dill
salt
3 tablespoons sour cream
4 eggs, separated

Elegant and subtle. *Serve with rice; Belgian endive and watercress salad with oil-and-vinegar dressing; hot flaky rolls; blueberry cheesecake.*

Arrange shrimp and grapes in buttered 1-quart soufflé or baking dish. Cook butter and flour together for 3 to 4 minutes, until dry and well blended. Add clam juice and beat with a wire whip until smooth and thickened. Add vermouth or sherry and dill. Cook until rather thick. Remove from heat, add salt to taste, and stir in sour cream and egg yolks. Beat whites until stiff and fold into the sauce gently, half at a time. Pour over shrimp and grapes. Bake in preheated 350° oven 45 to 50 minutes, until golden and puffy. Serves 4 or 5. Time: 1¼ hours.

Individual Lobster and Clam Pies

2 medium-sized potatoes, boiled and diced
1 medium-sized onion, minced fine
3 tablespoons butter
meat of 1 1½-lb. lobster, cooked, picked out of shell, and cut in hunks (or 1 6½-oz. can lobster meat, picked over)
1 dozen fresh clams, steamed and diced, or 2 7-oz. cans minced clams
1 cup heavy cream
salt and pepper
pie dough for 1 crust

This recipe stems partly from a memory of the very best of all clam chowders, made on a July night in Connecticut on the Sound, when there was a whole lobster left over from the night before, plus melted butter, well permeated—from repeated dunkings—with the flavor of the other lobsters. *Serve with salad of greens and chilled white grapes, with tart French dressing; hot biscuits.*

Sauté potatoes and onion in butter until brown. Mix lobster meat with clams, potatoes and onion, cream, salt, and pepper. Divide the mixture and put into four rather large individual casseroles. Top with circles of pastry cut to fit and slashed decoratively to allow steam to escape. Bake in preheated 425° oven 12 to 15 minutes, or until tops are brown and crisp. Serves 4. Time: 30 minutes.

Shrimp Frigideira

½ lb. fish fillets, preferably codfish
½ lb. shrimp, peeled and deveined
2 small onions, minced
½ clove garlic, minced
salt, pepper
1 teaspoon paprika
¾ cup milk
½ teaspoon vinegar
4 eggs
3 tablespoons chopped ripe olives

A Brazilian dish which always has eggs baked on top. In Brazil the codfish and shrimp would be dried. *Serve with sliced cucumbers, sliced radishes, oil-and-vinegar dressing; garlic bread; brownie pudding.*

Put fish and shrimp through a meat grinder, using the finest blade, or a food mill. Mix with half the onion, the garlic, salt, pepper, paprika, milk, and vinegar. This can also be done in a blender a little at a time, using milk for the liquid. Cook together for about 20 minutes. Beat 2 eggs. Remove fish mixture from heat and add beaten eggs, the rest of the onions, and chopped olives. Spread in a shallow casserole, about 9 to 10 inches in diameter. Beat the other 2 eggs and pour over. Bake in 400° oven about 10 minutes or until the eggs are brown and set. Serves 4. Time: 1 hour.

Shrimp with Feta and Dill

½ cup chopped onion
4 tablespoons butter
2 cups cooked rice
1 lb. shrimp, peeled and de-veined, preferably raw
1 loosely packed cup crumbled feta cheese
1½ tablespoons finely chopped fresh dill, or 1½ teaspoons dried dill
2½ cups (1-lb.-14-oz. can) tomatoes

Feta is a salty, pleasurably odd-tasting Greek cheese which may be bought in more and more places these days as cheese stores spring up in various cities and towns. Fresh dill is best, if available. *Serve with a salad of Belgian endive; pideh, the good flat crusty bread available in stores carrying foods from around the Mediterranean; glazed oranges.*

Sauté onion in butter. Spread cooked rice in a 1-quart casserole. Arrange shrimp and feta on top. Sprinkle with dill. There is no need for salt with feta, for most people. Pour in tomatoes. Bake in preheated 350° oven 35 minutes or until raw shrimp is opaque. Less time will be needed for cooked shrimp. Serves 4. Time: 50 minutes.

Shrimp, Green Bean, and Cheese Pie

pastry for one crust
1 lb. shrimp, cooked, shelled, deveined
¼ lb. natural Swiss or Cheddar cheese, diced
1 10-oz. package frozen green beans and mushrooms, partially cooked
4 eggs
2 cups half-and-half
1 teaspoon orégano
½ teaspoon dry mustard
salt, pepper

A robust and filling dish. *Serve with a sharply flavored salad such as tomato, grapefruit segments, and watercress with French dressing; French bread; pineapple sherbet sprinkled with shaved chocolate and grated orange rind.*

Line a 9-inch tin with pastry. Bake 5 minutes at 450°. Strew partially baked shell with shrimp, cheese, and green beans and mushrooms. Beat eggs with half-and-half, add seasonings, pour over the shrimp mixture. Bake 15 minutes, then reduce heat to 350°. Bake about 20 to 30 minutes more or until a knife inserted comes out clean. Serves 4. Time: 1 hour.

Shrimp Jambalaya with Barley

1 cup barley
2 cups (1-lb. can) tomatoes
1 medium-sized onion, chopped
1 teaspoon dried tarragon
salt and pepper
1 lb. fresh shrimp, peeled and deveined, or 2 cups frozen, or 2 cups canned
1 pt. fresh, or 1 7-oz. can frozen, oysters
1 teaspoon gumbo filé

This is an untraditional variation of a well-known New Orleans dish. *Serve with watercress salad; hot buttermilk biscuits.*

Put barley, tomatoes and juice, onion, tarragon, salt, and pepper in shallow casserole with 1 cup water. Cover tightly and cook in 350° oven 35 minutes. Add shrimp, oysters, and oyster liquid. Cover and cook 10 minutes longer. Before serving add gumbo filé (do not cook this) and fluff barley with a fork. Serves 4. Time: 1 hour.

Shrimp and Oyster Pie

2 tablespoons butter
2 tablespoons flour
1 cup milk
2 teaspoons chopped fresh parsley
1/4 teaspoon mace
salt and pepper
1/2 lb. fresh or frozen shrimp, peeled and deveined
1 pt. fresh, or 2 7-oz. cans frozen, oysters
1 tube pan-ready refrigerated biscuits

Best made, of course, from fresh oysters and shrimp, if you're fortunate enough to be near a waterfront. *Serve with salad of diced celery, green pepper cut in rings, marinated in French dressing, with finely chopped onion and a little dry basil; Italian bread sticks; macaroon soufflé (see index).*

Make a cream sauce by melting butter, blending in flour, adding milk, parsley, mace, salt, and pepper. Cook until smooth and thickened. Stir in shrimp and oysters and place in a low buttered casserole. Pull biscuits apart and arrange on seafood. Bake in 400° oven 15 to 20 minutes. Serves 4. Time: 45 minutes.

Shrimp Viennese

6 large mushrooms, diced
1 tablespoon finely chopped
  onion
¼ lb. sweet butter
1 tablespoon flour
2 tablespoons chopped fresh
  dill, or 2 teaspoons dried dill
½ cup chicken broth
½ cup light cream
juice of ½ lemon
salt and pepper
1 tablespoon white wine
1 lb. shrimp, cooked, peeled,
  and cleaned
2 cups cooked rice

This may be served in small amounts as a beginning course or in large quantities as a main course. *Serve with sliced avocado on a bed of watercress with French dressing (3 parts olive oil, 1 part fresh lemon juice, salt, pepper, and pinch of savory); hot biscuits.*

Cook mushrooms and onion in half the sweet butter until onions are pale yellow. Add flour and dill. Mix well and then add broth and cream. Bring to a boil, add lemon juice, salt, pepper, and wine. Simmer until barely thickened and add shrimp. Put rice in the bottom of a buttered casserole and pour the sauce on top. Distribute the rest of the butter in pieces over all, and bake in 325° oven 15 minutes. Do *not* overcook. Serves 3 or 4. Time: 45 minutes.

Shrimp More or Less Newburg

¼ lb. fresh, or 1 6-oz. package
  frozen, mushrooms, sliced
2 tablespoons butter
1½ lbs. fresh or frozen shrimp,
  peeled and deveined
2 cans frozen condensed cream
  of shrimp soup, thawed
⅓ cup cream or milk
¼ cup sherry
1 teaspoon dry mustard
pepper
grated Parmesan cheese

This can be prepared easily from a well-stocked freezer, with frozen shrimp and frozen condensed cream of shrimp soup. *Serve with rice cooked in chicken broth with a lump of butter; salad of 2 parts of lettuce, 1 part of parsley, torn up with French dressing; hot rolls; blueberries and sour cream.*

Sauté mushrooms in butter until pale yellow. Divide them into four parts, divide shrimp into four parts also, and put into the bottom of individual shallow baking dishes. Mix shrimp soup with cream, sherry, dry mustard, and pepper. Pour into the four casseroles. Top with grated Parmesan cheese and bake in 350° oven 20 to 25 minutes. Serves 4. Time: 35 minutes (not counting thawing time for the soup).

Creamed Shrimp in Individual Casseroles

1½ lbs. fresh or frozen shrimp
2 tablespoons butter
2 tablespoons flour
1¼ cups light cream
salt and pepper
⅓ cup catsup
pinch of nutmeg
breadcrumbs

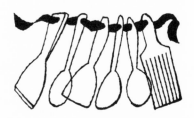

The fragrant and haunting flavor of shrimps that have been simmered lovingly, gently, and briefly is much, much better than that of canned or frozen ones, no matter how convenient the alternative. *Serve with baked potatoes; salad of romaine with canned hearts of artichokes marinated in French dressing; hot biscuits.*

Peel shrimp and remove the black veins. Melt butter and blend in flour. Add cream slowly, and salt and pepper, and cook until thickened. Add catsup and nutmeg—there should be just a suggestion of that spice. Check for seasonings and add more salt and pepper if necessary. Put shrimp in the sauce and pour into four individual buttered casseroles. Sprinkle the tops lavishly with breadcrumbs. Bake in preheated 325° oven 20 to 25 minutes. Serves 4. Time: 1 hour.

Shrimp and Fish Pie

2 lbs. frozen fish fillets or steaks
small pieces of lemon peel
9-inch baked pie shell
3 or 4 large mushrooms, sliced lengthwise through the caps and stems
7 or 8 large cooked shrimp, shelled and cleaned, or 1 4½-oz. can shrimp, rinsed and drained.
1 can frozen condensed cream of shrimp soup, thawed
2 tablespoons dry white wine
finely chopped fresh parsley, for garnish

Frozen fish fillets are inexpensive, convenient to buy and use, and good as the basis for many dishes. This is very pretty with symmetrical slices of mushrooms surrounding the pink shrimp. *Serve with cold cooked broccoli marinated in olive oil, salt, and lots of freshly ground pepper; hot biscuits; whipped strawberries (thaw and mash 1 package frozen strawberries, mix with powdered sugar and 1 egg white stiffly beaten.)*

Poach fillets in a small amount of water with some pieces of lemon peel until the fish is a beautiful white—5 to 15 minutes, depending upon the fish used. Drain and arrange in baked pie shell. Arrange mushroom slices in a circle on top with shrimp in the middle. Mix soup with wine and pour into the pie. Bake in preheated 350° oven about 15 to 20 minutes. Sprinkle with parsley. Serves 6. Time: 40 minutes.

Zucchini Baked with Shrimp and Tarragon Butter

5 small or 3 large zucchini or yellow squash, sliced thin but not peeled
1 lb. fresh or frozen shrimp, peeled and deveined
6 green onions, tops and bottoms chopped fine
¼ lb. butter
1 tablespoon dry tarragon, or 2 tablespoons chopped fresh tarragon
salt and pepper

Serve with radishes, sliced thin, with salt; hot toast; rice baked with honey and almonds (see index).

In a shallow casserole arrange a layer of zucchini slices on the bottom—about ⅓ of the zucchini—overlapping them somewhat. Sprinkle with shrimp and chopped onions and dot with ⅓ of the butter, cut in pieces. Sprinkle with tarragon, salt, and pepper. Repeat. There should be three layers. Cover and bake in 350° oven 20 to 25 minutes, or until shrimp is cooked and zucchini is tender. Serves 4. Time: 45 minutes.

Scalloped Oysters, Scallops, and Shrimp

1 pt. fresh, or 2 7-oz. cans frozen oysters
½ lb. fresh or frozen scallops
½ lb. fresh or frozen shrimp, peeled and deveined
breadcrumbs
1 tablespoon finely chopped parsley or chives
salt and pepper
¼ lb. butter
1 cup cream
¼ cup sherry

A delicate dish, simple to prepare, yet easily ruined by too long cooking. *Serve with risi pisi (rice cooked in butter, then in chicken broth, with fresh green peas added); Bibb lettuce with French dressing, sprinkled with chopped hard-cooked eggs; hot poppy-seed rolls (brown-and-serve).*

Put half the oysters on the bottom of a shallow buttered casserole, then half the scallops, then half the shrimp. Sprinkle with breadcrumbs, chopped parsley, and seasoning; dot with butter and repeat. Pour cream and sherry over all and bake in 350° oven 15 to 20 minutes. Serves 4. Time: 25 minutes.

Seafood Binge in Curry Sauce

4 tablespoons butter
1 tablespoon, or more, curry powder
4 tablespoons flour
1 cup chicken broth
1 cup cream
1¼ teaspoons salt
pinch of pepper
1 pt. fresh, or 2 7-oz. cans frozen, oysters
½ lb. fresh or frozen shrimp, peeled and deveined
½ lb fresh, or 1 6½-oz. package frozen, or 1 6½-oz. can, crabmeat, flaked
diced pimiento

This is a colorful, highly seasoned mishmash of seafood. Other combinations would be good — for instance, lobster instead of crabmeat, clams or mussels instead of oysters — but the shrimp always should be in it. *Serve with pilaf (rice cooked first in butter, then in broth); avocado halves filled with thinly sliced chilled cucumbers that have been marinated in vinegar and then mixed with chopped chives, minced garlic, and sour cream; hot toast points; fresh plums and* crème Chantilly.

Melt butter in a saucepan with curry powder, add flour, and stir until smooth. Add chicken broth first and then cream gradually, stirring constantly. Cook slowly over low heat, stirring all the time, until thickened. Add salt and pepper. Add oysters, shrimp, crabmeat, and pimiento to the cream sauce. Mix thoroughly and pour into individual casseroles. Bake in 350° oven until brown and bubbly, about 15 minutes. Serve immediately. Serves 4. Time: 40 minutes.

Shrimp Pilau

4 slices bacon, diced
1 small onion, chopped
1 cup uncooked rice
3½ cups (1-lb.-12-oz. can) tomatoes
1 small bay leaf
salt and pepper
1 lb. fresh shrimp, peeled and deveined but not cooked

An old-fashioned Charlestonian dish for those with leisure tastes but no leisure time. *Serve with salad of romaine, sliced avocado, grapefruit segments with bland French dressing; hot biscuits; macaroon soufflé (see index).*

Sauté bacon until almost crisp. Drain on paper towels. Add onion and rice to bacon fat. Cook over low heat 5 to 8 minutes. Pour into a medium-sized casserole, add tomatoes, 1 cup water, and seasoning. Cover and bake in 350° oven 25 minutes. Remove cover, add bacon and shrimp. Cover and bake 5 to 8 minutes longer, until shrimp are pink. Serves 4. Time: 1 hour.

Smelts Baked in Sherry

1 lb. cleaned smelts
1 teaspoon salt
3 tablespoons olive oil
½ cup medium dry sherry
2 tablespoons Italian-seasoned
    breadcrumbs
¼ cup slivered almonds

Smelts are the small, neat slate-blue fish cleaned and packaged in 1-lb. trays or pliofilm bags and selling for a small neat sum in most supermarkets. Usually they are pan- or deep-fried. Here a frugal fish is given a festive treatment. *Serve with Italian green beans; broiled tomato halves; poppy seed rolls; pear sherbet.*

Arrange the fish neatly, back to back, in a shallow oiled baking dish. Sprinkle with salt and dribble oil on top. Pour in half the sherry. Mix crumbs and nuts together and strew over the top of the fish. Bake in an oven preheated to 350° for about ½ hour or until the fish flakes. Add the rest of the sherry after half the baking time. Serves 3 or 4. Time: 45 minutes.

Eggs
and
Cheese

Eggs and Cheese

Swedish Omelet

8 slices bacon, cut in pieces
5 eggs
3 tablespoons flour
½ teaspoon salt
dash of pepper
2 cups milk

More substantial than most omelets, and simple to make, this custardy Swedish version is ample for Sunday breakfast, or as a luncheon or supper dish. To be authentic, serve it with lingonberries, somewhat like cranberries, obtainable at Scandinavian delicatessens, although any tart jelly or jam tastes good with it. *Also serve grapefruit halves with a dash of port wine; toasted English muffins with jam.*

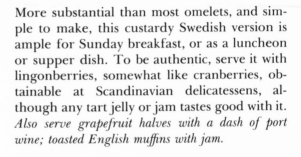

For this you need either a decorative and practical oval copper pan that can go on top of the stove, in the oven, and then on the table, or one of the enameled ironware skillets now available. Sauté bacon until crisp. Pour off all the fat except for 2 to 3 tablespoons. Leave bacon in the pan and keep it warm while getting the eggs ready. Beat them until light and fluffy. Add flour, beat some more, and then add seasonings and milk or buzz briefly in electric blender. When well blended, pour beaten eggs over hot bacon fat and bacon, and bake in 375° oven about 35 minutes, or until puffy and firm. Serve in the pan, accompanied by a separate dish of lingonberries or cranberries as a relish. Serves 4. Time: 50 minutes.

Hard-Cooked Eggs in Soubise Sauce

2 cups sliced onions
2 tablespoons butter
¾ cup milk or chicken broth
1 tablespoon flour
salt, white pepper
1 tablespoon French prepared
   mustard
pinch of nutmeg
2 or 3 tablespoons cream
4 hard-cooked eggs, shelled and
   quartered
dry breadcrumbs
butter

A delicate and lovely mixture. *Serve with hot biscuits; watercress salad with sliced cucumbers, oil-and-vinegar dressing; fresh pears and cheese.*

Cook onions in butter until soft. Add milk or broth and cook until tender. Purée in an electric blender, or put through a food mill. Stir in flour. Season with salt and pepper to taste. Cook over low heat and stir in mustard and nutmeg. Add cream a tablespoon at a time until the sauce is thick and smooth but not runny. Arrange egg quarters in a shallow casserole and spoon the sauce on top. Sprinkle lightly with breadcrumbs and dot with butter. Bake in 350° oven until lightly browned, about 25 to 30 minutes. Serves 4 at a light meal. Time: 1 hour.

> *Plunge hard-cooked eggs into cold water immediately to keep yolks from turning dark.*

Eggs Poached in Clam and Watercress Sauce

3 tablespoons butter
3 tablespoons flour
1 12-oz. can minced clams and
   juice
salt
1 bunch watercress—or sorrel,
   if available—simmered 15
   minutes, drained, and
   chopped fine or puréed in
   blender
4 eggs

A simple yet distinctive lunch or supper dish. *Serve with salad of cucumbers, radishes, and raw onions, sliced thin, with French dressing; hard rolls; canned pears with mashed fresh raspberries.*

Melt butter, add flour, cook a minute or two until brown. Add clams and clam juice slowly, stirring until smooth and thickened. Add a little salt. Add well-drained and chopped watercress or sorrel. Spread the mixture in a shallow buttered casserole and make 4 slight indentations with a spoon. Slide a raw egg into each indentation and put in 350° oven 15 to 20 minutes or until the eggs are set. Serves 4. Time: 45 minutes.

Baked Eggs with Mushrooms

4 eggs
2 cups half-and-half
salt and pepper
½ cup sliced fresh, or 1 6-oz. package frozen, mushrooms
3 pieces cooked bacon, crumbled

For Sunday breakfast. *Serve with honeydew melon or frozen melon balls with a split of champagne; English muffins, split and toasted, with strawberry jam or orange marmalade.*

Beat eggs with half-and-half, salt, and pepper. Add mushrooms. (They may be sautéed in butter first, but the flavor is more intriguing if they are put into the mixture raw.) Put a part of the crumbled bacon in each of four individual buttered casseroles and pour the mushroom-and-egg concoction over it. Bake in 350° oven about 20 to 25 minutes, or until the eggs are set. Serves 4. Time: 30 minutes.

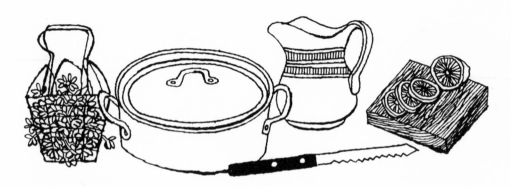

Baked Mushroom Omelet Soufflé

1 lb. fresh or frozen mushrooms, sliced
4 tablespoons melted butter
4 eggs, separated
3 tablespoons flour
2 cups milk
¼ cup dry sherry
salt, freshly ground black pepper
¼ teaspoon cayenne

Actually this is not exactly an omelet or a soufflé, but it's a nice well-behaved and well-flavored dish. *Serve with marinated hearts of artichokes; hot biscuits; lime pie.*

Cook mushrooms in 2 tablespoons of the butter and let brown. Put egg yolks, flour, milk, sherry, and 1 tablespoon melted butter in the electric blender and buzz a few seconds. Mix with mushrooms and their butter, season to taste with salt and pepper. Add cayenne. Beat egg whites until stiff and fold into the mushroom mixture. Put into a buttered 1½-quart baking dish and dribble remaining butter on top. Bake in preheated 350° oven 45 minutes. Serves 4. Time: 1 hour.

Baked Eggs with Chicken Livers

1 lb. chicken livers, cut in
   quarters
3 tablespoons butter
8 eggs
½ cup milk
salt and pepper

For a Sunday morning when you want to pamper yourself. *Serve with fresh peaches and cream; hot biscuits with bitter orange marmalade.*

Sauté chicken livers about 8 minutes in butter in a hot skillet. Divide chicken livers into four parts and place in individual casseroles. Beat eggs and milk, add salt and pepper, pour over livers, and bake in 350° oven about 25 minutes, or until the eggs are set and custardy. Serves 4. Time: 40 minutes.

Sliced-Egg Pie

1 pie shell, baked 5 minutes
6 hard-cooked eggs, sliced
salt and pepper
⅔ cup heavy cream
⅔ cup grated Parmesan cheese
⅓ cup finely chopped parsley

Serve with tomato aspic with hearts of artichoke embedded in the jelly, mayonnaise; corn bread; broiled grapefruit.

Arrange the slices of hard-cooked egg on the partly baked crust. Beat together slightly salt, pepper, cream, cheese, and parsley. Pour over the eggs and bake in 400° oven 15 to 20 minutes or until the cheese is melted and browned. Serves 4. Time: 45 minutes.

Quick Lunch

8 large firm tomatoes
8 eggs
salt and pepper
¼ teaspoon thyme
¼ teaspoon basil
⅓ cup grated cheese

Just what the name says, only a little less dull than what usually comes under that heading. *Serve with salad of diced cucumber, chopped sweet pepper, and French dressing; toasted English muffins.*

Scald tomatoes in boiling water a minute and remove skin. Cut a hollow center in each tomato and drop a whole raw egg in each. Sprinkle the top with salt, pepper, thyme, basil, and cheese. Place in a shallow buttered casserole and bake in 350° oven 20 minutes. Serves 4. Time: 45 minutes.

Stuffed Eggs au Gratin

4 eggs
½ teaspoon dry mustard
1 tablespoon vinegar
olive oil to make a smooth paste
salt and pepper
anchovies or anchovy paste,
    Smithfield ham, or capers
2 tablespoons butter
2 tablespoons flour
½ teaspoon basil
1 cup milk
½ cup grated Parmesan cheese

By varying the ingredients, this casserole may be adapted to many individual tastes. *Serve with raw vegetable salad (carrots, cauliflower, onion, green and sweet red pepper, all chopped) with French dressing; Melba toast.*

Hard-cook the eggs. Peel and halve them. Remove yolks to a bowl, mash, and mix with mustard, vinegar, olive oil, salt, pepper, anchovies, or whatever else you care to use. Pile mixture into halves of whites. Place in bottom of a shallow buttered casserole. Melt butter; blend in flour, salt, pepper, and basil. Add milk gradually, stirring until smooth and thick. Pour over the eggs. Sprinkle top with grated cheese. Bake in 350° oven 10 minutes or until cheese is melted. Serves 4. Time: 45 minutes.

Eggs Rattrap

1 whole spring onion, top and
    bulb chopped, or 1 small
    onion, chopped
1 teaspoon butter
1 can condensed tomato soup
½ lb. Cheddar cheese, diced
½ teaspoon mustard
¼ teaspoon dried basil
½ cup milk
3 eggs
4 pieces French or Italian bread,
    2 inches thick
salt and pepper
⅓ cup finely chopped parsley

Any good natural cheese will do; the processed ones have unpredictable and unpleasant consistencies. *Serve with salad of shredded celery, grated raw carrots, green pepper, French dressing; French or Italian bread.*

Cook onion in butter until yellow. Add soup, cheese, mustard, and basil, and cook slowly, stirring until cheese is blended with other ingredients. Remove from stove, let cool slightly. Beat milk and eggs together and add. Toast bread lightly in oven, arrange in buttered casserole, and pour sauce over it. Heat 15 minutes in 350° oven. Sprinkle with finely chopped parsley. Serves 4. Time: 40 minutes.

Cheese and Egg Casserole

1 cup uncooked rice
2 cups chicken broth
2 tablespoons butter
2 tablespoons flour
1 cup milk
1 teaspoon dry English mustard
salt and pepper
¾ cup grated sharp Cheddar
    cheese
4 eggs

Frugal, but not dreary, and simple enough for a bride to toss off casually for a Sunday-night supper. *Serve with salad of chicory with herb and sour-cream dressing (½ cup sour cream, 1 teaspoon lemon juice, ¼ teaspoon rosemary, and salt); hot buttered toast.*

Put rice in pan with chicken broth, bring to a boil, cover, turn heat down and cook 20 to 30 minutes. Uncover and fluff with a fork. Make a sauce by melting butter, blending in flour, and cooking thoroughly so there will be no floury taste. Add milk and seasonings slowly, stirring and cooking until thick. Stir in cheese and cook over very low heat until melted. Place rice in a low buttered casserole and make four dents or nests for the eggs. Break the eggs into the holes. Pour the cheese sauce on top, and bake in 350° oven until eggs are set and cheese is brown and bubbling, about 20 minutes. Serves 4. Time: 1¼ hours.

Ham and Egg Casserole

3 tablespoons butter
3 tablespoons flour
1½ cups milk
pinch of nutmeg
salt, pepper
⅔ cup grated Swiss or Cheddar
    cheese
2 cups cooked rice (done in
    chicken broth)
¼ lb. cooked ham, diced
2 hard-cooked eggs, quartered
finely chopped parsley
grated lemon rind
butter

Day-in-day-out provender. *Serve with cold cooked Italian green beans marinated in oil-and-vinegar dressing; onion rolls; rhubarb Betty.*

Make a sauce by cooking 3 tablespoons butter and flour together for 3 to 4 minutes before adding milk, a little at a time. Stir with wire whip or a wooden spoon until smooth and thickened. Add nutmeg, salt, and pepper. Add cheese and stir until melted. Arrange cooked rice in a shallow buttered casserole. Strew over it the ham and arrange pieces of egg on top. Pour sauce over all. Mix parsley and lemon rind and sprinkle over the top. Dot with small pieces of butter and bake in preheated 400° oven about 20 minutes or until lightly browned and bubbling. Serves 4. Time: 45 minutes.

Parmesan Cheese Soufflé

3 tablespoons butter
3 tablespoons flour
salt and pepper
1/2 teaspoon dry English
  mustard
1 cup milk
2/3 cup grated Parmesan cheese
3 egg yolks
4 egg whites

At Pierre's restaurant on East 53rd Street in New York his cheese soufflé is one of the best-loved specialities. It is made with grated Parmesan cheese, which Pierre insists tastes better, but he called it on his menu Swiss Cheese Soufflé for many years. Now it is called, rightly, "Parmesan." This is my version, not his. His is baked very fast at high heat. *Serve with tossed green salad with sliced cucumbers and radishes liberally doused with French dressing; French bread; open-face blueberry pie.*

Melt butter, blend in flour and seasonings. Cook for a minute or two before adding milk slowly. Stir until smooth and quite thick. Remove from stove. Add cheese; stir until melted. Add egg yolks and blend. Beat whites until stiff, fold in gently, pile into a baking dish with straight sides, and bake in 350° oven 40 to 50 minutes or until the top springs back when lightly touched. Serves 4. Time: 1¼ hours.

Quiche Lorraine

CRUST
1/4 lb. butter
1 3-oz. package cream cheese
salt
1 cup sifted flour
FILLING
2 cups light cream (or milk, or
  half cream and half milk)
3 eggs
2 slices cooked ham, cut julienne, or 5 slices cooked diced
  bacon
1/2 cup grated cheese, preferably
  a dry, nutty Swiss
salt and pepper
pinch of nutmeg

This ham and cheese custard pie may be served either hot or cold as a main dish for a light meal. One-fourth pound fresh mushrooms sliced thin and sautéed in butter may be substituted for the cheese. *Serve with hearts of celery and lettuce with a light French dressing; hot drop biscuits.*

Blend butter, cream cheese, salt, and flour with a pastry cutter until the lumps are about the size of peas. Pat together and chill thoroughly (about 12 hours). Roll dough out to fill a 9-inch pie plate. Bake in a 500° oven for 10 minutes. Remove just long enough to add the filling and cool the oven to 350°. For the filling, scald cream. Beat eggs and add cream, beat until mixed, and then add ham, cheese, and seasonings. Pour into the partly baked shell and bake 30 minutes, or until a knife inserted in the custard comes out clean. Serves 4. Time: 1½ hours, not counting chilling time for crust.

Potato Eggs with Lemon

3 cups mashed potatoes, plus 2 tablespoons finely grated onion, salt, and pepper; or 2 cans frozen condensed cream of potato soup, thawed but not diluted

⅓ cup finely chopped parsley

4 eggs, separated

1 tablespoon grated lemon peel

An old combination with a different presentation. Good for Sunday breakfast. *Precede with fresh fruit — say, pineapple chunks and melon balls — and accompany with hot poppy-seed rolls, coffee, and broiled ham steak on lavish days.*

Mix seasoned mashed potatoes or potato soup (which has onion and seasoning) with parsley. Pour into shallow buttered casserole. Beat egg whites until stiff, add about ¼ teaspoon salt, and add lemon peel, a bit at a time, beating all the while. Spread egg whites lightly over the potatoes, patting into peaks, meringue fashion. With a half-eggshell make four depressions and slide the egg yolks into them. Bake in 325° oven about 12 minutes or until the eggs are set. Serves 4. Time: 25 minutes.

Cottage Cheese Soufflé

4 tablespoons butter

4 tablespoons flour

¾ cup milk

salt and pepper

1 cup cottage cheese

2 whole canned pimientos, coarsely chopped

1 tablespoon finely minced onion

4 eggs, separated

Serve with lettuce, torn in pieces, with hot crumbled bacon and the hot bacon fat, mixed with a squirt of lemon juice; hot butterflake rolls.

Melt butter and blend in flour. Stir over heat until smooth and add milk gradually. Stir until smooth and very thick. Remove from stove and add seasonings, cottage cheese, pimientos, onion, and egg yolks. Mix thoroughly. Beat egg whites until stiff and fold them into the mixture. Bake in a buttered casserole with straight sides, in 350° oven 45 to 50 minutes, or until the top springs back when lightly touched. Serves 4. Time: 1¼ hours.

Pizza

1 box yeast-roll mix, prepared according to directions
olive oil
3½ cups (1-lb.-14-oz. can) Italian plum tomatoes, drained
mozzarella, or Cheddar cheese, sliced thin
orégano or marjoram
anchovies or tiny highly spiced sausages

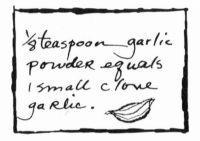

⅛ teaspoon garlic powder equals 1 small clove garlic.

Few Italians agree with the food companies that pizza can be made at home. It is true that most home ovens will not heat to the intensity that an Italian considers necessary, and the recipes in food advertisements have been much bastardized. This is an authentic Italian version adapted to home use. *Serve with salad of broccoli, steamed, chilled, and marinated in oil and garlic-vinegar dressing; Tipo red wine.*

Divide dough in two and roll out to ½-inch thickness to fit two 9-inch pie pans. (Use copper ones if possible.) Fit dough into well-oiled pans. Brush the inside of the pie dough with oil. If you are using anchovies on one of the pies, use the oil from them for this. Arrange tomatoes on the pies. Sprinkle well with orégano or marjoram. Embellish one pie with anchovies or sausages and the other with thin slices of cheese, or just leave them sprinkled with the herbs. Put them in the hottest oven you can achieve—500°, if possible—for 10 to 12 minutes, or until the crust is brown. Serves 4. Time: 1¼ hours.

Pissaladière

3 cups sliced onions
3 tablespoons olive oil
1 8-inch pastry shell, baked 5 to 8 minutes
1 2-oz. can flat anchovy fillets
small pitted black olives (dry wrinkled type)
salt, pepper

This is the pizza of Provence, made with a pie crust rather than the heavier yeast dough. It may be served as a hot hors d'oeuvre or as a dish for lunch or a light supper. *Serve with a salad of cold cooked broccoli with an oil-and-vinegar dressing; French bread; melon balls with blackberries and Cointreau.*

Cook onions very slowly in olive oil in a heavy skillet or heavy-bottomed pan until pale yellow, about ½ hour. Transfer to pie shell, sprinkle with salt and pepper, and arrange anchovy fillets on top in a fan design or in lattice fashion, with black olives in between. Bake in preheated 400° oven 15 to 20 minutes. Serves 4. Time: 1 hour.

Dutch Cheese Casserole

¼ cup butter
6 slices good-quality bread
6 thick slices Edam or Gouda
  cheese (a little more than
  ½ lb.)
2 eggs
1 cup milk
¼ teaspoon salt
pinch of nutmeg

A simple and perfect dish. *Serve with broiled tomatoes; watercress salad; blueberry tarts.*

Butter the bread and arrange in buttered casserole, overlapping the slices. Arrange cheese in the same way. Beat eggs with milk, salt, and nutmeg. Pour over bread and cheese. Bake in preheated 350° oven 30 to 40 minutes or until lightly browned and puffy. Serves 4. Time: 1 hour.

Green Chili and Cheese Dish

½ 4-oz. can green chilis, diced
½ lb. sharp Cheddar cheese,
  diced
2 eggs
1½ cups milk
½ cup flour
1 teaspoon salt

An enticing combination, very simple to prepare from ingredients that might be on hand in kitchens of those as addicted to green chilis as I am. *Serve with sliced tomatoes sprinkled with freshly chopped basil; French bread; fresh peach shortcake.*

Mix chilis and cheese together in the bottom of a small buttered casserole. Mix eggs, milk, flour, and salt in an electric blender, or beat the eggs while adding the milk, flour, and salt. Pour over cheese. Bake in preheated 350° oven 35 to 40 minutes. Serves 4. Time: 1 hour.

Cheese and Parsley Pie

1 loosely packed cup (¼ lb.)
  feta cheese
1 cup cottage cheese
1 9-inch pie shell, baked 5
  minutes
3 tablespoons chopped parsley
4 eggs
2 cups half-and-half
¼ teaspoon grated nutmeg
salt, freshly ground pepper

If the Greek feta cheese is not available, some other sharply flavored diced cheese may be used. Feta has a piquant, positive flavor that is unusual and delightful when mixed with the cottage cheese. *Serve with a salad of Bibb lettuce; hot biscuits; greengage sherbet and thin, crisp chocolate cookies.*

Mix feta, cottage cheese, and parsley. Strew over partially baked pie shell. Buzz eggs, half-and-half, and seasonings in the blender, or beat together, and pour over the cheese in the pie shell. Bake in preheated 450° oven 10 minutes, reduce heat to 350°, and bake 20 minutes or more, until a knife inserted comes out clean. Time: 1 hour.

Cereals
and
Pasta

Cereals and Pasta

Italian Baked Rice

½ cup chopped green onions
½ cup sliced fresh or frozen
  mushrooms
3 tablespoons butter
¾ lb. Italian sweet or hot sausage, cut in small pieces
3 cups slightly underdone
  cooked rice
½ 6-oz. jar marinated artichoke
  hearts, diced, with part of the
  juice
salt, pepper
½ cup beef bouillon or chicken
  broth
⅓ cup breadcrumbs
⅓ cup freshly grated Parmesan
  cheese
more butter

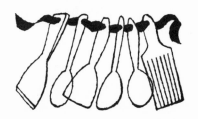

An amenable dish, infinitely variable. Sometimes the miscellaneous ingredients are put
between two layers of rice, sandwich fashion;
other times they are stirred with the rice before
baking. Either way is good. Try different combinations: tiny meatballs, tomato sauce, diced
cheese, and mushrooms; or diced cooked
chicken, hard-cooked eggs, green peas, cheese,
and tomato sauce; and so on. Chicken giblets
are a frequent ingredient. *Serve with green
salad; hot biscuits; lemon sherbet sprinkled with
fresh raspberries.*

Sauté onion and mushrooms in 3 tablespoons
butter until wilted. Add sausage and cook very
briefly. Spread half the rice in a medium buttered casserole and add a layer of onions,
mushrooms, sausage, cooking juices, and artichoke hearts with some of the marinade.
Sprinkle with salt and pepper, if wished. Top
with the rest of the rice. Pour in bouillon or
broth. Sprinkle the top with breadcrumbs and
grated cheese and dot with small pieces of butter. Bake in preheated 350° oven about 30
minutes or until the top is lightly browned and
crusty. Serves 4 to 6. Time: 50 minutes.

Polenta Pie (Polenta Pasticciata)

1 cup fine polenta meal or
    yellow corn meal
1 tablespoon salt
4 tablespoons butter
4 tablespoons flour
3 cups milk
salt, pepper
pinch of nutmeg
½ cup grated Swiss or Cheddar
    cheese
½ lb. fresh or frozen
    mushrooms, sautéed in butter,
    or 1 1-lb. can white Algerian
    truffles, sliced (use the liquid
    in place of part of the milk)
¼ cup freshly grated Parmesan
    cheese

In the north of Italy polenta, made from yellow corn meal that comes in several grinds, is eaten as bread or pasta is eaten elsewhere. By itself it is as dull as our corn-meal mush, but served with sauces it can be something else again. This is a fine dish in its everyday version, made with fresh or frozen mushrooms. Made with white truffles, even the comparatively inexpensive Algerian ones, it is a splendid and exciting dish. The Italians use the choice Piedmont white truffles, which are costly there and here. The Algerian, which are good but less choice and therefore less expensive, are available in New York in 1967 for around $1.60 for a 1-pound can. *Serve with raw spinach salad with hot bacon dressing; lemon mousse.*

Add 1 tablespoon salt and half the polenta to 1 quart boiling water over medium heat and stir with a wooden spoon until well mixed. Turn heat down before adding the rest of the polenta; sometimes it goes *plop* in your face. Stir well until smooth and thickened. Pour into buttered loaf pan or onto buttered platter. Make béchamel sauce by cooking butter with flour for 3 or 4 minutes until dry and well mixed. Add milk or milk and truffle liquid a little at a time, beating briskly with a wire whip, until smooth and thickened. Add seasonings, then cheese. Stir until melted and blended. Stir in sautéed mushrooms or sliced truffles, which do not need sautéeing. Cut polenta in slices. Arrange layer of slices in a medium buttered casserole. Pour some sauce on that, add another layer of polenta, then a layer of sauce, and so on until all ingredients are used, ending up with sauce. Sprinkle with grated Parmesan. Bake in preheated 400° oven about 30 minutes or until the top is golden and bubbling. Serves 6 or 7. Time: 1 hour.

Mamaliga with Bacon and Cheese

1 cup yellow corn meal
1 tablespoon salt
¼ lb. thick sliced bacon, cut in
  short pieces
1 cup grated cheese, Rumanian
  cascaval or Cheddar

In Rumania, as in the north of Italy, corn meal is as basic as bread, as pasta, as rice, and, like pasta and rice, rather boring without its sauces and embellishments. They can be plain or fancy. Most of the sauces for pasta are good with what we call corn-meal mush, the Italians polenta, and the Rumanians mamaliga. They have special kettles, usually copper, for cooking, and intricately carved stirring sticks that are heirlooms and a kind of status symbol, but any kettle and a wooden spoon will do. *Serve with cold dilled beans; watermelon.*

Add 1 tablespoon salt and a handful of corn meal to 1 quart boiling water. Stir and turn heat down before adding the rest; otherwise it may jump up at you. Stir until smooth and thick. Pour into greased loaf pan or spread on platter to cool, then cut into slices or squares. Cook bacon slowly, starting in a heavy cold skillet, pouring off fat as it appears. When crisp, drain on paper towels. In a shallow casserole put a spoonful of bacon fat and a few pieces of bacon, then a layer of mamaliga. Sprinkle generously with cheese and then with some pieces of bacon and spoonfuls of fat. Repeat until all ingredients are used, ending with a layer of cheese. Bake at 350° about 20 minutes. Serves 4. Time: 1 hour.

Hominy and Almond Soufflé

1 can condensed cream of
  mushroom soup
4 tablespoons flour
½ teaspoon cayenne pepper
1 teaspoon Worcestershire
  sauce
salt
freshly ground black pepper
1 1-lb.-13-oz. can hominy
3 eggs, separated
½ cup almonds, blanched,
  toasted, and slivered coarsely

Guaranteed to startle conventional Southerners. *Serve with turkey, ham, or tongue; watercress with French dressing.*

Mix soup and flour into a smooth paste; then add cayenne, Worcestershire sauce, salt, pepper, hominy, and egg yolks. Beat egg whites until stiff. Fold in gently. Pile into a buttered casserole and sprinkle top with almonds. Bake at 350° 45 to 50 minutes, or until top springs back when touched gently. Serves 4. Time: 1 hour.

Migliaccio

3½ cups milk
½ cup instant farina
⅓ cup sugar
2 tablespoons butter
4 eggs, beaten
⅓ cup walnuts, broken up (untraditional and not obligatory)

This lightly sweetened egg and farina loaf is one of the few dishes that can make me vary my usual breakfast of coffee, juice, and eggs. Addicts even like it for a between-meal snack. It is good hot or cold, and can be made the day before. Serve it plain, cut in slices like pound cake, or in a bowl with milk, a sprinkling of sugar, and some chopped walnuts. (The nuts are my contribution to this traditional dish. No Italian is responsible for this whim.) *Serve with large beakers of frozen orange juice; crisp bacon; coffee.*

Bring milk to a boil and add farina. Cook 2½ minutes. Add sugar (½ cup or more for those who have a sweet tooth) and butter. Let cool. Add beaten eggs and walnuts and pour into a buttered loaf-shaped casserole. Bake in 350° oven 50 minutes to 1 hour, or until brown and puffy. Will serve lots. Time: 1½ hours.

Kasha

1 whole egg
1 cup kasha
2½ cups hot bouillon or chicken
broth
3 tablespoons butter

The good buckwheat grain eaten instead of rice in many countries used to be found only in foreign groceries and, regrettably, health-food stores. Now it is on the shelves in most supermarkets. *Serve with duck cooked in red wine (see index); bitter greens (dandelion and mustard leaves) with egg dressing (mash the yolk of 1 hard-cooked egg with olive oil and vinegar, salt and pepper); French bread; apricot soufflé (see index).*

Put egg and kasha in a dry skillet and stir and cook over very low heat until all the grains are coated and slightly toasted. Transfer to a casserole, with hot bouillon. Cover and bake in 350° oven 40 minutes or until the liquid is all absorbed. Remove the top and bake 15 to 20 minutes longer to brown still more. Just before serving, stir in butter, or, if you have some good yellow chicken fat, it tastes even better. Serves 4. Time: 1¼ hours.

Baked Rice Pilaf

1 plump clove garlic, minced
1 cup uncooked rice, preferably
  long-grain rice
²/₃ stick (5¹/₃ tablespoons) butter
2 cups beef bouillon or chicken
  broth
salt in cautious amounts—the
  bouillon has some
¹/₃ cup freshly grated Parmesan
  cheese

Serve with roast duck basted with butter and ver-mouth; cucumber and sweet red onions, sliced thin, with French dressing; hot popovers.

Sauté garlic and rice in butter until pale yellow. Pour, butter and all, into a casserole. Add bouillon, and salt if necessary. Cover and bake in 350° oven 20 minutes or until the liquid is absorbed. Remove from oven. Add cheese and stir with a fork until cheese is mixed and melted and the rice fluffy. Serves 4. Time: 40 minutes.

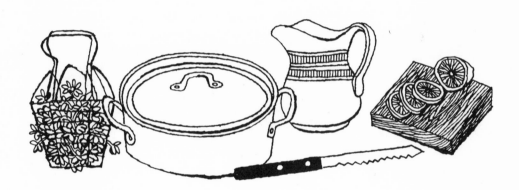

Rice Pilaf with Almonds

1 medium-sized onion, minced
3 tablespoons butter
1 cup uncooked rice
2 cups bouillon or broth
¹/₂ cup toasted slivered almonds
3 strips bacon, cut in 1-inch
  pieces and cooked until very
  crisp
1 teaspoon salt

Rice is a bland little grain that can be enhanced by almost any sauce or seasoning, preferably a rather positive one. *Serve with broiled steak; mixed greens with tomato quarters and thin rings of milky sweet red onions, sprinkled with olive oil, finely chopped parsley, lots of freshly ground pepper; French bread.*

Cook onion in butter until transparent. Add rice and cook until rice is pale yellow. Transfer to a shallow buttered casserole. Add bouillon. Stir in nuts, bacon, and salt. Cover and bake ³/₄ hour in 350° oven. Serves 4. Time: 1¹/₄ hours.

Anchovy, Rice, and Parsley Casserole

½ cup chopped onion
1 clove garlic, minced
1 tablespoon butter
2 cups cooked rice
1 2-oz. can anchovies, cut in
  pieces
1 teaspoon salt
½ cup finely chopped parsley
2 tablespoons melted butter
2 eggs
1 cup milk

Down around Naples a mixture like this of rice and eggs is called *sformato di riso*. It can, like so many simple and good dishes, vary according to mood and what is on hand. Tiny meat balls called *polpetti* might be added with some sliced cooked mushrooms instead of the anchovies. Let your imagination stray, within decent limits. *Serve with sliced tomatoes, sprinkled with finely chopped chives and basil, lemon-and-oil dressing; hot sesame rolls; rhubarb pie.*

Cook onions and garlic in 1 tablespoon butter until limp but not colored. Remove from heat and add rice, anchovies, salt, and parsley. Stir well and put into a small casserole with the melted butter. Beat eggs and milk together or buzz in a blender and pour in. Bake in preheated 325° oven 40 minutes or until the dish is set. Serves 4 to 5. Time: 1 hour.

Egyptian Rice (Rosz Masri)

¼ lb. butter
1 cup uncooked rice
2 cups meat stock or beef bouillon
2 medium-sized yellow onions,
  sliced thin
6 lamb kidneys, split, white part
  removed, and sliced
½ 6-oz. can Italian tomato paste
2 tablespoons minced parsley
salt and pepper

This recipe came from the Egyptian Embassy in Washington long ago when it was mostly distinguished for its parties. *Serve with escarole and avocado with French dressing (2 parts olive oil, 1 part lime juice, salt, pepper); hot rolls; lemon pudding (see index).*

Melt two-thirds of the butter and cook rice in it until pale yellow. Transfer butter and rice to a casserole. Add meat stock or bouillon. Cover and bake in 350° oven 25 to 30 minutes or until rice is tender and liquid absorbed. Meanwhile sauté onions and kidneys in the rest of the butter, add tomato paste, 2 cups water, parsley, and a little salt and pepper (the bouillon has some). Simmer and stir for about 15 minutes. Pour in casserole over rice and heat together before serving. Serves 4. Time: 1 hour.

Green Noodles with Sour Cream and Pot Cheese

½ lb. noodles, preferably the
  green spinach ones
salt and pepper
½ pt. sour cream
½ pt. pot cheese or cottage
  cheese
½ cup seedless raisins, soaked
  in rum
toasted slivered almonds

The simplicity of this mildly tangy dish is right for a pleasantly austere evening. There is a soothing mingling of foods, bland in texture and flavor, that is somehow intriguing. *Serve with watercress, sliced radishes, and cucumbers with French dressing; onion rolls (1 teaspoon minced onion sautéed in butter put in the folds of Parker House rolls made from a ready mix).*

Cook noodles in lots of briskly boiling salted water until almost tender. Drain, rinse with cold water, drain again, and place in a deep buttered casserole. Add salt, if necessary, and pepper. Mix sour cream with pot cheese and raisins. Pour over noodles and toss together slightly. Sprinkle the top with almonds. Bake 15 to 20 minutes in 350° oven. The almonds are extra—and extra special—but then I like any food, almost, with nuts in it. Serves 4. Time: 40 minutes.

Neota's Corn-Bread Stuffing, Baked Separately

1 batch plain corn bread, crumbled into large pieces
2 slices white bread, diced
2 cups turkey broth
¼ cup melted butter
3 cups chopped celery and
  onions, about half and half
salt
lots of pepper
4 eggs

There is a pleasant Southern custom of baking the turkey stuffing in a separate pan rather than in the bird. Somehow, when the bird is roasted unstuffed, it tastes turkeyer and crisper—and yet the dressing is there too. *Serve with roast turkey basted with butter and turkey broth (made by simmering the giblets and neck with 1 large onion, quartered, 2 stalks celery, chopped, ¼ cup parsley, in 4 cups water with salt and pepper); whole-cranberry sauce; celery, olives, and sweet burr gherkins.*

Mix all the ingredients together in the order given and put into a large shallow buttered casserole. Bake in 350° oven about 1 hour, or until brown and puffy. This serves about 6. Time: 1½ hours.

Spoon Bread

1 tablespoon butter or bacon
  drippings
salt
1 cup white corn meal
1 cup milk
1 to 3 eggs

This is the moist corn-meal pudding baked and served in a casserole in the South. It is served with a spoon onto the dinner plate and liberally doused with butter and used in place of potatoes or rice and hot bread. There are many different ways of making it, with varying amounts of eggs, but it is always made with white corn meal, preferably water-ground. *Serve with crisp oven-fried chicken; watercress with Roquefort cheese dressing; apricot nut pudding (see index).*

Heat fat in a casserole. Bring 1 cup water and a pinch of salt to a boil and pour over corn meal. Beat milk into the mixture until smooth. Break eggs into that, stir, and pour into casserole. Bake in 400° oven about 45 minutes. Serve with plenty of butter. Serves 4. Time: 1 hour.

A Blintz Flood with Sour Cream

BLINTZ BATTER
1 egg, beaten
¾ cup flour
¾ cup water
1 teaspoon salt

FILLING
3 large onions, sliced thin and
  sautéed in butter
½ lb. mushrooms, sliced and
  sautéed in butter
4 hard-cooked eggs, chopped
lots of paprika and salt
more butter
extra batter from the blintzes

This is the family name for a fascinating dish made by the Russian grandmother of a scholarly friend of mine. *Serve with raw broccoli with garlic mayonnaise; baked rhubarb.*

For the batter, beat the ingredients together and let stand several hours to "ripen." Make, one at a time, 5 very thin 8-inch blintzes. Keep them warm.

Put a blintz on the bottom of an 8- or 9-inch casserole and cover with fried onion slices, sautéed mushrooms, hard-cooked eggs, and lots of paprika and salt. Repeat in layers, ending with a blintz on top. Dot the top with butter and paprika and pour in the extra batter so that it covers the top and seals the sides. Bake in 350° oven 20 minutes or until the top is crisp and sounds like a hollow shell when tapped. Cut in wedges and serve with sour cream. Serves 4. Time: 45 minutes.

François' French Toast

1 egg
1½ cups light cream
1 tablespoon powdered sugar,
plus more for sprinkling
pinch of salt
½ teaspoon vanilla
⅓ cup rum, brandy, or curaçao
8 slices French bread, cut in
thick slices on a slant
butter
¼ cup applesauce
¾ cup thin custard sauce

While François Gouron was at the Plaza Hotel
in New York (and maybe now) you could get
this French toast for Sunday breakfast. *Serve
with large beakers of tangerine juice (from frozen
concentrate) and lots of good coffee.*

Beat egg, cream, sugar, salt, vanilla, and rum
together. Dip slices of bread in this and sauté
in butter until golden brown. Arrange slices
of sautéed bread in an earthenware casserole.
Mix applesauce and custard and pour over
toast. Sprinkle with powdered sugar and bake
in 400° oven until brown and bubbly, about
15 minutes, or put under the broiler briefly,
watching all the while. Serves 4. Time: 45
minutes.

½ cup evaporated milk plus ½ cup water make 1 cup milk for cooking.

Baked Pasta

½ lb. pasta—sea shells, bows,
spirals, etc., cooked according
to directions until barely tender, and drained
1 large onion, chopped
2 tablespoons butter
1 sweet green pepper, seeded
and diced
2 canned pimientos, diced
2 tablespoons chopped parsley
3 eggs
1 cup milk
3 tablespoons grated Parmesan
cheese
salt, pepper
breadcrumbs
butter

*Serve with watercress and white-grape salad with
oil-and-vinegar dressing; corn toast; pear sherbet
with shaved chocolate.*

Put drained cooked pasta in a medium casserole. Cook onion in butter until limp and
lightly colored. Add, with cooking butter,
green pepper, pimientos, and parsley, to the
pasta and stir until well mingled. Buzz in a
blender eggs, milk, grated cheese, salt, and
pepper, or beat together by hand, and pour
over rest of the ingredients. Sprinkle top with
breadcrumbs and dot with butter. Bake in
preheated 350° oven 40 to 50 minutes or until
the dish is custardy. Serves 4 to 6. Time: 1
hour.

Pasta with Fresh Tomato Sauce

1 large sweet red onion, sliced

4 tablespoons oil

1 small hot red pepper, crumbled

7 slices bacon, cut in pieces

¼ cup dry white wine

2 medium tomatoes, skinned, seeded, and chopped

½ teaspoon marjoram

salt, freshly ground black pepper

1 lb. small pasta shells, bows, etc.

freshly grated Parmesan cheese (if you wish)

Americans who have taken Italian cooking seriously in past years have been inclined to make an Italian meat sauce of the traditional kind that took 3 or 4 hours and ended up as a thick, velvety smooth, and rich sauce. There is a pleasing tendency the other way now, and Italians have always used both short and long methods. The short method, using fresh tomatoes, skinned, seeded, and diced, ends in an entirely different and delightful sauce, whether with or without meat. To skin a tomato, put it on a fork and dip briefly into boiling water, or hold it over a flame, also briefly, then pull off the skin. *Serve with spinach salad sprinkled with riced hard-cooked egg; Italian bread and mantecca cheese (the one that looks like a shmoo and has a center of fresh butter); fresh cherries.*

Cook onion in oil. Add 2 tablespoons water and the red pepper. Simmer 2 or 3 minutes. Add bacon pieces and cook until crisp, pouring off some surplus fat but not all. Add wine and cook down 3 or 4 minutes. Add tomatoes and marjoram and cook about 7 minutes; the tomatoes should be firm and not mushy. Meanwhile boil the pasta according to directions on the box, but not the full time. Drain, rinse with cold water, and put into a shallow casserole. Add the sauce. Heat together in preheated 375° oven about 20 minutes. Serve with freshly grated Parmesan cheese, if desired, but the sauce is good without it. Serves 5. Time: 50 minutes.

Norma Zamboni's Pasta

1 lb. ditalini, or other fine spaghetti
2 eggs
⅓ cup grated Parmesan cheese
salt
lots of freshly ground pepper

This honest Italian dish keeps the seasoning simple and sharp. *Serve 'with salad of romaine, quarters of tomatoes, and hearts of artichokes, with French dressing; Italian bread.*

Cook ditalini in salted boiling water until barely tender—definitely not until squishy. Drain, rinse with cold water, and drain again. Place in a medium-sized buttered casserole. Beat eggs slightly and pour over ditalini. Sprinkle with grated cheese, salt, and pepper. Toss slightly. Bake in 350° oven 20 minutes or until brown and crusty. Serves 4 amply. Time: 35 minutes.

Lasagne with Ricotta

½ lb. sausage or pork, cut in
  small pieces
2 plump cloves garlic, minced
2 tablespoons olive oil
1 1-lb.-3-oz. can Italian plum tomatoes
½ 6-oz. can Italian tomato paste
salt and pepper
½ lb. lasagne noodles, 1 inch
  wide
1 lb. ricotta (Italian cottage
  cheese)
1 cup sliced or cubed mozzarella, or Swiss cheese (somewhat different but equally
  good)
⅔ cup grated Parmesan cheese

Lasagne are the wide flat noodles, somewhat chewy, that give real substance to a dish. *Serve with mixed bitter greens with a tart French dressing.*

Brown sausage or pork in olive oil with garlic. Add tomatoes, tomato paste, salt, and pepper, and let them simmer while the noodles are cooking; add 1 cup water if the mixture gets too thick. Drop noodles into a very large pot of boiling salted water, one by one, letting them soften as they go in; otherwise they stick together and get gummy. Cook until almost tender. Don't let them get soft and squashy. Drain. Put a layer of sauce in the bottom of a deep casserole. Then add a layer of lasagne and a layer each of ricotta, mozzarella, Parmesan cheese. Repeat until all ingredients are used, ending with the Parmesan. Heat together in 350° oven until the dish bubbles and trembles. Serves 4. Time: 1¼ hours.

Tufoli Stuffed with Smithfield Ham in Tomato Sauce

1 pound tufoli or other large
  pasta
2 3-oz. jars Smithfield ham
  spread
4 8-oz. cans tomato sauce
1 cup grated Parmesan cheese
2 tablespoons anchovy paste

The tufoli may be boiled and stuffed ahead of time, ready for the last-minute cooking. *Serve with cucumber and watercress salad; garlic bread; wine sherbet.*

Cook tufoli in a large pot of boiling salted water until barely tender. Because this is a large size of pasta, allow plenty of time. It will vary according to the size of your pan, etc. Drain and let it cool enough for handling. With a pastry tube or demitasse spoon, fill each tube with ham spread but do not pack. Arrange filled tubes in a large casserole. Mix tomato sauce with cheese, anchovy paste, and seasonings. Pour over the tufoli. Bake in 350° oven about 1 hour or until brown and bubbly. Serves 4. Time: 1½ hours.

Cannelloni with Ricotta and Spinach

1 lb. fresh spinach, chopped, or
  1 10-oz. package frozen spinach, chopped
1 cup ricotta, or 1 cup creamed
  cottage cheese
1 egg
½ cup grated Parmesan cheese
salt and pepper
12 6-inch crêpes (see index)
2 or 3 large tomatoes, skinned,
  seeded, and cut in chunks
1 tablespoon melted butter or
  olive oil

Cannelloni may be made with noodle dough but frequently are made with crêpes as in this recipe. *Serve with chopped cucumber, mint, and yogurt that have chilled together for at least 2 hours; Italian bread; glazed oranges.*

Cook spinach until barely tender. Drain and press dry. Mix with ricotta or cottage cheese, egg, and 2 tablespoons grated Parmesan. Add salt and pepper. Fill and roll crêpes. Place side by side in a rectangular casserole. Tuck pieces of tomato around and sprinkle rolls and to-mato pieces with melted butter or olive oil. Sprinkle with the rest of the cheese. Bake in 450° oven 20 minutes. Serves 4 to 6. Time: 1 hour.

Vegetables

Vegetables

Stuffed Green Chilis

3 4-oz. cans green chilis, or 12
   fresh ones, peeled and seeded
1 pound mozzarella, cut in 12
   chunks, or 1 pound Monterey
   jack cheese
3 eggs, separated
3 tablespoons hot water
¼ cup flour
½ teaspoon salt
fat for frying

SAUCE

2 cups (1-lb. can) tomatoes
¼ teaspoon orégano
1 onion, chopped
2 cloves garlic, minced
3 tablespoons butter
3 tablespoons flour
salt, pepper

Green chilis are hot and wonderful, and when I spent several months in Santa Fe I became hooked on this dish. *Serve with sliced tomatoes and cucumbers with a vinaigrette dressing; hot popovers; lemon pudding (see index)*

Wrap a chili around each chunk of cheese. Make a batter of egg yolks, water, flour, and salt by buzzing in a blender or beating. Beat egg whites until stiff and fold into the batter (this is nice but not absolutely necessary; the eggs may be used whole). Dip each chili in the batter and fry a few at a time in fat 2 inches deep heated to 375°, until golden brown. This may be done in an electric skillet. Drain and keep warm. For the sauce, cook tomatoes with orégano for about 15 minutes and put through a sieve or purée in a blender. Brown onion and garlic in butter. Remove with a slotted spoon and add to tomatoes. Add flour to garlic butter and cook together for a few minutes. Add to tomato mixture. Salt and pepper. Arrange stuffed chilis in a shallow casserole. Pour in sauce and heat in preheated 350° oven 15 to 20 minutes. Time: 1 hour.

Stuffed Artichokes

4 fat round artichokes
1/3 cup freshly grated Parmesan
   cheese
2/3 cup breadcrumbs, homemade
   if possible
1 large clove garlic, minced
2 tablespoons finely chopped
   parsley
salt and pepper
3 tablespoons olive oil

When artichokes are stuffed, somehow the bother of eating them is more worth while. *Serve with sliced tongue with horseradish sauce (sour cream mixed with horseradish); small cherry tomatoes; French bread.*

Pull off the outside leaves of the artichokes and cut off the stems and thorny tips of the leaves. Turn artichokes upside down and press leaves open. Mix cheese, breadcrumbs, garlic, parsley, salt, and pepper together. Sprinkle lavishly between the leaves of the artichokes. Stand artichokes in a casserole with about 1 inch of salted water in the bottom. Sprinkle with olive oil, being sure most of the surfaces are moistened. Cover tightly and bake in 325° oven about 2 hours, depending upon the size of the artichokes. They are done when the bottom leaves will pull free easily. Pour off water (if there is any left) and serve the artichokes in the casserole. Serves 4. Time: 2¼ hours.

Asparagus Parmesan

1 bunch, or 2 lbs., fresh asparagus (the bunches run about
   2½ lbs.)
4 tablespoons butter
½ cup freshly grated Parmesan
or Romano cheese
salt and freshly ground pepper

Serve with broiled lamb chops; French bread; apricot nut pudding (see index).

Wash asparagus and break off tough ends. If they are broken instead of cut, they will break naturally at the tender point. Cook in boiling salted water, either upright in the bottom of a double boiler or flat in a large skillet, until tender. Drain and save some of the water. Melt butter in the bottom of a shallow casserole. Arrange asparagus in this, turning it around until all of it is coated with butter. Pour in three tablespoons of the asparagus water and sprinkle cheese over all. Grind black pepper generously over the cheese and salt lightly. Bake in 400° oven 10 to 15 minutes. Serves 4. Time: 30 minutes.

Black Beans in Red Wine

1 lb. black beans
1 onion, minced fine
¼ lb. salt pork, diced and
    scalded
1 cup beef bouillon
1 cup red wine
salt and pepper
1 cup sour cream

Black beans are among the most beautiful of all beans in shape and color, and have a definite and meaty taste. *Serve with baked ham; watercress with 2 parts sliced cooked beets, 1 part diced celery, French dressing; French bread; lemon sherbet sprinkled with blueberries.*

Soak beans overnight. Put them in a saucepan in the same water, with onion and scalded pork. Simmer until the skins curl back when a few in a spoon are blown upon. Drain. Put beans, onion, and salt pork in a bean pot or deep casserole with bouillon and red wine. Salt and pepper and bake 2 hours more or less in a 350° oven. Serve with a bowl of sour cream to spoon over the beans. Serves 6 to 8. Time: 12 hours, more or less.

Brazilian Baked Black Beans

2 cups cooked and seasoned
    black beans
beef bouillon
½ teaspoon orégano
½ bay leaf, crumbled
flour
salt and pepper
1 large onion, sliced and pulled
    apart
2 large tomatoes, peeled, seeded,
    and quartered
2 tablespoons bacon fat or other
    fat
3 hard-cooked eggs, sliced

It is possible that undiluted canned black-bean soup, thickened, could be used as a base for this. Traditionally the dish is accompanied by pork chops or spareribs.

Put beans in a blender with a little of their own liquid or a little bouillon. Or put through a food mill. Heat the puréed beans with orégano and bay leaf and thicken with a little flour mixed with cold water. The mixture should be about the consistency of a very thick white sauce. Check for seasoning and add salt and pepper if necessary. Spread in a low casserole 9 to 10 inches in diameter. Cook onion rings and tomatoes in bacon fat, being careful not to break them. When they are tender spread on top of mixture. Then arrange sliced hard-cooked eggs in a nice design on top. Bake in 350° oven 25 to 35 minutes. Serves 6 to 8. Time: 50 minutes.

Compromise Succotash

1 lb. fresh green beans, broken, or 1 9-oz. package frozen cut green beans
1 pt. fresh, or 1 10-oz. package frozen, lima beans
4 ears corn, cut from the cob, or 1 10-oz. package frozen cut corn, thawed
1 can condensed cream of mushroom soup, undiluted

There is no compromise in the flavor of this. But in some places in New England succotash is green beans and corn, and in the South it's lima or butter beans and corn. This has all three—and the mushroom soup, which I do not think is used anywhere. This is a dish that waits gracefully for your convenience. *Serve with fried chicken; cream slaw (1 small head cabbage, shredded and salted, tossed just before serving with ½ cup heavy cream, three tablespoons vinegar, ½ cup sugar); hot poppy-seed rolls.*

Simmer the green beans and the lima beans separately until tender. Drain. Mix the corn and mushroom soup. Pile into a shallow casserole and bake in 350° oven 15 to 20 minutes. Serves 4 to 6. Time: 30 minutes.

Hungarian Green Beans Baked in Sweet Cream

1½ lbs. fresh, or 2 9-oz packages frozen, green beans, frenched
1 tablespoon butter
½ teaspoon salt
pepper
½ cup heavy sweet cream
¼ teaspoon nutmeg
¼ cup breadcrumbs

To me green beans are among the most boring of the vegetables, but they are also among the most variable and popular with others. *Serve with fried chicken; spoon bread (see index); baked pears with shaved chocolate (see index).*

Simmer beans in water until barely tender. Drain and arrange in a shallow baking dish. Dot with butter, add salt, pepper, nutmeg, and cream. Top with breadcrumbs and bake 15 to 20 minutes in 350° oven or until top is lightly brown. Serves 4. Time: 30 to 35 minutes.

Swiss Peasant Beans

¼ lb. salt pork, diced
1 medium onion, chopped
1 clove garlic, chopped
bacon fat
1 lb. green beans, broken into pieces, or 2 packages frozen cut beans, cooked
12 tiny new potatoes, boiled, or 4 medium-sized potatoes, boiled and cubed
1 cup beef bouillon
1 slice bacon, minced and slightly cooked

This is a simple, sturdy dish such as you will find in small peasant inns in Switzerland, though not in glittering tourist places. *Serve with celery, radishes, small wrinkled black olives; pumpernickel.*

Simmer salt pork 10 minutes. Cook onion and garlic in bacon fat. Transfer to a casserole with salt pork, beans, potatoes, and bouillon. Sprinkle the top with minced bacon. Cover and bake in 350° oven 20 minutes. Garlic frankfurters may be added if desired. Serves 4. Time: 45 minutes.

The Beaniest Dish

1 plump clove garlic, minced
⅓ cup olive oil
1 lb. dried beans, soaked and simmered until tender, or 2 1-lb. cans cooked dried beans
1 lb. fresh, or 1 9-oz. package frozen, green beans, cooked until tender
2 cups beef bouillon
1 tablespoon grated lemon peel
salt and lots of freshly ground black pepper

Naturally, this should be served only to those really fond of beans. Any type of dried bean may be used—navy, marrow, lima, kidney, black, or even, to stretch a point, black-eyed peas. The beans may be soaked and simmered until tender, or canned ones may be used. *Serve with grapefruit segments with chicory and French dressing; corn sticks; honeydew melon.*

Cook garlic briefly in olive oil. Mix cooked dried beans and cooked green beans in a casserole. Add olive oil, garlic, bouillon, grated lemon peel, salt, and pepper. Stir around, cover, and bake 30 minutes in 350° oven. Serves 4 to 6. Time: 1 hour if canned beans are used.

Kidney Beans in Sour Cream

1 lb. dried red kidney beans, or
  2 1-lb. cans kidney beans
  (without sauce and drained
  thoroughly)
3 large or 4 medium-sized
  onions, sliced thickly
3 tablespoons butter
1 cup sour cream
salt and lots of freshly ground
  black pepper

One of the few foods I could eat happily and blissfully every day of the week is dried beans—any kind that I have tasted so far in a long, curious, and enthusiastic search. *Serve with raw spinach salad with grated raw carrots and canned pimientos cut in pieces, dressed with olive oil, salt, and lots of freshly ground black pepper; corn bread.*

Soak dried kidney beans overnight, then simmer until the skins curl back when blown upon, or cook in a pressure cooker according to directions. Drain and place in a casserole or bean pot with a lid. (If you are using canned beans, just drain and put in the pot.) Sauté onions in butter until pale yellow. Mix butter, onions, sour cream, salt, and pepper together. Stir the mixture into the beans. Cover and bake in 350° oven 15 to 20 minutes. Serves 4. Time: 30 minutes for canned beans, 2 to 3 hours for dried, plus time for soaking.

Kidney Beans and Red Wine

3 small spring onions, tops and
  bulbs chopped
½ green pepper, chopped, without seeds
1 cup diced cooked ham
3 tablespoons butter
1 6-oz. can Italian tomato paste
1 cup red wine
salt and pepper
2 1-lb. cans kidney beans,
  drained
8 bacon strips

Any good red wine, domestic or imported, does here, and we find it helps to serve the same wine before, during, and after dinner. *Serve with escarole with French dressing, Italian bread sticks.*

Sauté onions, pepper, and ham in butter. Add tomato paste to wine and seasoning. Cook 5 to 10 minutes. Put, with kidney beans, in low buttered casserole and cover with bacon strips. Bake 30 minutes in 350° oven or until the bacon is cooked. Serves 4 or more. Time: 55 minutes.

Baked Beans

2 lbs. marrow-fat beans, or other
   large white beans of good
   quality
1¼ lbs. lean salt pork
2 medium-sized onions
2 cups dark molasses
2 teaspoons salt
2 teaspoons dry mustard

You might just as well bake a lot at a time—home-baked beans are so nearly extinct that they are very, very popular. *Serve with baked or stewed rhubarb; endive with French dressing; Swedish bread.*

Wash and pick over beans, soak overnight in 3 cups of water, then simmer below boiling point until skins begin to loosen and pop. Add more water if needed. Cut salt pork in 2-inch cubes and scald in 3 cups actively boiling water. Use two 2-quart heavy bean pots with covers. Place an onion in bottom of each pot, divide beans and other materials equally, and place half in each pot with pork near the surface. Add enough water nearly to fill pots, cover, and bake in 325° oven 5 or 6 hours, adding water about twice nearly to fill pots again. Remove covers and bake 1 hour longer. Reheat in the same bean pots. Serves about 20, depending on the assembled appetites. Time: 24 hours, plus time for soaking.

Beans Baked with Honey

2 cups, or 2 1-lb. cans cooked,
   navy beans, black-eyed peas,
   or dried lima beans, drained
1 medium-sized onion, minced
6 slices bacon, diced
1 teaspoon salt
pepper
1 teaspoon dry mustard
¼ cup chopped preserved ginger or chutney
¾ cup honey

Baked beans with a Southern accent. *Serve with slaw with sour-cream and caraway dressing (½ cup sour cream, dash of lemon juice, 1 teaspoon caraway seeds); pumpernickel and sweet butter; lemon pudding (see index); beer.*

Soak beans overnight. Simmer until tender (check by blowing on a few in a spoon, the skins should burst and curl) or cook in the pressure pan according to directions. Sauté onion with bacon. Mix with beans, salt, pepper, mustard, and ginger or chutney. Put in a deep casserole with a lid, and pour honey over all. Cover and bake 1½ hours at 325°. Uncover the last ½ hour. Serves 4. Time: 4 hours for dried beans, plus time for soaking; 2½ hours for canned.

Fresh Lima Bean Soufflé

1 cup fresh, or 1 10-oz. package
  frozen, lima beans (either baby
  or Fordhook)
1 can condensed dried-lima-
  bean soup, undiluted
4 tablespoons flour
1 jigger rum
¼ cup sour cream
3 eggs, separated
salt and pepper

Pale green, and as light as the puff of an April breeze, a lima bean soufflé makes a fragile and dramatic vegetable course. *Serve with pan-broiled lamb chops; watercress with sour-cream mushroom dressing (½ cup sour cream, 1 teaspoon lemon juice, 2 raw mushroom caps, finely chopped); corn muffins.*

Put lima beans through the meat grinder, using the coarsest attachment, or purée them in the blender with the rum. Mix them with undiluted soup, flour, sour cream, rum, and yolks of eggs. Beat egg whites until fluffy, and fold into bean mixture very gently. Pat into a greased casserole. Bake in 350° oven 45 minutes to 1 hour, or until the top springs back when lightly touched. Serves 4. Time: 1¼ hours.

Dried Lima Beans and Tomatoes

4 spring onions, tops and bulbs
  chopped, or 1 medium-sized
  onion, chopped
¼ cup olive oil
1 lb. dried lima beans, soaked
  and simmered until tender, or
  2 1-lb. cans cooked dried lima
  beans
½ green pepper, chopped, without seeds
½ teaspoon sugar
salt
cayenne pepper
3½ cups (1-lb.-12-oz. can) tomatoes
grated Parmesan cheese

Serve with lettuce and chopped parsley with crumbled cooked bacon, tossed thoroughly in a sweet French dressing (2 parts olive oil, 1 part vinegar, 1 teaspoon sugar, salt and pepper); whole-wheat muffins.

Cook onions in oil until yellow; add drained beans and green pepper. Toss a few minutes in pan to add flavor, then put in deep buttered casserole with sugar, salt, and cayenne. Cover with tomatoes. Sprinkle liberally with Parmesan cheese. Cook uncovered in 350° oven 40 minutes. Serves 8. Time: 1 hour (allow 3 hours for cooking dried beans).

Dried Lima Beans Baked in Sour-Cream Sauce

1 lb. dried lima beans, soaked and simmered until tender, or 2 1-lb. cans cooked dried lima beans, drained

2 tablespoons maple syrup or ⅓ cup brown sugar

1½ teaspoons dry English mustard

½ pt. sour cream

salt and pepper

6 strips bacon, cooked and crumbled, or 4 slices thin ham, cut into small squares

½ teaspoon thyme and rosemary, mixed

Serve with watercress with grapefruit segments and French dressing; hot corn muffins; apricot soufflé (see index).

Put drained beans in a casserole and make a paste of syrup, mustard, sour cream, salt, and pepper. Add to beans and mix gently. Sprinkle the top with ham or bacon and herbs. Bake in 350° oven 20 minutes—or longer if you want another drink. Serves 4. Time: 40 minutes.

Jagasee

2 large Bermuda onions, sliced thin

2 tablespoons fat, preferably bacon fat

2 cups dried lima beans, soaked overnight and simmered until tender, or 3 1-lb. cans cooked dried lima or butter beans, drained

½ lb. salt pork, cubed and scalded with boiling water

3½ cups (1-lb.-12-oz. can) tomatoes

¾ cup diced green pepper, seeds removed

¾ cup diced celery

2 cups uncooked rice

salt and pepper

This is a lusty New England version, apparently, of the frugal bean and rice combination so popular around the Mediterranean and Caribbean. *Serve with salad of pieces of raw cauliflower, green pepper, celery, and so on; hot corn bread.*

Sauté onions in fat until pale yellow. Transfer to a casserole with a tightly fitting top. Add cooked beans, scalded pork, tomatoes, green pepper, celery, rice, seasoning, and 3 cups water. Cover tightly and bake in 350° oven 2 or 3 hours. Add more water when the dish starts to dry out. Serves 6 to 8 generously. Time: 3½ hours.

Carrots and Yellow Squash

1 lb. young carrots
1/4 cup melted butter
3 tablespoons lemon juice
1 1/2 tablespoons sugar
1 lb. yellow squash, sliced but
  not peeled
1 teaspoon poultry seasoning
salt and freshly ground black
  pepper

A cheerful-looking dish, as springlike as the first daffodils. *Serve with roast leg of lamb; baked sweet potatoes; watercress salad with Roquefort dressing; orange sherbet and almond cookies.*

Trim ends off carrots and cut in 1-inch pieces. Put in electric blender with butter, lemon juice, and sugar; blend at high speed until puréed; they can be more laboriously grated by hand or put through food mill. Put carrot purée into a buttered shallow medium casserole, and pour over the sliced squash. Sprinkle with poultry seasoning and salt and pepper. Bake 50 minutes at 350°, or until the carrot loses its raw taste. Serves 4. Time: 1 1/4 hours.

Baked Celery au Gratin

2 cups celery cut in 3/4-inch
  pieces
2 tablespoons butter
2 tablespoons flour
1 cup chicken broth
1 cup milk
salt
1/2 cup grated Parmesan cheese
1/2 cup blanched slivered almonds

Celery is always plentiful, in season, and usually in the bottom of your refrigerator. Cooked in a casserole this way, it is elegant *and* different. *Serve with fried chicken or roast pork; green salad with French dressing; poppy-seed rolls; baked pears with shaved chocolate (see index).*

Blanch cut celery in boiling salted water 8 minutes; drain and set aside. Melt butter and blend in flour. Stir over low heat until smooth. Add chicken broth and milk and cook, stirring, until mixture thickens. Taste for seasoning and add salt if necessary. Combine celery and sauce in shallow buttered baking dish. Sprinkle with Parmesan cheese and almonds. Bake at 350° for 1/2 hour or until brown and bubbly. Serves 4 to 6. Time: 45 minutes.

Dried Lima Beans Baked with Pears

1 lb. large dried lima beans, soaked and simmered until tender, drained; or 1 1-lb.-14-oz. can cooked dried lima beans, drained
1 6-oz. can pear halves, quartered
⅓ cup pear juice
¼ cup brown sugar
½ cup chopped onion
1 cup chicken broth
½ teaspoon salt

A subtle and sublime combination of flavors and textures, at least to a lover of beans and pears. *Serve with baked ham; watercress and endive salad; cornsticks; strawberry sherbet.*

Pour lima beans into greased baking dish, scatter pear pieces through them, sprinkle with pear juice, brown sugar, and chopped onion. Stir in chicken broth and season. Bake at 350° for 45 or 50 minutes. Serves 6. Time: 1 hour.

Mushroom Pudding

1 lb. fresh mushrooms, sliced
salt and pepper
1 onion, chopped
4 tablespoons butter
⅓ cup flour
2 cups milk
4 egg yolks, beaten
2 tablespoons grated Parmesan cheese
1 chicken bouillon cube dissolved in ½ cup water
4 egg whites, beaten until stiff
3 tablespoons breadcrumbs

A pleasing variant on the usual rice, potato, or noodle dish. *Serve with roast baby turkey; watercress, orange, and white grape salad with oil-and-vinegar dressing; vanilla ice cream with chopped soft citron; thin chocolate cookies.*

Sprinkle mushrooms with salt and pepper, sauté them lightly with onion in 2 tablespoons butter. In another saucepan, melt 2 tablespoons butter, stir in flour until smooth, add milk, and cook over low heat until the sauce thickens, stirring all the while. Remove from heat and add beaten egg yolks and Parmesan cheese. Add mushrooms and onion and let cool. Stir in bouillon, fold in egg whites, and put in a well-greased shallow baking tin. Sprinkle with breadcrumbs. Bake at 350° for 30 to 40 minutes. It is done when a knife inserted comes out clean. Serve with melted butter. Serves 4. Time: 1 hour.

Broccoli and Cheese Custard

1 bunch fresh broccoli, trimmed, and bottoms cut off, or 1 10-oz. package frozen broccoli
3 eggs
²/₃ cup milk
1¼ cups grated sharp Cheddar cheese
salt and pepper

Serve with broiled ham slices; salad of escarole, cooked celery cut in 2-inch pieces and marinated overnight in a tart dressing (2½ parts olive oil, 1½ parts vinegar, salt, pepper, and 1 teaspoon capers), canned pimientos cut in squares; hot poppy-seed rolls.

Cook broccoli until tender. Drain and place in the bottom of a shallow buttered casserole. Beat eggs, add milk, cheese, and seasoning, and beat until thoroughly mixed. Pour over broccoli. Set baking dish in a pan with about 1 inch of water. Put in 325° oven about 25 to 30 minutes, or until the top is brown and a knife inserted in the custard comes out clean. This is good either hot or cold and may even be re-heated in a moderate oven. Serves 4. Time: 45 minutes.

Cabbage with Rice

3 thick slices bacon, cut in 1½-inch pieces
1 large onion, chopped
½ lb. fresh or frozen mushrooms, sliced
1 small head cabbage, shredded
2 cups slightly undercooked rice
1 large tomato, peeled, seeded, and diced.
3 tablespoons white seedless raisins or currants
2 or more cups beef bouillon
pinch of nutmeg
½ teaspoon thyme
2 lumps sugar
1 piece lemon peel
1 clove garlic, minced
salt and pepper to taste

Cabbage, when cooked with rice and seasoned subtly in the Greek manner, is pleasing to those who like its rather powerful aroma and flavor somewhat muted and diluted. *Serve with some good crusty bread and finish with cheese and fruit.*

Cook bacon, onion, and mushrooms together in bacon fat until wilted. Put a layer of shredded cabbage in a deep but not large casserole. Mix rice, bacon and bacon fat, onion, mushrooms, tomatoes, and raisins or currants together. Put a layer of the mixture on the cabbage, add another layer of cabbage then rice mixture and so on until all are used. Mix 2 cups bouillon with the seasonings and pour into the casserole, adding more bouillon if necessary to reach almost to the top. Cover tightly and bake in 200° oven 2 hours, although it will not hurt the dish if it waits a longer time. Serves 6. Time: 2½ hours.

Robinson Cabbage

3 tablespoons melted butter
2 medium-sized onions,
  chopped
3 green peppers, chopped, without seeds
6 stalks celery, diced
6 medium-sized fresh tomatoes,
  diced
1 small head cabbage, shredded
1 teaspoon sugar
salt and freshly ground black
  pepper
2 cups coarsely diced cooked
  tongue

Serve with French bread and cheese.

Put melted butter in the bottom of a large casserole and add all the rest of the ingredients, shuffling them around a bit to mix. Cover tightly and bake 30 minutes in a 350° oven. It can go on longer without getting mushy. The recipe is assumed to serve 6, but some feel extra greedy around this. Time: 45 minutes.

Carrots Baked in Parsley Cream

2 bunches young carrots,
  scraped and slivered with
  potato-parer or cabbage-
  shredder
1/3 cup finely chopped parsley
2/3 cup heavy cream
4 tablespoons melted butter
salt and lots of freshly ground
  black pepper

A plain-Jane vegetable in a glamour guise. *Serve with veal loaf (see index); chicory with French dressing; hot rolls; fresh or frozen pineapple chunks, marinated in rum.*

The carrots may be puréed in the electric blender in several batches with 1/4 cup water each time. Drain before adding to the casserole. Put carrots in a casserole with parsley, heavy cream and butter. Sprinkle with salt and pepper. Bake in 350° oven 15 to 20 minutes or until carrots are tender and the top is browned. Serves 4. Time: 30 minutes.

Cauliflower Baked in Cheese Sauce with Poppy Seeds

1 medium-sized head cauliflower
1 cup heavy cream
1 cup grated Cheddar cheese
1 tablespoon poppy seeds
salt and pepper

Serve with tomato wedges, sprinkled with lime juice and salt; Swedish bread; fresh or frozen raspberries with custard sauce (a jar of custard for babies diluted with light cream and a good dash of curaçao).

Boil cauliflower until almost tender, and separate into flowerets in a shallow buttered casserole. Mix cream and cheese. Spread over cauliflower and scatter poppy seeds on top. Bake in 350° oven 20 minutes. Serves 4. Time: 50 minutes.

Celery Pie

2 bunches celery, leaves
   discarded, cut in 1-inch pieces
2 tablespoons butter
2 tablespoons flour
1/2 teaspoon basil
salt and pepper
1 cup milk
2 tablespoons chopped
   pimiento
1 lb. fresh, or 1 package frozen,
   peas
1 tube prepared refrigerated
   buttermilk biscuits
1/4 cup grated cheese

Light, simple, and different — a good luncheon dish. *Serve with salad of lettuce, shrimp, hard-cooked eggs, French dressing; crackers.*

Parboil celery 15 minutes. Meanwhile make cream sauce, melting butter, blending in flour, adding seasonings and milk. Stir in drained celery, pimiento, peas. Pour into a low buttered casserole and top with buttermilk biscuits. Sprinkle cheese around and on top of biscuits and bake in 400° oven 15 to 20 minutes or until biscuits are done. Serves 4. Time: 35 minutes.

Celery Baked in Cheese Sauce

1 bunch celery, cut in 1/2-inch
   pieces, leaves discarded
4 tablespoons butter
1 teaspoon olive oil
1/2 teaspoon salt
1/2 cup beef consommé
1/2 cup sour cream
3 tablespoons freshly grated
   Parmesan cheese

A nice accompaniment to a roast. *Serve with roast lamb; baked sweet potatoes; sliced orange-and-onion salad with oil-and-vinegar dressing; coffee ice cream with shaved chocolate.*

Put celery in a small casserole that will take top-of-the-stove heat, with butter, olive oil, salt (very little because of that in the consommé), and consommé. Bring to a boil, cover, and put in preheated 350° oven about 25 minutes or until celery is tender. Remove, stir in sour cream and cheese, and serve. Serves 4. Time: 45 minutes.

Baked Corn Custard

1 tablespoon minced onion
2 leeks, chopped
3 tablespoons butter
3 tablespoons flour
2 cups milk
1 cup grated Cheddar cheese
1/2 teaspoon marjoram
salt and pepper
1 pimiento, chopped
1 teaspoon sugar
2 7-oz. cans whole-kernel corn, or 1 10-oz. package frozen cut corn
2 eggs, slightly beaten
breadcrumbs
more butter

This is the version for people who do not have access to fresh corn. *Serve with salad of lettuce, shrimp, chopped green pepper, with French dressing; toasted finger rolls.*

Sauté onion and leeks in butter, blend in flour, add milk and cheese slowly. Add seasonings, pimiento, sugar. Stir in corn and eggs. Put in a low buttered casserole, sprinkle top with breadcrumbs, and dot with butter. Bake in 350° oven 30 to 35 minutes. Serves 4. Time: 1 hour.

Add a little sugar to water when cooking peas, corn, or sweet potatoes to improve flavor.

Pennsylvania Dutch Corn Pie

pastry for 2 crusts (made according to your favorite basic recipe or from a ready mix)
2 cups fresh corn, cut from the cob
1/2 cup milk
1 tablespoon butter
2 teaspoons salt
lots of freshly ground black pepper
1 teaspoon sugar

Serve with ham; cream slaw (1 small head cabbage, shredded and salted ahead of time, then tossed with 1/2 cup heavy sweet cream, 4 tablespoons vinegar, 1/2 cup sugar); hot corn sticks; lemon sherbet sprinkled with blueberries.

Line an 8-inch ceramic pie pan with pastry. Mix other ingredients, fill pan, and top with a crust. Pierce top of the crust all over with a fork in a symmetrical design. Bake 10 minutes at 400°, reduce heat to 325° and bake 35 minutes more. Serve hot with the main course. Serves 4. Time: 55 minutes.

Moussaka

1½ lbs. ground beef
1 medium onion, minced
2 tablespoons butter
salt, freshly ground black
   pepper
1 teaspoon cinnamon
1 8-oz. can tomato paste
1 large eggplant, cut in chunks
   and salted but not peeled
½ cup grated cheese (Cheddar
   or Swiss is all right)

SAUCE

4 tablespoons butter
5 tablespoons flour
2 cups milk
salt, freshly ground pepper
1 egg
freshly grated Parmesan cheese

All around the Mediterranean, eggplant is cooked lovingly and often with meat. The dishes are called by many names, have minor regional differences, and of course vary from cook to cook within a country. The Greek version called moussaka is one of the best loved. The meat mixture usually contains cinnamon and, unlike others, is topped with an egg-and-cheese sauce. This recipe, from a friend who once lived in Greece for a long while, is lighter than most versions because the eggplant is not fried. *Serve with the good crusty flat round bread found in stores catering to those from Mediterranean countries and usually called pideh; fresh fruit.*

Brown meat and onion in butter. Salt and pepper to taste and add cinnamon. Dilute tomato paste with two cans of water and add. Simmer 15 to 20 minutes. Rinse and drain eggplant. Simmer in boiling water for 10 minutes. Drain. Arrange a layer of eggplant pieces in a shallow casserole. Add a layer of meat sauce, sprinkle with cheese, add another layer of eggplant, then the rest of the meat mixture and the rest of the cheese. Make sauce by melting butter, stirring in flour, and cooking for a few minutes before adding milk, little by little, beating with a wire whisk until smooth and thickened. Salt and pepper to taste, remove from heat, add egg and beat until well mixed. Pour half over eggplant-and-meat casserole, letting it seep through the interstices of the mixture. Bake in 350° oven 10 to 15 minutes. Cook the rest of the sauce until much thicker. Remove casserole from oven, add the rest of the sauce, and sprinkle lavishly with grated Parmesan cheese. Bake 45 to 50 minutes or until golden brown. Cut in squares to serve. The meat-and-eggplant mixture may be made the day before and refrigerated, but make the egg sauce just before baking. Allow more time for baking if the dish is taken right from the refrigerator. Serves 4 or 5. This may be easily doubled and tripled, if you allow more baking time. Time: 2 hours.

Eggplant Susie

1 eggplant, peeled and diced
2 hard-cooked eggs, chopped
1 raw egg, beaten
1 cup milk
1/4 teaspoon dry English
  mustard
2 tablespoons sherry
salt and pepper
1/2 cup herb-seasoned stuffing or
  breadcrumbs
2 tablespoons melted butter

SAUCE

3 fresh tomatoes, peeled, seeded,
  and diced
1 tablespoon grated onion
1/4 cup parsley, finely chopped
salt
pinch of sugar

Serve with chef's salad of crisp mixed greens, sliced cucumbers, sweet red onion rings, and thin slivers of ham and Swiss cheese with anchovy dressing (3 parts olive oil, 1 part wine vinegar, 1 teaspoon anchovy paste); toasted halves of English muffins.

Salt eggplant and boil it until tender. Drain and put through a ricer or purée in a blender. Mix with chopped hard-cooked eggs, beaten egg, milk, mustard, sherry, salt, and pepper. Put into a buttered casserole and top with stuffing or breadcrumbs. Pour melted butter on top and bake in 350° oven 35 minutes. For the sauce, cook all ingredients together until thick. Serve in a small fat pitcher, to be poured over the eggplant. Serves 4. Time: 1¼ hours.

Baked Eggplant with Almonds

1 large eggplant or 2 medium-
  sized ones, peeled and cubed
1/2 teaspoon salt
2 eggs
salt and freshly ground black
  pepper
1 small onion, finely chopped
3 tablespoons finely chopped
  parsley
1/2 cup blanched almonds,
  slivered
3 soda crackers or 5 saltines,
  crumbled by hand
butter

Delicate and different. Don't tell the difficult ones what they are eating until they have finished. *Serve with Swiss meat loaf (see index); watercress; hot salt sticks (brown-and-serve).*

Simmer eggplant in boiling salted water until tender. Drain. Mash in a bowl. Add unbeaten eggs, salt, pepper, onion, parsley, and all but 2 tablespoons almonds. Mix and put in a shallow buttered casserole. Sprinkle the top with cracker crumbs and the rest of the almonds and dot with butter. Bake 20 minutes in 350° oven. Serves 4 amply. Time: 45 minutes.

Eggplant Parmesan

2 medium-sized eggplants, peeled and cut into uniform slices
salt and pepper
flour
2 egg yolks, beaten
¼ cup olive oil
2 8-oz. cans tomato sauce
1 tablespoon sherry or red wine
1 lump mozzarella cheese, sliced
¼ cup freshly grated Parmesan cheese

Mozzarella is a mild Italian variety of cream cheese, with a gently zippy flavor. It is slightly and pleasantly stringy when cooked. If there is no Italian store near you, try a Monterey jack. *Serve with bitter greens with French dressing; Italian or French bread; fruit*

Sprinkle eggplant slices with plenty of salt and place in a colander with something heavy on top (say, a plate and a heavy can) for about ½ hour, to eliminate the bitterness that some dislike. Rinse in fresh water and pat dry with a clean towel. Dip into flour and then into beaten egg yolks, then in flour again. Heat half the olive oil and start sautéing the slices of eggplant. Cook until golden brown, then drain on paper towels. Add the rest of the oil to the skillet as needed. When all the eggplant is done, slosh tomato sauce around in the skillet with wine. Put some of the tomato sauce in the bottom of shallow greased casserole, then a layer of eggplant slices, then a layer of mozzarella slices, and sprinkle with Parmesan cheese, salt, and pepper. Repeat until all ingredients are used. Place in 350° oven 15 minutes, or until mozzarella is brown and bubbling. Serves 4. Time: 1 hour.

Eggplant Mediterranean

3 tablespoons olive oil
2 onions, peeled and sliced
1 medium-sized eggplant, peeled and quartered
1 stalk celery, cut in small pieces
4 green peppers, sliced
10 green olives, pitted
3 medium-sized tomatoes, quartered
about 10 capers
salt and pepper

This recipe, a savory and exciting combination of foods, comes from Felix Ruvolo, who is both cook and artist. *Serve with broiled lamb chops; escarole with French dressing; French bread.*

Heat olive oil in enameled ironware casserole. Brown onions in oil, add eggplant, celery, peppers, and olives. Sauté about 5 minutes, or until nicely browned. Add tomatoes, capers, and seasoning. Cover tightly and bake in 350° oven about 30 minutes. Serves 4. Time: 45 minutes.

Souffléd Eggplant

1 large eggplant or 2 smaller
  ones, cut in half
6 tablespoons butter
3 tablespoons flour
1 cup chicken broth
⅔ cup grated sharp cheese
3 eggs, separated

The beautiful dark and satiny eggplant shell makes a handsome dish within a dish. *Serve with bacon and dandelion salad (dandelion greens dressed with hot bacon, a little of the hot fat, and 1 tablespoon warm vinegar); hot rolls; lemon pudding (see index).*

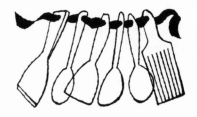

Scoop the flesh gently out of the eggplant with a melon scoop. Sauté briefly in 3 tablespoons butter. Make a sauce by melting 3 more tablespoons butter, blending in flour, adding broth gradually. Cook over low heat until smooth and thickened, stirring all the while. Add cheese and stir until that is melted. Chop sautéed eggplant fine, mix with cheese sauce, and add yolks of eggs. Beat whites until stiff. Fold in gently. Pour the mixture into the eggplant skins. Place in a shallow casserole and bake in 350° oven 15 to 20 minutes, or until the top springs back when lightly touched. Serves 4. Time: 45 minutes.

Egyptian Eggplant (Bedingane Masri)

1 large eggplant or 2 small ones,
  peeled and sliced thin
salt and pepper
2 onions, chopped
½ cup butter
1 lb. round steak, ground
1 6-oz. can Italian tomato paste
1 cup hot water
flour
salad oil – not olive oil this time

Graciously contributed by Ostah Abdul Rahim Selim, distinguished former chef of the Egyptian Embassy at Washington, which, nostalgically, was once famous for food and parties rather than politics. *Serve with tossed mixed greens, chopped hard-cooked eggs, and anchovies with French dressing; Italian bread, cut in hunks.*

Sprinkle eggplant slices with salt and let stand 30 minutes. Sauté onions in butter until brown, add ground meat. Brown meat, then add tomato paste and hot water. Season with salt and freshly ground black pepper and simmer for 15 minutes. Rinse eggplant well and pat each piece dry with a towel. Flour, and sauté eggplant slices in salad oil. Butter a deep casserole and place half of the eggplant on the bottom. Then add the meat mixture and repeat until all ingredients are used. Bake 1 hour in 325° oven. Serves 4. Time: 2 hours.

Green Pepper Pudding

4 large green or red sweet peppers, seeds, stem ends, and white part removed
2 cups seasoned *cubed* bread stuffing (bought)
½ 2-oz. can flat anchovies, cut in small pieces
3 eggs
2 cups milk
a little salt
butter

It takes character for people to see peppers and not want to stuff them every time. They start thinking, like Pooh, that peppers are "a useful pot to put things in." Well, they are, but the tendency is to stuff them too tightly and too often. Here the stuffing is all around instead of inside. *Serve with broiled ham slice; onion salad with oil-and-vinegar dressing; poppy-seed rolls; greengage sherbet with thin ginger snaps.*

Cut the prepared peppers in inch-wide strips. Put in a shallow buttered casserole with the stuffing and anchovies and stir around so they are well intermingled. Buzz eggs, milk, and a very little salt in the blender, or beat together by hand. Pour over pepper mixture. Dot the top with small pieces of butter. Bake in preheated 350° oven 40 to 50 minutes or until the dish looks crusty and puddingy. Serves 4. Time: 1¼ hours.

Stuffed Grape Leaves

2 medium-sized onions, chopped
¼ cup olive oil
1 cup uncooked rice
⅓ cup pine nuts or pignolias
1 tablespoon chopped parsley or mint
½ teaspoon allspice
juice of ½ lemon
salt, pepper
1 can grape leaves, well drained, or 12 fresh leaves

Either buy canned grape leaves in a Greek delicatessen or drop fresh ones into boiling water for a minute or two to make them pliable. *Serve with broiled lamb chops (put ½ teaspoon tarragon vinegar on each chop before serving); wrinkled black green olives (buy the ones in a barrel, soak first in boiling water, then in French dressing); French bread;* crème Chantilly; *fresh dark sweet cherries.*

Brown onions in oil. Add rice, pine nuts, parsley, allspice, lemon juice, salt, and pepper. Add 1 cup warm water, cover, and cook until liquid is absorbed. Put a spoonful of the mixture on each leaf. Roll leaves up and secure with toothpicks. Place the tidy rolls side by side in a casserole. Add 1 cup water. Cover and bake in 350° oven until liquid is absorbed, about 45 minutes. Serves 4. Time: 1¼ hours.

Kedgeree

1 large onion, sliced thin
3 tablespoons olive oil
1 tablespoon curry powder
1 cup uncooked rice
1 cup lentils, simmered until
  tender
2 cups chicken broth
1 small bay leaf
salt and pepper
2 hard-cooked eggs, quartered

This is an English dish of Indian derivation. Like many much-traveled dishes it is made many different ways — usually as a mixture of seasoned lentils or boiled fish with rice, often decorated with hard-cooked eggs. In this version, Egyptian lentils are much the prettiest to use. They are rosy orange, and turn a deep saffron yellow when cooked. However pretty, they are not available in many stores. Any lentils may be used. *Serve with salted cucumber sticks; hot salt sticks (brown-and-serve); watermelon pickle.*

Sauté onion in olive oil, add curry powder, blend, and stir in rice until well coated with oil and onion and curry. Put in a casserole with lentils. Add chicken broth, bay leaf, and seasoning. Cover and put in 350° oven 30 to 40 minutes or until the liquid is all absorbed. Arrange quarters of hard-cooked eggs on top. Serves 4. Time: 3 hours.

Bermuda Onions Baked with Sour Cream

4 or 5 large Bermuda onions,
  peeled and sliced thin
1 pt. sour cream
½ lemon, juice and grated peel
salt and pepper
⅓ cup finely chopped parsley or
  watercress

Onions can be important in themselves, besides being a practically indispensable seasoning. This prideful dish earns them a place of honor on the menu. *Serve with sautéed chicken livers with bacon; salad of lettuce, watercress, and thin slices of green pepper with French dressing; hot biscuits.*

Arrange onion slices in a shallow buttered baking dish. Mix sour cream with lemon juice, grated rind, 1 cup water, salt, and pepper. Pour over onions and sprinkle lavishly with parsley. Bake in 350° oven until onions are barely tender and still retain some crispness — usually about 25 to 30 minutes. Serves 4. Time: 40 minutes.

Mushroom Soufflé

½ lb. fresh, or 1 6-oz. package
  frozen mushrooms, sliced, or
  ½ cup dried mushrooms,
  soaked
3½ tablespoons butter
salt, freshly ground black
  pepper
pinch of nutmeg
3 tablespoons flour
1 cup milk
4 egg yolks
5 egg whites

There is no place in my life or my cooking for canned mushrooms, which have no flavor at all. I like the wild ones that I can identify, the fresh ones in the markets, and if these are not available, the frozen or dried mushrooms have a superb concentrated flavor and are easy to keep on hand. *Serve with broiled hamburgers; broiled green tomatoes; French bread; Dobos torte.*

Sauté mushrooms in 1 tablespoon butter for 2 or 3 minutes or until limp. Purée in an electric blender, add seasonings, the rest of the butter, flour, milk, egg yolks, and blend all. If soaked dried mushrooms are used, omit the sautéing and use the liquid in place of part of the milk and proceed as with fresh ones. Cook in a heavy saucepan over low heat until smooth and thickened, beating with a wooden spoon or wire whip. Remove from heat and let cool slightly. Beat egg whites until stiff and fold into mushroom mixture, half at a time, very gently. Pour into a buttered 1-quart soufflé dish and bake in preheated 375° oven 35 to 45 minutes or until golden and puffy. Soufflés may be made with an equal number of yolks and whites, as directed elsewhere in this book, but there is an exciting puffiness when an extra white is added. Serves 4 to 6.

Mushroom Pie

1½ lbs. fresh mushrooms, sliced
  lengthwise through caps and
  stems
¼ lb. butter
4 tablespoons flour
salt and pepper
1 teaspoon paprika
1 cup cream
¼ cup sherry
1 tablespoon lemon juice
1 tube prepared buttermilk biscuits, or 10 biscuits made according to a basic recipe

We like mushrooms a lot of ways, and this is one of them. *Serve with salad of chicory and sliced avocado with French dressing (2 parts olive oil, 1 part lime juice, salt and pepper); hot biscuits (buy 2 tubes); lemon pudding (see index).*

Cook mushrooms in butter about 5 minutes or until pale yellow. Remove from pan. Blend flour, salt, pepper, and paprika into the drippings in the pan. Add cream and sherry slowly, stirring until smooth and thickened. Add lemon juice and mushrooms. Pour into a shallow casserole. Top with biscuits and bake in 400° oven until brown, about 15 minutes. Serves 4. Time: 40 minutes.

Stuffed Onions

8 large Bermuda onions
½ lb. uncooked ground veal
9 slices bacon (1 chopped fine)
2 tablespoons mixed chopped herbs (parsley, basil, and chives)
¼ cup cream
⅔ cup breadcrumbs
salt and pepper
1 cup beef bouillon

This one may try your patience, but it's worth the effort. We suggest scooping out the onions before (well before) your guests are on the doorstep. *Serve with Canadian bacon, roasted in a piece; salad of endive and hearts of artichokes with French dressing; Italian bread, cut in hunks; blueberry pie.*

Peel and parboil onions for 20 minutes, then scoop out centers. Sauté veal and chopped bacon, but do not brown. Add herbs, cream, breadcrumbs, salt, pepper, and a little bouillon. Stuff onions with mixture, place in casserole, place one folded slice of bacon on top of each onion, pour rest of bouillon in casserole, and bake in 375° oven 40 minutes, or until tender. Serves 4. Time: 1¼ hours.

Zwiebelkuchen

CRUST

1½ cups all-purpose flour, measured after sifting
½ teaspoon salt
¼ cup butter plus ¼ cup lard, or ½ cup shortening
3 tablespoons ice water (about)

FILLING

6 strips bacon, diced
4 large onions, chopped
2 whole eggs, plus 1 egg yolk
¾ cup sour cream
salt and pepper
1 teaspoon chives
pinch of caraway seeds

Zwiebelkuchen, the German onion custard pie that is a good main dish for a light meal, is a close relative of the French Quiche Lorraine. It may be made in very small tarts for a wonderful hot hors d'oeuvre. *Serve with avocado halves with salt and a dash of fresh lime juice; Holland rusks.*

For the crust, sift dry ingredients together. Work in butter-and-lard mixture or shortening with a pastry blender or your fingers until the mixture is crumbly. Add ice water, just enough to hold mixture together. Chill several hours. Roll to fit a 9-inch ceramic pie pan. Sauté bacon until crisp. Remove and drain on paper towels. Pour off most of the fat and sauté onions in remaining fat until pale yellow and limp. Beat eggs and egg yolk together and mix with sour cream, seasoning, chives, onion, and bacon. Turn onto pie shell and sprinkle with a few caraway seeds (not more than 12 even if you like them). Bake in preheated 400° oven 30 minutes. Serve hot or warm. Serves 4. Time: 50 minutes, plus time for chilling pie dough.

Baked Onions Stuffed with Black Walnuts

4 large fat onions, peeled
²⁄₃ cup coarse dried homemade
   breadcrumbs
¹⁄₃ cup chopped black walnuts
¹⁄₄ cup melted butter
salt

Black walnuts have a positive, almost acrid taste—a very special delight to those who like it, and horrid to those who don't. In this dish they make a kitchen staple the star of the meal. *Serve with cold roast lamb (basted while roasting with tarragon vinegar); garden leaf lettuce sprinkled with hickory-smoked salt; pumpernickel.*

Boil onions in salted water until almost tender. Hollow them out. Mix breadcrumbs with walnuts. Fill the cavities in the onions with this mixture and pour melted butter on top. Put onions in a shallow buttered casserole in 350° oven. Bake until tender, about 20 to 30 minutes. The time will vary according to the size of the onions and the tenderness. Serves 4. Time: 1 hour.

Soubise (as a Vegetable)

¹⁄₂ cup uncooked rice
1¹⁄₂ tablespoons salt
4 tablespoons butter
2 lbs. yellow onions, sliced thin
salt, pepper
¹⁄₄ cup heavy cream
¹⁄₄ cup grated Swiss cheese
2 tablespoons butter
1 tablespoon minced parsley

Sometimes this is served as a vegetable and sometimes, made by a slightly different technique, it is served as a sauce. That recipe is given elsewhere in this book (Hard-Cooked Eggs in Soubise Sauce; see index). Either way is a delectable way of cooking a vegetable that I hope never again to be without, as was the case when I first came to New York and found a shortage of onions. *Serve with roast lamb rubbed with rosemary; Belgian endive; lemon pudding (see index).*

Cook rice in a large pot of water (even for this tiny amount) 5 minutes. Drain. Heat butter in a large fireproof casserole and add onions. Stir until thoroughly coated with butter. Add rice and seasonings and mix. Cover and bake in preheated 300° oven 1 hour, stirring occasionally, until the onions are a light lovely yellow. This much may be done ahead of time. Transfer to a smaller dish (yes, this defeats or negates one of the blessings of a casserole but the onions cook down and look meager in too large a dish). Add cream, cheese, and butter. Taste for seasoning and add more if necessary. Sprinkle with parsley. Serves 6. Time: 1¹⁄₂ hours.

Curried Peas and Barley

6 slices bacon
2 medium onions, chopped
1 can condensed cream of pea
  soup, undiluted
1 tablespoon Madras curry powder
2 cups cooked barley
1 tablespoon chopped parsley

Serve with baked ham; sour pickles; lemon sherbet with chopped black walnuts.

Cook bacon over low heat until crisp, draining off fat into a jar as it accumulates. Drain bacon on paper towels and crumble. Sauté onions in enough of the bacon fat to cover the pan thinly. Mix pea soup with curry powder. Put a layer of cooked barley in a shallow casserole, then a layer of the curried pea soup. Sprinkle with crumbled bacon and parsley and repeat until all ingredients are used, ending with pea soup, bacon, and parsley. Bake in preheated 350° oven 30 minutes or until hot and bubbly. Serves 4. Time: 1 hour.

Walnut and Onion Soufflé

1 cup milk
1 cup chopped onions
3 tablespoons butter
4 tablespoons flour
salt, pepper
⅓ cup chopped walnuts
5 eggs, separated
1 tablespoon chopped parsley

Delicate and different. Serve with roast pork tenderloin; hot rolls; watercress salad; coffee jelly with whipped cream.

Simmer milk and onions 8 to 10 minutes. Meanwhile melt butter and add flour. Cook together 3 to 4 minutes until dry and well blended. Add part of the milk and onions and stir until well blended. Add the rest of the milk and onions, beating with a wire whip until smooth (except for the onions) and thickened. Season with salt and pepper to taste and add walnuts. Remove from heat, cool slightly, and add egg yolks and parsley. Beat whites until stiff, then fold the other mixture in gently, part at a time. Turn into a greased 1-quart straight-sided casserole or a soufflé pan or charlotte mold. Bake in preheated 350° oven 45 minutes or until the top, lightly touched, springs back. Serves 4. Time: 1¼ hours.

Red Peas and Rice Cooked in Coconut Milk, Jamaican Style

½ lb. raw ham, diced
1 cup milk
1 cup shredded coconut
2 cups cooked Mexican pink beans or 1 1-lb. can red kidney beans
1 cup raw rice
salt, pepper

What the Jamaicans call red peas are the small Mexican pink beans. Canned cooked kidney beans may be used when the Mexican ones are not available. *Serve with mixed green salad; hot rolls; pineapple upside-down cake.*

Simmer ham in water for 10 minutes. Scald milk, pour over coconut, and let stand until cool; then strain or buzz in blender. Drain ham and put in a casserole with cooked beans, coconut milk, and rice. Add 3 cups water, salt, and pepper. Cover and bake in 350° oven about 50 minutes to 1 hour or more, until the rice has absorbed the liquid and become acquainted with the beans and ham. Fluff with a fork. Serves 4. Time: 1½ hours.

Shell Macaroni with Peas

2 cups large shell macaroni
1 cup fresh, or ½ 10-oz. package frozen, peas
1 8-oz. can tomato sauce
salt
freshly grated Parmesan cheese

Serve with wilted slaw (fine shredded cabbage dressed with hot cooked crumbled bacon with a little of the hot fat and a dash of lemon juice); French bread, cut in chunks and toasted on the end of a long fork over a gas flame.

Cook shells in briskly boiling salted water until tender but not mushy. At the same time cook peas in another pan until barely tender. Drain and rinse macaroni with cold water. Put macaroni and peas in a shallow buttered baking dish and shake slightly. Most of the peas will roll into the shells. Pour in tomato sauce, add salt, and sprinkle the top generously with cheese. Bake in a 350° oven 15 to 20 minutes, or until bubbling. Serves 4. Time: 40 minutes.

1 cup uncooked macaroni makes 2 to 2¼ cups cooked.

Stuffed Peppers in Tomato Sauce

4 fat green peppers, tops, white membrane, and seeds removed
2 cups diced stale bread
⅓ cup finely chopped parsley
4 anchovies, finely chopped, and the oil from the anchovies
½ plump garlic clove, minced
½ cup tomato juice
1 8-oz. can tomato sauce

Serve with raw spinach leaves with grated raw carrots and a very oily dressing (5 parts olive oil, 1 part vinegar, salt, and lots of freshly ground black pepper); Italian bread sticks.

Drop peppers into boiling water for just 1 minute, then drain. Mix bread cubes with parsley, anchovies, anchovy oil, and minced garlic until well intermingled. Stuff into peppers. Dribble 2 tablespoons tomato juice into each pepper. Put peppers in a shallow baking dish and pour tomato sauce around them. Bake in 350° oven 20 to 25 minutes. Serves 4. Time: 40 minutes.

Potato Pancake with Sour Cherries

1-lb. can sour red pitted cherries, drained
2 cups mashed potatoes (instant may be used)
2 eggs, beaten
2 tablespoons flour
1 teaspoon cinnamon
1 cup small-curd cottage cheese
salt, pepper
2 tablespoons melted butter

Rather freely adapted from a Viennese dish, this is a good accompaniment for roast duck, turkey, pork, or lamb; or an entrée for lunch or a late leisurely breakfast. *Serve with roast duck; watercress, Belgian endive and oil-and-vinegar dressing; profiteroles (cream puffs filled with ice cream and topped with chocolate sauce).*

Strew the cherries in a shallow buttered casserole. Mix seasoned mashed potatoes with eggs, flour, cinnamon, and cottage cheese. Check seasoning and add more salt and pepper to taste. Spoon over cherries and dribble melted butter on top. Bake in preheated 375° oven 45 to 55 minutes or until light brown and puffy. Serves 4. Time: 1¼ hours.

Potatoes with Bacon and Parsley Sauce

2 tablespoons butter
2 tablespoons flour
1 cup milk
pinch of sugar
salt
⅓ cup finely chopped parsley
12 tiny new potatoes, boiled in their skins, then peeled, or 4 large potatoes, peeled, diced, and boiled
6 pieces bacon, diced and cooked

Use parsley—that spicy and pungent herb, available all year round practically everywhere —for more than trimming a roast. Put large handfuls in food. It has the nutritional equivalent of a bowl of green vegetables and gives the dish a flavor unknown to mere garnishers. *Serve with salad of chicory with thin slices of fresh orange and raw sweet onion with French dressing; poppy-seed rolls.*

Make sauce by melting butter (bacon fat can be used, but butter is better to give this dish a more delicate flavor), blending in flour, and adding milk and seasonings gradually. Cook sauce until smooth and thickened. Add parsley. Arrange potatoes in a shallow casserole and pour sauce over them. Sprinkle cooked bacon on top. Bake in 350° oven 20 to 25 minutes. Serves 4. Time: 1 hour.

Kugula

6 to 8 raw medium-sized potatoes, peeled and grated coarsely
1 small onion, grated
4 or 5 pieces of bacon, fried crisp and crumbled
¼ cup bacon fat
2 eggs
2 tablespoons flour
salt and pepper
sour cream

Potatoes may be grated in an electric blender, about two at a time, diced, with water. Drain after grating. *Serve with Caesar salad (torn romaine or escarole with crumbled wedge of Roquefort cheese, ½ cup freshly grated Parmesan cheese; 2 parts olive oil, 1 part lemon juice, salt, pepper, Worcestershire sauce; croutons, tossed in ½ cup oil containing 1 clove garlic; raw egg or 1-minute egg is usual but not essential); garlic bread; fruit macédoine (sliced fresh fruit, marinated in sugar syrup with a jigger of brandy, fruit brandy, or Cointreau).*

Mix all ingredients except sour cream together and put in a shallow flat casserole greased with bacon fat. Bake in a 350° oven for 50 to 60 minutes, until brown and crusty on top. Serve with a pitcher of sour cream. Serves 4. Time: 1¼ hours.

Potato and Salami Casserole with Cheese Sauce

3 tablespoons butter
3 tablespoons flour
salt and pepper
2 cups milk
1 cup grated sharp cheese
5 medium-sized potatoes,
    boiled, peeled, and cut in ½-
    inch slices
5 hard-cooked eggs, sliced
1 lb. salami, sliced

Serve with cucumber-and-onion aspic (use un-flavored gelatin and chopped raw vegetables) with mayonnaise; poppy-seed rolls; fresh strawberries chilled in red wine.

Make cream sauce by melting butter, blending in flour, salt, and pepper, and adding milk slowly. Stir and cook until smooth and thick. Remove from stove and stir in grated cheese. Arrange a layer of potato slices, slightly overlapping, in the bottom of a buttered casserole. Then add a layer of hard-cooked eggs, then a layer of salami slices. Pour in some of the cheese sauce and repeat until all ingredients are used. End up by blanketing the top with cheese sauce. Bake in 350° oven until brown and bubbling—about 20 minutes. Serves 4. Time: 45 minutes.

To slice hard-cooked eggs without crumbling yolks, first dip knife in water.

Potato Soufflé

2 cups potatoes mashed with
    butter, salt, and milk (frozen
    whipped or instant potatoes
    can be used, but the long way
    is best for this)
⅔ cup grated sharp Cheddar
    cheese
¼ cup finely chopped chives
salt
lots of freshly ground black pepper
3 egg yolks
4 egg whites

Potatoes, sometimes a drab and routine vegetable, become a noble dish when mashed and made into a rich, golden, savory soufflé, flecked with bits of green chives. *Serve with pork chops baked with rhubarb; chicory and white seedless grapes with a French dressing made of 2 parts olive oil, 1 part garlic vinegar—very good with the grapes—salt, pepper; French bread.*

Mix potatoes, cheese, chives, salt, and pepper with egg yolks. Beat whites until they are fluffy. Fold into potatoes mixture and pile in a buttered loaf-shaped casserole. Bake in 350° oven until golden brown and puffy, about 40 to 45 minutes. Serves 4. Time: 1½ hours—less with frozen potatoes.

Potatoes Baked with Sour Cream and Mushrooms

½ lb. fresh, or 1 6-oz. package
frozen, mushrooms, sliced
lengthwise
3 tablespoons butter
4 medium-sized boiled potatoes,
peeled and cut in ¼-inch
slices
1 pt. sour cream
salt
lots of freshly ground black pepper
2 tablespoons lemon juice
1 tablespoon grated lemon peel

Serve with avocado halves filled with frozen or canned pineapple chunks, with a dash of fresh lime juice added to that of the pineapple; hot bacon biscuits (Bisquick mixed for drop biscuits, with crumbled cooked bacon added to the batter).

Sauté mushrooms in butter (the flavor is different but still good if they are put in the casserole raw). Arrange a layer of potatoes in a shallow buttered casserole, then a layer of mushrooms, and so on until both these ingredients are used up. The top layer should be mushrooms. Season sour cream with salt and pepper. Add lemon juice, 2 tablespoons water, and grated lemon peel. Pour over potatoes and mushrooms. Bake in 325° oven 15 to 20 minutes, or until barely heated. Serves 4. Time: 45 minutes.

Mashed Potatoes with Apples and Onion

4 large boiled potatoes, or 1 4½-
or 5½-oz. package instant
mashed potatoes
butter
milk
salt and pepper
2 cups applesauce or sliced pie
apples
½ cup diced onion
⅓ cup chopped parsley

The Danes, who are truly imaginative about their plentiful and beloved foods, bake mashed potatoes with layers of prunes or apples. Apples appeal more to Americans. *Serve with pork roast; sliced fresh tomatoes sprinkled with dill; salty rye bread.*

Mash potatoes with butter, milk, salt, and pepper. Put a layer of mashed potatoes on the bottom of a well-buttered small deep casserole. Next spoon in a layer of applesauce or apples, sprinkle with onion and parsley, dot with butter. Add another layer of potatoes, one more layer of apple, onions, and parsley, and top with mashed potatoes. Bake in 350° oven 20 to 25 minutes, or until brown and crusty on top. Serves 4. Time: 1 hour.

Danish Potato Pie

1 strip bacon, cut into pieces
½ lb. chopped pork
½ lb. chopped beef
3 cups mashed potatoes, or 2
  cans frozen condensed potato
  soup, thawed but undiluted
salt and pepper (none for frozen
  soup)
4 medium-sized tomatoes,
  skinned, seeded, and sliced in
  1-inch slices

This Danish recipe has been somewhat stream-lined since Svend Fennow gave it to me. *Serve with red cabbage slaw, sprinkled with caraway seeds and dressed with 1 cup sour cream mixed with 1 tablespoon lemon juice and 1 teaspoon dry English mustard; dark pumpernickel and sweet butter; sponge cake, spread with whipped cream mixed with Droeste cocoa before whipping, and dusted with more cocoa.*

Partly cook bacon and then add pork and beef. Stir and sauté until lightly browned. Put a layer of mashed potatoes about 1 inch or 1½ inches thick on the bottom of a small deep well-buttered casserole. Salt and pepper this and each succeeding layer generously. Then spread a layer of about half the meat. Top that with overlapping slices of tomatoes. Add another layer of half the remaining mashed potatoes, the rest of the meat, and another layer of mashed potatoes and bake in 350° oven about 45 minutes. Serves 4 amply. Time: 1¼ hours.

Cheese and Spinach

4 pieces bacon, chopped fine
2 lbs. fresh spinach, chopped, or
  2 10-oz. packages frozen
  chopped spinach, thawed
4 eggs, hard-cooked, quartered
salt and pepper
2 tablespoons butter
2 tablespoons flour
1 cup milk
½ lb. sharp Cheddar cheese,
  grated or chopped fine

Serve with broiled calves' liver; endive with long strips of green pepper, thin onion slices, sprinkled with wine vinegar; cheese corn sticks.

Cook bacon until crisp. Drain on paper towels. Place spinach in a shallow buttered casserole and arrange a layer of hard-cooked eggs on top. Salt and pepper. Make a sauce by melting butter, blending in flour, adding milk, salt, and pepper slowly. Stir until smooth and thickened. Add cheese and cook slowly until cheese is melted. Pour over eggs and spinach. Cover the top with crumbled bacon and bake 25 minutes in 350° oven. Serves 4. Time: 1 hour.

Spinach Baked with Mushrooms and Cream

2 lbs. fresh spinach or 2 10-oz.
  packages frozen spinach
2 tablespoons butter
salt and pepper
¼ lb. fresh or frozen mushrooms, sliced through the caps
  and stems
2 more tablespoons butter
1 jigger sherry
½ cup heavy cream
⅓ cup coarse breadcrumbs
4 tablespoons grated Parmesan
  cheese

Serve with baked slice of ham; watercress and 2 parts sliced cooked beets, 1 part diced celery, with French dressing; French bread; honeydew melon.

Cook spinach in its own liquid until barely tender (5 to 10 minutes). Chop fine or purée in a blender. Mix with 2 tablespoons butter, salt, and pepper. Sauté mushrooms briefly in the other butter. Mix with puréed spinach. Add sherry, cream, and put into a shallow casserole. Top with breadcrumbs and grated cheese. Bake in 350° oven 15 to 20 minutes or until cheese has melted and browned. Serves 4. Time: 45 minutes.

Summer Squash with Chili

1½ cups cubed stale bread
salt and pepper
1 lb. round steak, ground
3 tablespoons olive oil
2 small white onions, minced
½ green pepper, chopped, without seeds
1 tablespoon chili powder
1 tablespoon chopped fresh basil, or 1 teaspoon dried basil
grated peel ½ lemon
2 8-oz. cans tomato sauce
2 lbs. small yellow squashes,
  cubed but not peeled
3 tablespoons butter

Serve with escarole, chicory, French dressing; Italian bread.

Brown bread cubes in a hot oven, but do not burn. Salt and pepper round steak and sauté in olive oil with onions and green pepper. Mix chili powder, basil, grated lemon peel, and tomato sauce with the mixture in the skillet. Take a deep buttered casserole and place half of the squash and bread cubes on the bottom. Dot with half of the butter. Spread with half of the meat mixture and repeat. This needs no other liquid because the squash will cook down. Cover tightly and bake in 350° oven 35 minutes. Serves 4. Time: 1 hour.

Acorn Squash with Brazil Nuts

2 acorn squash
1/2 cup Brazil nuts, coarsely
  chopped
4 tablespoons brown sugar
4 tablespoons butter
salt

Tidy round squash halves—such a proper size for serving—with a filling of chopped Brazil nuts make a simple yet festive dish. Bake and serve them in individual round covered casseroles. The casseroles should fit the halves of squash, with a slight clearance for the water. *Serve with raw cauliflowerets, thin strips of green pepper, raw carrots scraped and cut julienne fashion, and julienne strips of Swiss cheese, marinated in French dressing; hot biscuits.*

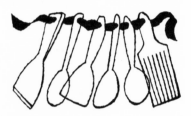

Cut squash in half lengthwise and scoop out seeds. Mix chopped nuts, brown sugar, butter, and salt together. Divide into four parts and fill each squash half. Put halves of squash into casseroles with 1/2 inch water in the bottom. Cover and bake in 375° oven 1 hour, uncovering the last 1/2 hour. Pour out water from casseroles before serving, being careful not to get it inside the squash. Serves 4. Time: 1 1/2 hours.

Sweet-Potato Pudding with Whisky

1 pt. medium cream
3 medium-sized sweet potatoes,
  peeled and grated
3 eggs
2/3 cup brown sugar
2 teaspoons cinnamon
1/8 lb. butter, melted
1/2 cup blanched almonds,
  slivered
1/2 cup whisky or rum

One of the best of the Southern dishes. The grating takes time, but the rest is simple, and now the electric blender can do the grating. It is usually served with roast turkey or chicken, though it would be suitable for a heavy dessert. *Serve with roast turkey; cream slaw (1/2 head shredded salted cabbage, tossed with 1/2 cup heavy cream, 1/2 cup sugar, 3 tablespoons vinegar); hot biscuits.*

Put cream in a medium-sized shallow casserole and grate potatoes into the cream to keep them from darkening. Beat eggs until lemon-colored and add sugar and cinnamon gradually. Stir into sweet potatoes and cream. The potatoes, cream, and eggs may be blended in a blender, using half these ingredients at a time. Scatter almonds over all and pour melted butter on top. Bake in 300° oven until firm and lightly browned. Before serving pour the whisky or rum on top. Serves 6 to 8. Time: 1 1/2 to 2 hours.

Sweet-Potato and Apricot Casserole

1-lb. can whole sweet potatoes, or 4 medium-sized sweet potatoes, boiled and peeled
3 tablespoons undiluted frozen concentrated orange juice
3 tablespoons melted butter
1 tablespoon brown sugar
salt
pinch of nutmeg
2 eggs
½ cup chopped dried apricots

This is a change from the usual sticky, sweet concoctions. *Serve with cold sliced ham, roast pork, or veal, basted with vermouth; escarole with French dressing; Triscuits.*

Mash sweet potatoes with a fork. Mix them with concentrated orange juice, butter, sugar, and seasonings. Stir in unbeaten eggs and, last, pieces of apricot. Spoon into a shallow buttered casserole and bake in preheated 350° oven 20 to 25 minutes or until brown and puffy. Serves 4. Time: 40 minutes.

Bacon and Sweet-Potato Soufflé

4 medium-sized boiled sweet potatoes, peeled and mashed, or 1 l-lb. can sweet potatoes, mashed
2 tablespoons undiluted frozen concentrated orange juice
2 tablespoons bacon drippings
salt and pepper
3 eggs, separated
3 strips cooked bacon, crumbled

Delicate, robust, and somewhat unexpected. *Serve with lettuce with thin slices of onion and orange with French dressing; hot poppy-seed rolls (brown-and-serve); thin, crisp ginger cookies.*

Mix mashed sweet potatoes with concentrated orange juice, bacon drippings, salt and pepper, egg yolks, and bacon. Beat egg whites until stiff. Fold in gently and pile into a buttered baking dish with straight sides. Bake in 350° oven until the top springs back lightly when touched—40 to 45 minutes. Serves 4. Time: 1 hour.

Tomato Pilaf

¼ cup butter
1 cup uncooked rice
1 cup chicken broth or beef bouillon
1 cup tomato juice
2 fresh tomatoes, skinned, seeded, and chopped
⅓ cup finely chopped parsley
salt and pepper

A simple and flavorful way of cooking rice. *Serve with Parmesan cheese soufflé (see index); watercress; coffee ice cream sprinkled with chocolate bits or macaroons.*

Melt butter in a heavy skillet and add rice. Stir until grains are well coated and pale yellow. Transfer to a casserole. Heat chicken broth and tomato juice together and add. Add tomatoes, and sprinkle parsley, salt, and pepper on top. Cover and cook in 350° oven about 30 minutes or until liquid is absorbed. Fluff with a fork. Serves 4. Time: 45 minutes.

Cheese with Tomatoes and Okra

4 medium-sized fresh tomatoes
1 pt. fresh, or 1 10-oz. package
frozen, okra
1 pound Cheddar cheese, diced
1 bunch spring onions, chopped
salt and pepper

From our Southern cousins. Very inexpensive.
Very easy to prepare. *Serve with hot potato salad
(warm boiled potatoes and raw onions sliced thin,
chopped hard-cooked eggs, dressed with raw egg
beaten with mustard, cream, salt, pepper, and enough
vinegar to moisten; let stand in oven a few minutes);
Italian bread cut in hunks.*

Butter a deep casserole. Slice but do not peel
tomatoes. Cut tips and stems from okra pods.
Dice cheese and chop onion. Arrange in layers
in casserole—first a layer of tomatoes, then a
layer of okra, then a sprinkling of onion, salt
and pepper, and finally cheese. Repeat until
all ingredients are used, cover, and bake in
350° oven 40 minutes. Serves 4. Time: 1 hour.

To cut butter cleanly, heat knife blade
in hot water or cover with
waxed paper.

Tomatoes Stuffed with Spinach

½ 10-oz. package frozen
chopped spinach, thawed
½ can condensed cream of
mushroom soup, undiluted
4 large perfect tomatoes, with
centers scooped out, drained
upside down
2 strips cooked bacon, crumbled

Tomatoes stuffed with spinach are colorful
and delectable, even though the dish may
sound as if concocted by someone carried away
by an infatuation for vitamins. *Serve with pan-
broiled calves' liver with onions; escarole with thin
slices of avocado, sprinkled with lime juice and salt;
garlic rolls—rolls browned with a lump of garlic
butter in the top (mix 1 minced clove garlic and 1
small minced onion with 1 stick butter; add 1 teaspoon mayonnaise to keep it from hardening).*

Mix spinach with mushroom soup and stuff it
into the tomatoes. Sprinkle bacon on top. Place
in a shallow casserole and bake in 375° oven
about 15 to 20 minutes. Fresh spinach may be
used if you really like to get sand out. Serves 4.
Time: 30 minutes.

Zucchini Baked with Cheese and Bacon

6 small or 3 large zucchini or yellow summer squash, sliced thin but not peeled
salt
1½ cups grated Cheddar cheese
4 slices bacon, diced and partly cooked to remove excessive fat
⅓ cup chopped parsley

Zucchini, the green striped Italian squash, and our yellow summer squash that used to be crooknecked until the busybodies in the Department of Agriculture started fussing, may be used interchangeably in recipes. *Serve with red sweet onion rings chilled in French dressing; French bread; broiled grapefruit halves.*

Arrange a layer of overlapping slices of zucchini or yellow squash in a shallow casserole. Salt and sprinkle with part of the cheese. Sprinkle with partly cooked bacon and parsley. Add layers of zucchini, cheese, bacon, and parsley, and repeat until ingredients are used. It is best if the casserole is large enough and shallow enough so that all ingredients may be used in just two layers. Bake in 350° oven 30 minutes or until zucchini is tender. Serves 4. Time: 45 minutes.

Chakchouka

4 large onions, sliced
2½ cups diced zucchini
4 tablespoons oil
4 large tomatoes, skinned, seeded, and diced
2 sweet Bell peppers, green or red, seeded and diced
1 medium eggplant, cut in chunks but not peeled
chopped tarragon
salt, pepper
2 cloves garlic, minced
1 tablespoon chopped parsley
4 eggs

This is the lusty and variable vegetable mélange from the South of France called ratatouille, but it's chakchouka when baked with eggs. Ratatouille may be served hot or cold, and so may chakchouka if you don't mind your eggs cold. The French don't, although to an American, the first time, the cold poached eggs of *oeufs en gelée* are a surprise, usually a good one. *Serve with French bread and a rich bland dessert such as cheesecake.*

This is just a suggested list which may be varied. Cook onions and zucchini in oil for a few minutes. Add tomatoes and peppers and cook a few minutes more before adding eggplant, tarragon, salt, pepper, garlic, and parsley. Cook these until somewhat thickened and saucelike. Put into a casserole and make four depressions with a spoon. Slip an egg into each one. Sprinkle with more salt and pepper. Bake in preheated 375° oven until eggs are set. Serves 4. Time: 1 hour.

Vegetable Casserole with Cheese Sauce

1 small cauliflower, pulled
  apart, or 1 10-oz. package
  frozen cauliflower, cooked
1 lb. fresh, or 1 10-oz. package
  frozen, lima beans, cooked
4 carrots, scraped and slivered
  with potato peeler
3 tablespoons butter
3 tablespoons flour
salt and lots of freshly ground
  black pepper
1½ cups milk
⅔ cup grated Cheddar cheese

This may be done the long way with fresh cauliflower, lima beans, and carrots, or the slightly shorter way, using frozen cauliflower, frozen limas, and canned diced carrots. *Serve with ham; French bread; brandied peaches.*

Put cooked cauliflower and lima beans in a shallow buttered casserole with the slivered raw carrots. Melt butter and blend in flour. Cook a few minutes, add seasoning and milk slowly, and stir until smooth and thickened. Add cheese and stir until melted. Pour over the vegetables and put in 350° oven about 30 to 35 minutes or until the sauce is brown and bubbling. Serves 4. Time: 1 hour.

To keep parsley fresh for several days, wash thoroughly, cut clusters from stems, and store in refrigerator in tightly covered jar.

Cheese and Tomato Soufflé

4 tablespoons butter
4 tablespoons flour
1 cup beef bouillon
½ teaspoon basil
salt and pepper
1 cup Cheddar cheese, grated
½ 6-oz. can Italian tomato paste
4 eggs, separated

One more sound argument that a good soufflé is not the hardest thing you can do. *Serve with escarole with French dressing; Italian bread sticks; brownie pudding (see index).*

Make sauce by melting butter, blending in flour, and adding bouillon and seasonings slowly. Cook and stir until smooth and thickened. Add cheese and tomato paste and stir until cheese is melted. Remove from stove, cool slightly, and add egg yolks. Beat egg whites until stiff but not dry. Fold the whites into the sauce, pour into a low buttered casserole with straight sides, and bake in 350° oven 40 to 45 minutes or until top springs back when lightly touched. Serves 4. Time: 1 hour.

Curried Fruit Casserole

4 cups mixed fruit, such as:
  1 cup dried apricots, soaked 1
    or 2 hours
  2 oranges, peeled, seeded,
    sliced thin
  1 8-oz. can pear halves
  1 9-oz. package frozen dark
    sweet cherries
⅓ cup butter
1 tablespoon curry powder
about ⅔ cup brown sugar

Any pleasing combination of fruits of contrasting colors, textures, and flavors, fresh, frozen, dried or canned, may be used. *Serve with roast pork; baked kasha (see index); French crêpes rolled around sweetened whipped cream flavored with Cointreau and topped with chocolate sauce.*

Drain fruit and arrange in a shallow casserole. Melt butter with curry powder and pour over the fruit. Sprinkle with brown sugar. The amount of sugar needed will vary according to the fruit used. Bake uncovered in preheated 325° oven 45 minutes. Remove from oven and let stand for at least 2 hours to let the flavors ripen. Reheat for 15 minutes before serving. Serves 4 to 6. Time: 1 hour, not counting time for ripening.

To enhance flavor of bottled olives, green or black, pour off the brine and cover with olive oil, with or without such seasonings as garlic or herbs, and let stand in refrigerator for several days. Let come to room temperature and drain before serving. Oil may be used again for more olives, or for salad dressing.

Desserts

Desserts

Apple Charlotte

5 slices bread or toast
butter, softened
⅓ cup bitter orange marmalade
3 cups sliced cooking apples
 (about 1 lb.)
about ½ cup granulated sugar
½ cup orange juice
1½ tablespoons lemon juice
2 egg whites
pinch of salt
pinch of cream of tartar
3 tablespoons granulated sugar,
 or 4 tablespoons powdered
 sugar
½ teaspoon almond extract

Most charlottes are not cooked and not casseroles. This one is baked and thus included. The charlotte molds with straight sides which are available in many of the fancy culinary equipment stores are a good shape to use for soufflés. On the other hand, any good deep baking dish may be used. *Serve with broiled steak; baked potatoes; Caesar salad.*

Trim crust from bread and butter it on both sides. Spread marmalade on only one side. Place 1 slice, marmalade side up, in bottom of charlotte mold and stand the other slices, marmalade side facing in, around the sides, overlapping if necessary. Put a few slices of apple in the center, sprinkle with sugar, and continue until all apples are used. The amount of sugar will vary according to the tartness of the apples. Only cooking apples should be used. Mix orange juice with lemon juice and pour in. Bake in preheated 350° oven until apples are almost tender (30 to 40 minutes). Make meringue by beating egg whites until stiff, then adding salt, cream of tartar, and sugar, about a teaspoon or less at a time, beating until all has been added. Remove charlotte from oven and spread the meringue, being careful to spread to the edges or it will shrink back. Bake 10 to 15 minutes, or until lightly browned. The charlotte may be baked earlier, then chilled before the meringue is added, for a decidedly impure casserole but a good dessert. Serves 4 to 6. Time: 1½ hours.

Apples Baked in Maple Syrup

5 or 6 medium-sized cooking apples, peeled, cored, and quartered
½ to ⅔ cup maple syrup
pinch of salt
heavy cream or vanilla ice cream

This is a sort of sublimated applesauce, simple enough for the dinner suggested here, but good enough for a formal one of consequence. *Serve with Canadian split-pea soup with sliced garlic frankfurters; escarole, diced cucumber, and finely chopped sweet red onions with French dressing; French bread.*

Arrange apple quarters in a shallow buttered casserole. Pour in maple syrup (there should be enough to come halfway up on the apples; the amount will vary with the size of the dish). Add salt. Bake in preheated 350° oven about 30 minutes, or until apples are tender. Serve hot or cold with cream or vanilla ice cream spooned on top. Serves 4. Time: 40 minutes.

Baked Apples with Meringue Top

4 egg yolks
2 tablespoons sugar
¼ teaspoon salt
½ teaspoon ground cinnamon
1 tablespoon melted butter
4 large cooking apples, peeled and cored, with some of their centers cut out
1 egg white
1 teaspoon sugar

From the days when desserts were important and instant puddings were not known. *Serve with Kugula (see index); tossed greens with Roquefort cheese dressing.*

Beat egg yolks with sugar, salt, cinnamon, and melted butter. Fill apples, which should have much larger hollows than usual, with the mixture. Bake in 300° oven until apples are fork-tender, about 50 minutes to 1 hour. Beat egg white to a stiff froth and add the teaspoon of sugar gradually, beating after each addition. Drop a spoonful on each apple and return to the oven to brown, about 15 minutes. Serves 4. Time: 1½ hours.

Apple Cream

1/3 cup muscat raisins
muscatel
4 cooking apples, peeled and
  sliced
3 eggs
1 cup heavy cream
1/4 cup brown sugar

This dish is unusual and gives importance to a meal for special guests. *Serve with steak and oyster pie (see index); dandelion greens with sour-cream dressing (4 parts sour cream, 1 part tarragon vinegar, 1 tablespoon capers, salt, pepper); drop biscuits.*

Soak raisins in muscatel for 2 or 3 hours, or until they are plump. Place slices of apple decoratively in the bottom of a buttered casserole that is very shallow. Sprinkle wine-soaked raisins on the apple slices. Bake until apples are almost tender but not soft. Beat eggs with cream and brown sugar. Pour over partly baked apples. Put the casserole in a pan of water 1 inch deep and bake in a 325° oven. Cook until mixture is firm and custardy and a knife inserted comes out clean, which should be about 25 to 35 minutes. Chill. Serve very cold. Serves 4. Time: 50 minutes, not counting soaking time for raisins, or chilling.

For a tenderer piecrust, use less water than is called for.

German Apple Pudding

1 egg
1 cup milk
1/4 teaspoon salt
2 tablespoons melted butter
2 cups sifted flour
2 teaspoons baking powder
5 medium-sized cooking apples,
  peeled, cored, and quartered
brown sugar

This is a very old Pennsylvania Dutch version. *Serve with kidney beans and red wine (see index); watercress with French dressing; hot party rolls (brown-and-serve).*

Beat egg with milk, add salt, melted butter, and flour. Beat well and add baking powder. Beat thoroughly. Pour into a very shallow buttered pan. Press quartered apples decoratively and symmetrically into the dough. Dust thickly with brown sugar and bake in 350° oven 35 to 45 minutes or until the apples are fork-tender. Serves 4. Time: 1 hour.

Apples Bettleman, Viennese Version

2 cups fresh or canned applesauce
1½ cups dry rye breadcrumbs
¾ cup raisins, plumped in water
   for 1 hour, drained
½ cup chopped nuts (walnuts,
   filberts, almonds, or peanuts)
4 eggs, beaten

Many of the middle- and northern-European
countries make their version of this dish. The
constants are apples and rye breadcrumbs.
*Serve with chicken and green noodles (see index);
cucumber salad.*

Combine applesauce, breadcrumbs, raisins,
and nuts. Put into a shallow buttered casserole.
Pour beaten eggs on top and bake in preheated
350° oven 30 to 40 minutes. Serves 4. Time: 50
minutes.

Apricot Nut Pudding

1 12-oz. package tenderized
   dried apricots, soaked 2
   hours
3 tablespoons sugar
⅓ cup melted butter
1½ cups dried breadcrumbs,
   preferably coarse and homemade
½ cup chopped walnuts (or
   black walnuts, or slivered
   almonds)

This is somewhat like the much-loved apple
betty. *Serve with chicken pot pie (see index); chicory with French dressing.*

Drain apricots and save juice. Mix sugar, butter, breadcrumbs, and walnuts together with a
spoon or your fingers. Arrange a layer of apricots in a shallow casserole. Sprinkle with crumb
mixture. Repeat until all ingredients are used,
ending with crumbs on top. Pour in the juice
from the apricots and bake 30 to 40 minutes in
350° oven. Serves 4. Time: 1 hour.

Blueberry Puff Pudding

2 tablespoons quick-cooking
  tapioca
⅓ cup granulated sugar, or
  brown sugar firmly packed
salt
1 cup blueberries
1 cup sliced apples
1 tablespoon butter
1 tablespoon lemon juice
1 egg
pinch of cream of tartar
3 tablespoons sugar
¼ cup cake flour, sifted before
  measuring

Serve with chicken salad with lots of toasted chopped Brazil nuts; artichoke hearts marinated in French dressing; French bread.

Combine tapioca, ⅓ cup sugar, a pinch of salt, blueberries, apples, butter, and ½ cup water. Place over medium heat and bring to a full boil, stirring constantly. Remove from heat and add lemon juice. Pour into a large deep buttered casserole and keep hot. Beat egg with cream of tartar and a pinch of salt until thick and lemon-colored, adding 3 tablespoons sugar gradually. Add flour all at once and stir until smooth. Spoon over the fruit mixture. Bake in 325° oven 50 minutes, or until done. Serve warm. Serves 4. Time: 1¼ hours.

Apricot Soufflé

½ lb. dried apricots, soaked 1 or
  2 hours
2 tablespoons sugar
2 egg yolks, slightly beaten
2 tablespoons heavy cream
5 egg whites, stiffly beaten

It is wonderful and rare to find apricots or figs in their fresh-fragrant, sun-ripened, almost perfect state, but I have been fortunate. The mediocre simulacra in the market do not tempt me to almost certain disappointment. But dried apricots seem to be a constant, concentrated, and compact delight, adding a delicate aroma and delightful flavor to almost any dish. In a soufflé, with the puréed fruit acting as the sauce base, they are, I think, at their blissful best. *Serve with ham baked with endive (see index); new potatoes; chilled cucumber sticks; hot biscuits.*

Drain apricots and purée in electric blender or put through a food mill. Add sugar, egg yolks, and cream, and stir until thoroughly mixed. Fold in stiffly beaten egg whites gently, put into a buttered 1-quart casserole or soufflé dish with straight sides, and place on a cookie sheet in preheated 350° oven. Bake 25 to 35 minutes or according to the idiosyncrasies of your oven. When done, it should spring back when *lightly* touched. Serves 4 in small but rich portions. Time: 1 hour.

Lemon Pudding

1 cup sugar
3 tablespoons flour
pinch of salt
3 tablespoons fresh lemon juice
1 tablespoon grated lemon rind
2 eggs, separated
1 cup milk

For those who feel that there should be a dessert to put a period to a meal, but don't like it too sweet or too heavy. *Serve with Swedish stew (see index); mixed greens with sour cream dressing; Swedish bread.*

Blend sugar, flour, salt, lemon juice and rind, egg yolks, and milk in top of double boiler, mixing well. Stir and cook over hot water until smooth and thickened. Remove from stove, cool slightly, beat egg whites until stiff, and fold in. Pour into a small buttered casserole and set in a pan of hot water. Bake 1 hour at 300°. (This will separate at top and bottom, but that is according to plan.) Serves 4. Time: 1¼ hours.

Noodle Soufflé with Cherries and Nuts

2⅔ cups milk
dash of salt
½ lb. wide egg noodles
5 tablespoons butter, softened
5 tablespoons sugar
3 eggs, separated
1 teaspoon vanilla
⅓ cup ground nuts (almonds, walnuts, or filberts)
1 lb. dark sweet cherries, pitted (fresh, or canned and drained)

Middle European countries serve noodle puddings for dessert, as we serve bread puddings. They are best, of course, with freshly made noodles. *Serve with roast pork loin; salad of Boston lettuce; hot rolls; lemon sherbet; or as a robust dessert following a light main dish.*

Bring milk and salt to a boil. Add noodles and cook until thick and tender, stirring constantly so they do not stick together. Mix butter and sugar together, add egg yolks, and beat together until foamy. Add cooked noodles, their liquid, and vanilla. Beat egg whites until stiff and fold into noodle mixture with nuts. Put into a shallow buttered baking dish and arrange cherries on top. Bake in preheated 350° oven 35 to 45 minutes. Serves 6. Time: 1¼ hours.

Cherry Pudding

1 cup flour
1½ cups sugar
½ cup milk
1 teaspoon baking powder
pinch of salt
1 1-lb. can sour red pitted
   cherries
3 tablespoons butter

Bake this so that it comes out of the oven just when dinner is being put on the table. It should be served warm but not hot. *Serve with shrimp jambalaya; cucumber salad; poppy-seed rolls.*

Put flour, ½ cup sugar, milk, baking powder, and salt in a blender and buzz to mix, or beat together in a bowl. Spread on a shallow buttered baking dish. Drain cherries. Put the juice in a pan with the rest of the sugar and butter and bring to a boil. Sprinkle cherries over the batter and pour juice on top. Bake in preheated 350° oven 50 minutes or until done. Serves 4 to 6. Cold whipped cream or vanilla ice cream may be served with this. Time: 1¼ hours.

Pear Clafouti

3 cups peeled, cored, and sliced
   ripe pears
¼ cup sweet white wine or cognac
⅓ cup granulated sugar
1 cup milk
3 eggs
⅓ cup granulated sugar
1 tablespoon vanilla extract
pinch of salt
⅔ cup sifted flour
powdered sugar

In French, clafouti is an elegant name for very good fruit batter puddings that we sometimes call pan dowdies, or cobblers. *Serve with beef goulash with red and green sweet peppers and rice; mixed green salad.*

Soak pears in wine or cognac and sugar for at least 1 hour. Drain and put the sugared liquid in electric blender with milk, eggs, ⅓ cup sugar, vanilla, salt, and flour. Blend at top speed. Put a thin layer of batter in a shallow buttered baking dish that will take top-of-stove heat. Cook over medium heat for a minute until the batter has set. Remove from heat and arrange pears on batter. Pour the rest of the batter on top and sprinkle lightly with powdered sugar. Bake in preheated 350° oven about 1 hour. It is done when brown and puffy and when a cake tester comes out clean. Serve warm. It will sink a little. Serves 6 to 8. Time: 2½ hours.

Baked Pears with Shaved Chocolate

6 medium-sized pears, quartered and cored, but not peeled
3 tablespoons sugar
1 to 2 squares semi-sweet chocolate, shaved (chocolate bits
   may be used, but with less sub-
   tlety)

Baked pears are as pleasing and as variable as baked apples, but less often remembered. Pears not entirely ripe are best, and of course some varieties are better for baking than others. Ask your fruit store which ones to use. *Serve with baked ham slice; spoon bread (see index); asparagus vinaigrette salad (cooked or canned asparagus with French dressing and garnished with chopped pimientos.*

Arrange pear quarters on the bottom of a very shallow casserole. Sprinkle with sugar and then with chocolate shavings. Pour in ⅓ cup water. Bake in 350° oven 45 minutes or until pears are fork-tender. Serves 4, hot or cold. Time: 1 hour.

Chestnut Soufflé

½ lb. dried chestnuts
2 cups milk
¼ cup sugar
4 tablespoons heavy cream
4 egg yolks, beaten
1 teaspoon vanilla extract
¼ cup cognac
5 egg whites, beaten stiff
confectioner's sugar

You may go through that tedious business of boiling and skinning fresh chestnuts, or buy them from a man on the streets of New York or elsewhere. But the dried ones keep well and are blessedly simple to use. *Serve with chicken breasts with sesame seeds (see index); broiled rice; sliced orange, onion, and watercress salad.*

Soak dried chestnuts overnight. Simmer in milk until tender, drain, and mash thoroughly with fork or in blender. Add sugar and cream to the purée and stir over low heat until mixture is thick and smooth. Remove from heat and stir in beaten yolks, vanilla extract, and cognac. Fold in egg whites, turn batter into buttered and sugared baking dish, and bake in preheated 350° oven 35 to 45 minutes. Sprinkle with confectioner's sugar and serve with sweetened whipped cream flavored with vanilla. Serves 6. Time: 1½ hours.

Baked Pears with Ginger Marmalade and Almonds

1 lb. cooking pears, peeled and
    sliced
½ cup ginger marmalade,
    melted
½ cup dry white wine
½ cup slivered blanched
    almonds

I think pears are delectable any way they are presented, from fresh ripe pears eaten in the hand to pear sherbet with shaved chocolate. I also like ginger marmalade and any kind of nuts. Obviously, this dish is designed for me, and, I hope for many others. *Serve with turkey loaf Michel (see index); creamed spinach; French bread.*

Arrange pears in a shallow casserole. Mix melted marmalade with white wine and pour over the pears. Sprinkle the top with slivered almonds. Bake in preheated 350° oven 20 to 30 minutes or until the pears are tender. Serve either hot or cold. Serves 4. Time: 50 minutes.

To peel or squeeze oranges or grapefruit easily, have them at room temperature.

Italian Cheesecake

1½ cups fine zwieback or
    graham-cracker crumbs
¼ cup confectioner's sugar
6 tablespoons melted butter
3 lbs. ricotta
1½ cups granulated sugar
6 eggs
1 teaspoon vanilla
4 teaspoons orange-flower water
    (nice if you can find it)
¾ cup cream
½ cup chopped citron
1½ squares bitter chocolate,
    shaved

Serve with chili con carne (see index); bitter greens (dandelion and mustard) with watercress and French dressing; hot corn bread.

Mix zwieback crumbs with confectioner's sugar and melted butter and pat on the sides and bottom of a 9-inch shallow ceramic casserole with straight sides, saving ½ cup of the mixture for later. Mix ricotta with sugar, eggs, vanilla, orange-flower water, cream, citron, and chocolate and pour into the crumb shell. Sprinkle the other crumbs on top. Bake in 325° oven 1 hour and let the cheesecake cool in the oven. Open the door and turn off the heat before chilling. Serves 8. Time: 1½ hours.

Rice Pilaf Baked with Honey and Almonds

⅓ cup uncooked rice
⅔ stick (5½ tablespoons) butter
½ cup honey
2½ cups fresh orange juice,
   heated
½ cup blanched almonds,
   slivered

In Turkey and the Near East they have a sweetened pilaf that is just about as far as you can get from the drab rice pudding of your childhood. They often add water to the pilaf while cooking, but the orange juice seems more delicate and delicious to me. *Serve with lamb chops baked with tarragon and butter; kasha (see index); chilled strips of peeled cucumber; French bread.*

Cook rice in butter until brown and opaque. Put both in a casserole. Add honey. Bake in 350° oven about 20 minutes or until rice is toasted. Add orange juice. Cover casserole and put back in the oven for 45 minutes or until rice is tender. Add more hot juice if it starts to dry out. Sprinkle with almonds. Serve hot or cold. Serves 4. Time: 1¼ hours.

Raspberry or Strawberry Soufflé

2 3-oz. packages Philadelphia
   cream cheese, softened at
   room temperature
½ cup sour cream
3 egg yolks
4 egg whites
1 cup fresh berries, slightly
   mashed and sweetened with 1
   tablespoon honey, or 1 10-oz.
   package frozen raspberries or
   sliced strawberries, thawed
   and drained
1 tablespoon Cointreau, Grand
   Marnier, or Triple Sec

As fragrant and delicate as the air of a spring day. Impressive to serve and simple to prepare. *Serve with chicken baked in cream (see index); mixed greens with artichoke hearts in a bland French dressing (4 parts olive oil, 1 part tarragon vinegar, salt, freshly ground black pepper); hot biscuits.*

Mix cream cheese, sour cream, and egg yolks until smooth and creamy. Stir in berries and Cointreau. Beat egg whites until stiff and fold in gently. Put into a small buttered casserole with straight sides. Bake in 350° oven 50 to 60 minutes or until top springs back when lightly touched. For good timing, put this in the oven a few minutes before serving the main course. Serves 4. Time: 1¼ hours.

Black-Walnut Pudding

4 eggs, separated
1 cup zwieback crumbs
1 cup chopped black walnuts
⅔ cup powdered sugar
1 teaspoon vanilla
½ cup heavy cream, whipped

Black walnuts are definitely an acquired taste, but, once the taste is acquired, the usual English walnuts seem rather characterless. Transplanted Southerners and other black-walnut lovers can now find them in vacuum tins in specialty shops, with the familiar acrid and pungent flavor and none of the tedium of cracking them. *Serve with Zuppa da Pesce (see index); baked rice pilaf (see index); chicory with French dressing; hot biscuits.*

Beat egg yolks slightly. Mix zwieback crumbs with chopped nuts, egg yolks, sugar, and vanilla. Beat whites until stiff, fold in gently, and pile into a buttered shallow casserole. Bake in 350° oven 20 to 25 minutes. Let stand overnight before serving. Top with whipped cream. Serves 4. Time: 45 minutes.

Canadian Rhubarb Cobbler

1½ cups sugar
1 cup apple juice
1 teaspoon vanilla
2 cups diced fresh or frozen
  rhubarb
2 cups sliced strawberries

BATTER

1 cup all-purpose flour
2 tablespoons sugar
1½ teaspoons baking powder
¼ cup butter
½ teaspoon mace
¼ cup milk or cream
sugar
nutmeg

There are people, like me, who love rhubarb's fascinating sharp flavor and beautiful color. Others, like a very nice editor, who winces when she even sees it listed on a menu, hate rhubarb. *Serve with beef stew; sliced tomatoes with vinaigrette dressing; hard rolls.*

Bring sugar, apple juice, ½ cup water, and vanilla to a boil, stirring until sugar is dissolved. Remove from heat, add fruit, and put into a buttered baking dish. For batter, sift flour, sugar, and baking powder together. Work in the butter with a pastry blender or two knives or your fingers. Add mace and milk or cream. Stir. Drop by the tablespoon, evenly spaced, on the fruit, like soft dumplings. Sprinkle the tops of the dumplings with sugar and a pinch of nutmeg. Bake in preheated 450° oven 25 to 30 minutes. Serves 6 to 8. Time: 50 minutes.

Rhubarb Custard Pie with Meringue

2 egg yolks
1 cup sugar
¼ teaspoon salt
2 tablespoons flour
2 cups diced peeled rhubarb
1 8-inch unbaked pastry shell

MERINGUE

2 egg whites
3 tablespoons granulated sugar,
   or 4 tablespoons powdered
   sugar
½ teaspoon almond extract

Rhubarb in a fancy guise. *Serve with Braciuola (see index); baked risotto; chicory with French dressing; hot biscuits.*

Beat egg yolks with sugar, salt, and flour. Mix with rhubarb and put into pastry shell. Bake in 350° oven 35 minutes. For meringue, beat egg whites until stiff, adding sugar, a teaspoon at a time. Add almond extract. Spoon meringue on baked custard and return to oven 15 more minutes to brown. Serves 4. Time: 1¼ hours.

Macaroon Soufflé

1 cup crumbled almond macaroons
1 cup milk
3 eggs, separated
few drops vanilla
1 jigger brandy or rum
⅓ cup sugar
pinch of salt
⅓ cup chopped almonds

This is an elegant dish, but easy enough to make so that you can be very, very nonchalant about it. *Serve with oyster stew; tossed greens with French dressing (3 parts olive oil, 1 part fresh lemon juice, grated lemon peel, dash of nutmeg, salt, pepper); pilot biscuits.*

Soak macaroons in milk for ½ hour. Beat egg yolks slightly. Mix with macaroons and vanilla, brandy or rum, sugar, salt, and almonds. Beat egg whites until stiff, fold them in, and transfer to a buttered casserole. Set in a pan with about 1 inch of water. Bake in 350° oven 40 to 45 minutes, or until the top springs back when touched lightly with the fingers. Serves 4. Time: 1¼ hours.

Chocolate Soufflé

2 tablespoons butter
3 tablespoons flour
1 cup milk
1 teaspoon vanilla or brandy
½ cup sugar
3 squares bitter chocolate,
  melted
3 egg yolks
4 egg whites

The sauce for this may be prepared ahead of time and the beaten whites added just before dinner is served. Let it bake while eating the main course. *Serve with broiled swordfish steak, basted with butter and vermouth; fresh tender young okra, boiled and dressed with Hollandaise sauce; tiny new potatoes, boiled in their jackets; mixed green salad with French dressing; hot biscuits.*

Melt butter over a low flame, add flour, and stir until you have a smooth paste. Add milk slowly, stirring constantly until smooth. Add vanilla or brandy, sugar, and melted chocolate. Remove from stove and beat until smooth. When slightly cool, stir in egg yolks. Beat egg whites until stiff and fold gently into the chocolate mixture. Pour into a buttered quart casserole with straight sides. Set on a cookie sheet. Bake in 350° oven 40 to 45 minutes or until top springs back when lightly touched. Serve immediately. Serves 4. Time: 1 hour.

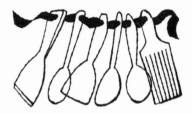

Brownie Pudding

½ cup sifted flour
1 teaspoon double-acting baking
  powder
½ teaspoon salt
⅓ cup granulated sugar
1 tablespoon breakfast cocoa
¼ cup milk
1 tablespoon melted butter
½ teaspoon vanilla
¼ cup chopped nut meats
½ cup brown sugar, firmly
  packed
2 tablespoons breakfast cocoa
⅔ cup boiling water

Serve with chicken baked in cream (see index); watercress and tomato aspic, with mayonnaise; hot rolls.

Sift flour once, measure, and add baking powder, salt, granulated sugar, and 1 tablespoon cocoa, and sift again. Add milk, butter, and vanilla. Mix until barely smooth. Add nuts and pour into a buttered casserole. For the sauce, mix together brown sugar and 2 tablespoons cocoa and sprinkle over the batter. Pour boiling water over the top—this makes the chocolate sauce go to the bottom of the casserole. Bake in 350° oven 30 to 40 minutes. Serve warm (not hot) or cold. Serves 4. Time: 1¼ hours.

Cream Pudding with Chocolate Meringue

3 cups milk
¾ cup sugar
4 tablespoons flour
3 egg yolks, beaten
1 tablespoon butter
1 teaspoon vanilla
3 egg whites
1 oz. chocolate, melted
4 tablespoons sugar

A combination so old that it seems new to the present generation. *Serve with Chicken George Murphy (see index); hot biscuits.*

Heat 2½ cups of milk with ¾ cup sugar. Make a smooth paste with the flour and the rest of the milk. Mix the paste with beaten egg yolks. Pour hot milk over egg mixture and beat with a whisk or spoon. Return to stove and cook over medium heat in the top of double boiler, stirring until thick. Add butter and vanilla. Pour into a shallow buttered baking dish. Beat egg whites until foamy, add 4 tablespoons sugar gradually, and beat until the whites stand in peaks. Add slightly cooled chocolate. Beat again until the mixture is the consistency of whipped cream. Top the pudding with the meringue and bake in 350° oven 15 minutes. Chill. Serves 4. Time: 45 minutes, not counting chilling time.

Ricotta Pudding

1 cup heavy cream
2 eggs, beaten
½ lb. ricotta
2 tablespoons chopped citron
1 tablespoon grated orange peel
2 tablespoons chocolate chips,
  or shaved chocolate
¼ cup sugar
1 tablespoon rum
½ teaspoon vanilla

Ricotta is the delicate yet characterful Italian version of cottage cheese, with much the best flavor and texture for this dish. If there is not an Italian store near you, try large-curd cottage cheese, but it is not the same. *Serve with salmon salad (mix and chill 2 cans flaked and boned salmon with 1 large cucumber, diced, 6 radishes, sliced thin, 1 finely chopped onion, 1 chopped green pepper, and ½ package frozen pineapple chunks, in French dressing; garnish with crisp greens); Swedish flat rye bread.*

Scald cream and pour slowly over beaten eggs. Add the rest of the ingredients and put in a shallow buttered casserole set in a pan of hot water 1 inch deep. Bake in 350° oven 25 to 30 minutes or until a knife inserted comes out clean. This may be served hot or cold. Serves 4. Time: 45 minutes.

Rhubarb Betty

2 tablespoons melted butter
2 cups soft breadcrumbs
1 cup sugar
½ teaspoon cinnamon
1 tablespoon grated orange peel
3 cups rhubarb cut in 1-inch
  pieces

In season from February until late August, rhubarb is one of the most beautiful of all fruits. Called by our ancestors "pie plant," it is usually eaten in pies or stewed. Baked in the oven, it is equally delectable. *Serve after chicken stewed in sherry (see index); boiled rice; green salad; French bread.*

Mix melted butter and breadcrumbs. Mix sugar, cinnamon, and orange peel. Put a quarter of the crumbs on bottom of buttered baking dish, cover with half the rhubarb, sprinkle with half the sugar mixture. Add another quarter of the crumbs, the rest of the rhubarb, the rest of the sugar and spices. Pour in ¼ cup water and sprinkle the rest of the crumbs on top. Cover and bake in a 375° oven 45 minutes. Uncover and brown 5 to 10 minutes more. Serve plain or with whipped cream. Serves 4. Time: 1¼ hours.

Danish Apple Cake

1 egg
¾ cup sugar
½ teaspoon vanilla extract
2 tablespoons melted butter
½ cup flour
½ teaspoon salt
1 teaspoon baking powder
1 cup chopped apple
½ cup chopped mixed nuts (not
  salted)

A tasty autumn dessert when apples abound — or whenever you want something hearty to top off a light meal. *Serve after egg and cheese casserole (see index); green salad with French dressing; hot rolls.*

Beat together the egg, sugar, vanilla extract, and melted butter. Stir in flour, salt, and baking powder. Add chopped apple and nuts and mix well. Put into greased pie plate and bake at 350° for 30 minutes. Serve warm and top with whipped cream or vanilla ice cream. Serves 4 to 6. Time: 1 hour.

Baked Apples in the German Manner

4 or 5 cooking apples, cored and
   sliced
½ cup sugar
⅓ cup diced citron
2 eggs, slightly beaten
1 cup sour cream
¼ cup bourbon or brandy
3 tablespoons sifted confectioner's sugar

Apples are America's most loved fruit and are plentiful, frugal, adaptable, and delicious in all their guises. *Serve after venison stew (see index); hot rolls; tossed green salad.*

Spread sliced apples in greased shallow baking pan. Mix ½ cup sugar, citron, and eggs together, add sour cream and bourbon or brandy, and pour over apples. Sprinkle with confectioner's sugar and bake at 350° ¾ hour or more. Serves 4. Time: 1 hour.

Peach Pie Almost

3½ cups (1-lb.-13-oz. can) home-
   style peaches
½ package pastry mix
1 heaping cup light brown sugar
4 tablespoons butter, melted

A wonderful hurry-up way to use canned peaches when you haven't any fresh fruit for dessert and don't like the idea of canned peaches unadorned. *Serve after pork chops and rice (see index); pickled beets; rye-bread toast.*

Drain peaches and arrange in a buttered shallow baking dish. Crumble the pastry mix and stir into it the brown sugar, mixing well. Sprinkle on peaches, dribble melted butter on top, and bake at 325° for 30 minutes, or until brown and bubbly. Serve with cream or ice cream. Serves 4. Time: 45 minutes.

Blueberry Bread Pudding

8 thick slices buttered French
   bread
1 pint fresh or frozen blueberries
1 teaspoon grated lemon peel
3 eggs
⅔ cup sugar
3 cups half-and-half or milk

An old-fashioned favorite with a new twist. *Serve with pork chops and rice (see index); marinated celeriac.*

Arrange buttered slices of bread in overlapping circles in shallow casserole. Strew blueberries on top, sprinkle with lemon peel. Beat eggs and sugar together, then add the half-and-half or milk. Bake in preheated 350° oven 45 minutes or until a knife inserted comes out clean. Serve warm. Serves 4 to 6. Time: 1 hour.

Index

Grape leaves, stuffed, 184